Spirit in Business

Spiritual Leadership For A New Era

Ginny West

Copyright © 2016 Ginny West
All rights reserved.

ISBN 978-0-646-95912-2

No part of this publication may be reproduced or transmitted in any form or by any means, electronic or mechanical, including photography, recording, or any information storage and retrieval system without the prior written consent from the publisher and author, except in the instance of quotes for reviews. No part of this book may be uploaded without the permission of the publisher and author, nor be otherwise circulated in any form of binding or cover other than that in which it is originally published.

The publisher and author acknowledge the trademark status and trademark ownership of all trademarks, service marks and word marks mentioned in this book.

The author of this book does not dispense medical advice or prescribe the use of any technique as a form of treatment for physical, emotional or medical problems without the advice of a physician, either directly or indirectly. The intent of the author is only to offer general information to help you in your quest for success, self awareness, emotional and spiritual wellbeing. In the event you use any of this information yourself, which is your constitutional right to do so, the author and the publisher assume no responsibility for your actions.

Contents

Introduction 1

Spirit 5
　Purpose 7
　Manifestation 13
　Conscious Co-Creation 21
　Receiving 25
　Finding Your Voice 28
　Being Soul Driven 32
　Authenticity and Integrity 36
　Creativity and Innovation 41
　Permission and Sovereignty 45
　Shining Bright 48
　Perfection and Excellence 53
　Leadership 56
　Success 59
　Money 63
　Time and Patience 68
　Self-Sabotage 73
　Competition 77
　Illusion 82
　The Wounded Healer 87
　Overcoming Disappointment 90
　Divine Helpers 96
　Light 100
　Grounding, Clearing and Protection 104

Ritual 110
Self-Care 115
Physical Vitality 121
Living Spirit 124
Honouring Yourself 128
Meditation and Visualisation 131
The Sweet Spirit 136
Generosity and the Giving Heart 139
Appreciation 142
The Essential Bridge between Spirit and Business 146
One Tribe 150
It's Not All Rainbows and Angels 153

Business 157
Marketing 159
Your Niche 165
Brand 179
Audience and Target Market 190
Business Model 194
Planning 198
Operations 204
Diversifying and Dilution 208
Website 212
Social Media and Content 220
Social Proof 244
Newsletters and Email Marketing 247
Blogging or Vlogging 253
Batch Your Work 260
Networking 263
Getting an Unknown Out There 267
Finding Work 270
Business Coaching 275
Speaking 278

Writing and Publishing	285
Consultations	291
Classes	296
Workshops	309
Running Retreats	314
Products	322
Packages	328
E-Courses	331
Transitioning from Work to Your Business	336
Pricing, Value, Generosity & Worth	339
Evaluate, Review and Respond	347
Mind Mapping and Soul Mapping	350
Customer Service	354
Difficult Clients	359
Professional Conduct and Ethics	369
Licensing	375
Business Names and Intellectual Property	380
Continuing Education	385
Collaboration and Partnerships	388
One Last Thing	393

Introduction

'With deep faith we light up the incense of our hearts'
- Thich Nhat Hanh

Spirit in Business is about holding a deep connection with spirit and creating a business that is an inspirational driving force in fulfilling your purpose. For some people business is a trigger word, carrying automatic presumptions about greed, competition and dishonesty. You may believe as soon as you use the word, all spirituality is lost. You may believe that there is a huge division between spirit and business, and you can live only one or the other, but not both. I beg to differ. To me business is the essential sacred vehicle to fulfilling your purpose. It is the dance of the soul on the earth. It carries the opportunity to express the manifest vision of your spirit. What a glorious opportunity to celebrate who you are in essence, and to serve humanity.

No matter what your business is, you need to write a list and check it twice to be absolutely sure that your spirit is totally, utterly supported in every way, so it can unleash the full, glorious vibrancy of its expression without hindrance or interference. Business has two fundamental tasks. The first is to create space, support and a clear path for your soul's authentic expression. The second is to let your tribe know you are here and ready to work in service for them.

Let's get one thing straight, being in business is going to bring up your stuff, because the intention of your business is to bring the full expression of your soul work out into the world. It is the driving force behind the soul. And that's scary for the ego. Super scary. So it will become fearful, competitive, take you off on crazy tangents, want to use fear based language, tell you everyone out there is better than you, manipulate your direction, have you worried about others' opinions, your professional capacity and so on. The ego will want to discredit the structures at every turn because if it can sabotage the pathway and the plan, if it can set out detours and distractions, the soul's expression is lost and the ego can relax back into its safe world. It will whisper to you that business is unholy and that if you were really spiritual you wouldn't touch it with a bargepole. It is not business that is the bad fellow, but the ego that will rub its hands with delight as it sees numerous opportunities to keep you away from fulfilling your purpose.

Do you need to be mindful of your business practices? Absolutely. Every business decision must have its roots in the soul, and be utterly aligned with your highest path. You will need to be avid in your daily meditation practice to keep every day a soul driven one. You can no longer consult the soul just in times of difficulty or doubt. You will need to hone your intuitive skills on a daily basis by dipping into that infinite pool of integrity, vision and wisdom, so you can be sure your purpose is generated and motivated from the inside out, not the outside in. You will need to set each day with the positive intentions of what you intend to achieve and consciously co-create each moment with spirit. You will need to follow through with action instead of just dreaming about your perfect life. More than knowing your audience, you will need to know your work.

Business is the humble servant who will wait outside the door of your meditation room for daily instructions to be carried out. Break that communication between the soul and your business and pretty soon the ego will peek around the corner calling 'pssst over here, I have another great project for you'. If you can stay centered and true, your path is assured. There has never been a more potent time for manifesting your dharma. If you are willing to take the role of active co-creator from a soul space, it is impossible to fail. You are destined to succeed. It is in your DNA. It couldn't be any easier.

There is not one spiritual practitioner out there that is not using business tools, whether they care to admit it or not, and they do that because it supports the work of spirit, and the fulfilment of their dharma; from large organisations like the Brahma Kumaris, to the Dalai Lama, to regular everyday practitioners like you and me. If you get judgement from other practitioners, let it slide and carry on with your highest work. Never, ever let your ego, or the ego of anyone else deter you from your deepest work. The truth is that right now most of us are holding back. And its time to raise the vibration of our work and get it out there, because now, more than ever, we need your glorious, joyful, divine spirit to stand up and be seen.

If at any time you feel overwhelmed by the amount of information here please stop, step back and take a deep breath. Take it one chapter at a time. This book is going to show you how to raise the vibration of your work to something that will astound you and bring you great joy. How to manifest your authentic soul desires easily and effortlessly. How to create a deep, authentic, daily spiritual connection that is going to get you thirsty for more. How to align with the deepest essence of your work, name it and hold fast, when everything around you is trying to pull you away. It is going to help you find your one true soul purpose. It is going to pull you away from illusion and get super clear on the nitty gritty daily tasks that need to be done to succeed. It is going to show you how to create a business and marketing plan that will take your deepest work out into your local or global community, in a way that is wholly, intrinsically tied to your soul. And so much more. 'One day' has gone, the time is now. So what are you waiting for?...

Spirit

Find the sacred in what you do.
The deepest, sweetest essence of your work.
Protect it, nourish it, honour it and take it out into the world
so it may be of benefit to yourself and others.

Together we can light the world.

Ginny West

Purpose

'Effort and courage are not enough without purpose and direction'
- John F Kennedy

How can you find your soul purpose? There are hundreds of books, seminars, workshops and consultations trying to help people find the answer to this question. The truth is there is one way you will find your purpose, and that is through a committed daily practice of meditation. It's that simple. There is also just one way you will be able to stay true to your purpose and not wander off course and that is; you guessed it, through a committed daily practice of meditation. And here's why. Meditation is where your soul hangs out. It is the interface between this world and the divine. It is where all wisdom and all answers reside. Your purpose is not out there, it's within you. It is who you are. Your purpose is simply to connect with who you are at the deepest level and express that in the world. The closer you can get to your soul, and the more deeply you can connect to your true self, the more your life will become living purpose. Your purpose is an extension of your inner being. My purpose is to empower, inspire and motivate millions of wellbeing practitioners and spiritual leaders. My personal journey bought me to work in wellbeing; my education and experience have now placed me in a position to help other leaders, but more than that, it is who I am. I have a deep pool of innate knowledge and wisdom within me I feel compelled to share. At some subtle and intrinsic level I understand energy and the spiritual path. I also have a unique capacity to translate business and spiritual information into language and advice that is real and practical. My information is best suited to other leaders or people working at a higher spiritual level. I didn't choose my audience from the outside. This is who I am, and who I am destined to serve.

The first step in finding your purpose is a dedicated daily meditation practice where you get to know your soul. Here you learn to love yourself, to listen and to be guided by the inner realms, not outer distractions. It can be tempting to go to meditation purely for instructions on what to do next, or when you're lost and confused, but this will never make sense or be as smooth and cohesive without first understanding who you are. You need to know *why* the actions suggested are important. Why you feel compelled to do what you do. This will help you understand how your soul can best express itself in the world. At a personal level I could say that I want to help other wellbeing practitioners because I struggled personally in the early days of my business, and this is true. The deeper reason is because I feel compelled to; because I can't refuse, because it is an inner calling that will not rest while it is unexpressed. You have that within you too. You just need to listen to it.

Once you become clearer about who you are, the second step is to receive further information on how to bring your purpose into being. That too should come from the higher realms. When you enter your meditation room in the morning, go to receive. Connect first to your soul or higher self, and then listen. All the information you need to fulfil your purpose will be downloaded in that space. It may come as a feeling sense, a direct message, vision or physical sensation to act on something. Creating a regular daily practice ensures you are soul driven, rather than ego driven. It will show you what to do, where to go, and what to look out for. It will consistently deepen your relationship with your soul. Signs and synchronicities occur more often, and most importantly you can actually see them. You must nourish your practice from the roots up every day to build on your knowledge and connection. The unravelling of your purpose is the direct responsibility of the soul. The job of the mind is to create the most efficient structures in the real world to ensure the fulfilment of the soul's instructions, nothing more. If you truly want to know your purpose, go straight to the source of all information and knowing.

You may want to avoid connecting with your soul daily out of fear that you will be asked to do something you don't want to do, or that will be too much for you, or that you won't like. You may not like the idea of someone or something else telling you what to do, but this is very much the fear of the ego. Please know that your purpose will be wholly, intrinsically tied to who you are in essence. It will bring you the greatest joy, ease, wisdom, fulfilment and deep satisfaction. You will be able to end each day in a state of profound peace and fulfilment. The questioning will go, the doubting will stop and your soul will blossom. Finding your purpose is a revelation. It is all about having a deep, unshakeable sense of faith that you will be guided by your soul and spirit, day by day, moment by moment, to the fulfilment of your dreams. Eventually people will look at you and see your soul. If we were all listening at this deep level, how much easier everything would be. How I wish I had connected to my soul earlier in my career, rather than letting my mind call the shots. It would have saved a whole lot of time, money, energy and angst. I can't believe how much easier my life has become with this one change. If there is one piece of advice I could give you it would be to dip into this rich pool of love today and everyday thereafter. You'll never look back.

Finding your purpose is not about finding a thing to tie yourself to, or put on your website. It's about how you can serve. And that's powerful. It is not something external; it is something deeply innate and intuitive within you. It will often seem too simple when you find it, because you will assume everyone knows and understands it. It's about what you have to say. It's about knowing who you are in essence and coming as close to that as possible in your words, your energy, your actions and your being. It's about radiating that out into the world. It is holding fast to the energy of your soul when your ego wants to take over. Purpose is not about what you can achieve, it's about who you are, and how that expresses itself in the world every moment of every day.

Ask Yourself

Could it be you know what your purpose is, but you're too scared to go there because you have let your fears take hold?

Why are you resistant to connecting deeply with your soul? What are your fears around this?

Can you make yourself a promise to meditate and connect with your soul for 28 days straight?

What if your life could be so much simpler and your purpose so much clearer, by just adding a daily meditation?

Can you silence the ego's excuses long enough to get down on that meditation cushion?

If you don't believe in spirit or soul, can you simply create a regular meditation practice to connect with the deepest part of your being?

Can you stop thinking of your purpose as something to achieve, and start thinking of your purpose as who you are?

How does your soul want to serve?

How can I best express my soul in the world today?

Try This

Before you begin your meditation, set the intention to connect deeply to your soul. Sit or lie quietly, become aware of your breath entering and leaving your body, allow the mind to become quiet and sit in that beautiful deep space of stillness. On every inhale breathe light into the body, on every exhale, let go. Ask your soul or higher self to come forth. Begin to feel or sense a deeper presence within your being. Rather than ask questions or demands of your soul, try to connect deeply instead. Feel a sense of presence becoming stronger and more loving. Feel your soul in your heart. Breathe your soul energy into your lungs. Feel the energy become stronger and simply sit with it. Feel the love. Say to yourself, this is who I really am. Listen, tune in, and wait. It is enough to sit in this energy and connect deeply with it, or you may hear, feel or sense wisdom coming through. The more you connect with the soul, the more clearly you will feel its presence, hear its voice and get a deeper sense of who you really are.

Ask spirit or your soul to reveal to you your greatest gifts for service to the world. Don't strain to find answers or the mind will make something up for you; simply sit in the space of peace and wait. Be quite prepared for nothing to happen. Ask questions like who am I, how may I serve, what is my divine role, how may I contribute? You may be lucky and hear, feel or sense an answer. Or there may simply be silence. Do not be disappointed. The request itself in a space of deep meditation and stillness is a powerful message to the universe that you are ready. You may be sure it has been heard. Stay as long as you can, focussing on the breath, and allow yourself to go deeper and deeper still. When the time is right allow the breath to become longer and deeper, gently wiggle your hands and toes and have a nice stretch. Take your time to come back into the waking moment. Finish your meditation with a sense of happiness and gratitude that your answer is on its way. Notice how you are now more conscious of the energy of your soul, and a higher vibration moving through and around you. During your waking hours, keep a good level of self awareness as you move through your day. Don't strain for answers, simply watch, wait and listen.

Once you have set the intention to connect deeply to your soul and find your purpose, look for pathways and synchronicities in your daily life. Keep your awareness soft and open. At the end of each day ask yourself if anything stood out to you. Carry on every day with your meditation and your daily awareness practice. You may even buy yourself a beautiful divine purpose notebook where you record sensations, hints and illuminations, quotes and so on that deepen your relationship to your soul and who you are. As you continue, a pattern will begin to emerge. Relax, explore, be open, invite, commit to a daily practice and your soul and the universe will respond with strength, clarity and joy at your willingness. That is exactly what it is waiting for.

If you like working with angels then Archangel Chamuel is great for clarifying your purpose and Archangel Michael is excellent for courage, clarity, direction and cutting through distractions. Invite these angels to be present in your meditation and help you connect deeply to your soul and look out for signs in your daily life.

Once you think you have found your purpose, before you birth it in the world, test it out in the body. How does it feel? The body doesn't lie. Put one hand on your heart and the other on your belly, and breathe your purpose in. If the body feels light, energized, and excited you're there. If it feels constricted, uncomfortable or hesitant, keep searching. You can use the body to check in with any choices, to ensure they are coming from the soul and not the ego.

Are you complicating things? Your purpose will be very simple in essence, and then it is up to you to extend it, deepen it, nourish it and flesh it out into something beautiful and true.

Spend a day as your soul rather than your personality. Begin with a meditation to connect to your soul, and then take a soft awareness into your day. Look around you from another perspective, soften your gaze and take in your environment from another level.

When you step into your craft, try to be there as your soul as much as possible. This means your wisdom, healing, advice or practice will operate from a whole new level and create incredible shifts in yourself and others.

Manifestation

'Once when we were discussing a world peace project with my teacher Maharishi Mahesh Yogi, somebody asked him "Where is all the money going to come from?" And he replied without hesitation "From wherever it is at the moment".
- Deepak Chopra

This is one of my all time favourite subjects. In the brave new world of social media marketing, we can sometimes forget the most powerful platform in the world to be seen and heard. It's called the universe. The power of manifestation, unbridled potential, pulsing energy and particles just waiting to burst forth and create whatever it is you want. Let's pause for a moment while you really consider that. You have been born into this world at this time for a purpose. The universe specifically sent you forth to fulfil your dharma, and to help others to fulfil theirs. You were given the unique skills, talent, path, and experiences to get you exactly where your heart and soul wants to go. The universe wants you to succeed; it's counting on it. It is oriented in every way for you to blossom.

You are a walking, talking navigation system for fulfilling your purpose. The moves are external, but the guidance is internal, ever present and always true. If you have ever felt misguided by your soul or spirit before, know that this was your mind or ego playing with you, not your heart, soul, spirit, or guides. If you're still not convinced go back to a time where you took a wrong turn and things didn't work out. Did you check in with your body, your heart, your soul? Did you take the time to sit in meditation and connect? Did you *feel* whether it was right or did you just push ahead because the idea sounded good?

Unconsciousness is a choice, and one I've made many times, don't worry about that! But how about making a new commitment to check in with every bright new idea *before* you book the venue? I have seen many brokenhearted practitioners in tears because they felt the universe or spirit didn't love or support them. Whilst the universe is magical, it is also pragmatic. Particles create form with life force energy and spirit, form doesn't create itself. Expecting to fill a retreat without a client base is like expecting form to create itself. However if you get clear on who you are, infuse it with love, send it out to your audience every single day until you create a following, build amazing programs, test it out in a few classes or one day workshops, network, increase your own spiritual practices, research the perfect venue, food and location, leave plenty of time for marketing and so on you will get there. Feel the difference in the love, energy and time going into that? That is life force energy at its best. Manifestation is the combination of a clear vision, a lot of work and keeping the faith. It's about making a soulful plan and following it through with the full force of your being. Then surrendering the rest to spirit...

Ask Yourself

Do you believe in manifestation?
    Can you trust the universe to guide you?
    Do you believe you deserve to receive?
    Are you open to guidance and discernment on what to manifest?
    Can you feel the energy of pure potential in you and around you?

Try This

Trust that the universe will bring your vision alive in the easiest, most joyful way possible if you can just let go, listen and be guided. If you make the effort to sit every day with your vision, the next steps to achieve success will become clearer and clearer. Everything in your life will align itself to your dream and you will start to become aware of signs, experience more synchronicity, and feel a deeper and deeper connection with who you are and where you are going. Make a sacred promise to yourself to follow through on your vision with a clear map to make it happen. Otherwise it's like having a secret plan to success in your back pocket and not bothering to take it out to see the way.

Visualising a goal that doesn't feel alive and joyful in the body creates a clash of intentions, so get really, really clear first on your vision.

No vision is any bigger or better than another. A grassroots practice is just as valid as an international career if it is your true calling. This is about living your spirit from the tips of your toes to the last hair on your head; a vibrant life that pulses through your being, so you are truly living heaven on earth. You are a living spirit. Your body is simply an energetic extension of the world around you, and you can pass through new gateways anytime you wish. You can go anywhere, do anything and be anyone. Ironically in this state there is no rush, and you are happy to experience the glorious world and people around you. As spirit all your connections are joyful. Conscious choice and manifestation is hands down the easiest and most joyful path to wellbeing, happiness and success. Every other activity should be done from the energy of this space. Not from the mind or the ego.

Manifestation Practices for Success

It is absolutely crucial that you check in with the heart, soul and body first to make sure your plan is in line with your purpose and spirit. Otherwise it doesn't matter how much manifestation you do, it won't happen. Or worse, it will happen and be a disaster. Take it from me; twenty minutes in meditation will save you hundreds of dollars, thousands of hours and a whole load of angst.

Check in

Find some quiet time and connect to the breath, the body, the moment. Settle in fully, take your time. Put your left hand on your heart, the right hand on your belly. Breathe into the heart, feel your palm there steadying you. Mentally say 'dear body and spirit, please give me clear indication if my plan is aligned with my soul's journey.' Then sit in silence as long as it takes. Visualise going ahead with your plan and notice how that feels in your body, then come back to neutral for a few breaths, then visualise cancelling your plans, and notice how that feels. If you feel energised, excited, light and expansive, you can move on to the next practices for your vision. If things feel tight, restricted or uncomfortable, you have some soul-searching to do.

Energising Your Intentions

Sit every day in the stillness of meditation. When you are in deep, connect to your dreams, not just visually, but also energetically. Feel the pulse of spirit in your body. It is a vibration that extends beyond the heartbeat to the whole body. Wait until you feel this energy becoming stronger and stronger. See yourself fulfilling your dreams, moving through your day, seeing clients, filling your diary, filling stadiums, selling your book, working overseas, or whatever it is you are called to do. Allow the energy to build. Remember to let it flow freely, releasing all resistance to hold on to it. Let go of form and feel the pulse becoming stronger. That is pure potentiality, the molecules of your dreams. Feels amazing doesn't it? Now ask that you be clearly shown the next step. Don't grasp, just relax and wait for a message or a feeling sensation. If it doesn't come to you in meditation you can rest assured if you move through your day with awareness, it will come to you via synchronicity. Keep your eyes and ears open. I recommend a daily visioning of your biggest picture. If you always keep this to the front of your mind, the next steps on your path will become very clear.

Filling a Workshop or Event

Decide on the number of people that you want to come to your event. Take a piece of paper and write down the event, the date, the venue and the amount of people you want to come. Then on the back of the paper write 'thank you spirit' (or universe or God or angels or whatever feels right to you). Put the paper up on your pin board, in your wallet or wherever you will most often see it. If you like you can hold it in your hands with a crystal, or tuck it in your bra when you are doing your visioning exercise. Keep visioning big, and let it evolve over time. Keep trusting. When I taught my first yoga class in Melbourne I had two people. I'm ashamed to say I felt embarrassed and cross at spirit for not bringing me more; I felt like giving up. Thankfully I didn't listen to my ego, those two beautiful people stayed with me and more people came. Five years later I was teaching nine classes a week with twenty people in each, with school, corporate and council classes on top. Classes filled from having a clear vision, a lot of work and keeping the faith. It might not happen straight away but it will happen if you keep up the work.

Manifestation Altar

A lovely way of manifesting your soul work is to create a small altar dedicated to its fruition. Place some beautiful flowers, candles and manifestation crystals on your altar. Place your intentions upon the altar and say a beautiful prayer over it. Truly connect to the work you want to bring into the world. Know that as you leave your altar the energy of your intentions is already pulsing out into the world.

Vision Board

Create a vision board of your dreams and intentions. This is a very powerful way of setting intentions at the beginning of the year. Gather magazines or brochures related to wellbeing, travel, nature, home, art, photography or anything else you are passionate about. Then sit down with your scissors and cut out any pictures, words or phrases that speak to you. You can get as creative as you like with your vision board, you can add feathers, ribbons or logos of companies you'd like to work with. You can add pictures of relaxation, good food and yoga amongst your work goals to remind you to take care of yourself. I have started using a pin board for my vision board, so at the end of the year I remove the goals I have achieved and paste them in my manifestation book. I don't do this as soon as they happen because when

I look at my vision board seeing goals next to things I have already achieved gives me a sense that all things are possible and that my vision is working. In the New Year I transfer the goals I have achieved, leave the goals I still want to achieve on the pin board and throw away the goals that no longer feel right. A vision board gives you a powerful visual experience of what your goals and dreams will look like. Every day stand in front of your board, breathe it in and give thanks for what you have already achieved, and what you *know* is coming

Manifestation Book

My manifestation book is filled with all the things that have been on my vision board over the last few years that I have achieved. Usually this is about eighty percent of what I wanted. It is a great inspiration if you ever feel overwhelmed or despondent about your journey. By going to your manifestation book, you can see that you have achieved so much of what you wanted, that the universe is behind you and that you are powerfully manifesting your purpose. In this sense it becomes a book of blessings.

Give Thanks

Every day give thanks for what you have achieved, who you are and the blessing of being able to serve in this lifetime. The more grateful you are, the more that comes your way, and the more capable you are of seeing opportunities in front of you. Giving thanks is both recognition for what you have been given, and an acknowledgement of what is to come. Act as if and it will be. Know that somewhere out there you have already achieved all your dreams; you just have to make your way to that point.

Energise a Crystal

Crystals have specific purposes like rose quartz for self-love, clear quartz for clarity, haematite for grounding and so on. I also believe that each crystal has its own unique vibration as well. For instance one particular rose quartz crystal may be for healing the mother wounds in relation to self-love. Another may help you to know yourself to love yourself and so on. This is why it is always important to choose your crystals energetically so they can work with you more specifically. You can find out what a crystal is for specifically by sitting quietly, closing your eyes, holding it in your hands and tuning in. You can also energise a crystal to help you manifest your vision. I would use a master crystal for my highest vision and some other crystal for specific goals along the way. The master crystal sits in my meditation room and if I feel lost I can sit in meditation with this crystal and remember who I am. It holds the energy for me. You can use any crystal for the master vision, so go with your instinct, but I find clear quartz works for me. If you want to work on something specific along the way, like getting more speaking gigs or opening your voice, you might choose a blue crystal like blue lace agate or sodalite.

My purpose is to inspire, empower and motivate millions of spiritual leaders and wellbeing practitioners, so that is the vision I infuse into my master crystal. I hold it and see myself speaking on stage to millions of practitioners, selling millions of books and so on. When I pick it up I am reminded of that energy and feel it moving through me. The idea is the crystal helps to attune you to your highest vision, energise it, hold it for you and clear any blocks on your path.

Ask

Ask the universe for what you want; ask for help, direction, synchronicity, and guidance. Ask people. Start to think of other people as the angels that are here to help you, and imagine every day as you wake up and go out into the world, everyone is ready, willing and able to serve you to fulfil your purpose. For that matter be an angel yourself, and open doors for others wherever possible. Every amazing thing I have ever done is just because I have asked. Apply for opportunities, pick up the phone, email, and connect. Action is the bridge by which manifestation is born into reality. Apply to the very best venues, businesses and people you want to work with or for. No one and nothing is above you or beyond you.

Flower Essences and Essential Oils

I am a big believer that we are surrounded by nature's pantry in terms of healing tools. You can use flower essences to shift your energy or attune you to a new vibration, sage smudge sticks to clear lower vibrations, and essential oils to shift your old perceptions. Manifesting your dreams is about clearing, aligning and increasing the vibration of your energy as much as anything else. Have a look at the Bach Flower, Bush Flower or other vibrational essences. Check out Robbi Zeck's amazing Aromatic Kinesiology work to heal and transform gently and powerfully with essential oils. Shift and cleanse anything in the way of your pure manifestation capabilities.

Destination and Character Goals

Focus on manifesting not just external goals but internal qualities. Internal alignment with outer goals is the true key to success. As you know it is much easier to welcome clients to a meditation workshop when you are clear yourself. It is much more likely that you will be a highly regarded teacher if you work on developing the highest qualities within. The inner always reflects the outer, so be sure and ask yourself who you want to be and focus on manifesting the highest qualities you admire, so they may radiate from you. Remember the closer you can get to who you are in essence, the more you increase your manifestation potential.

Make Bold Goals

Make a bold statement. Tell yourself and the universe what you intend to achieve. Make it big. Go to the highest level of your vision. Want to write for a magazine or online publication? Don't start small; send your work to the best out there. Want to work at retreats? Apply to the best retreats all around the world. There's nothing I like better than a good dare. Applying to the very best people or organisations builds your risk muscles, and you'd be surprised how few people do. Remember it's a numbers game, so keep asking, keep approaching and you'll definitely get a win.

Conscious Co-Creation

'If we ask, we should also be prepared to give.'
- Stephen Richards

Conscious co-creation is the master of all manifestation practices. It is also an incredibly beautiful, easy way to live a deeply enriching life. It is about joining your will with the will of the universe to ensure you are on track and on purpose. Conscious co-creation is about creating a life of intentional change and growth, which is as natural to your spirit as the changing seasons. It is where the living spirit is made manifest in your every waking moment. It is where your life becomes a natural part of the very breath of the universe. You sway with the trees, you rise with the sun, you move with the wind and you flow with the ocean. You no longer let the mind make the decisions for you, nor wait until change knocks upon your door to call you out. You do not wait for the rough tail end of the current, but dive willingly into the body of the ocean that carries your dreams to abundant shores, where they will thrive and prosper. Born of pure nature, your soul willingly aligns itself to the abundant natural flow of the universe.

You can make every day an act of conscious co-creation by waking each morning with a sense of joyful optimism, expectation and willingness. It is like leaping up in the morning to go to your dream job, in your dream life. Conscious co-creation is all about being deeply intentional in your every waking moment. There is no need to do more than what you are asked, as the universe will calculate the exact energy commitment required of each day, so you are kept in a state of physical, mental, emotional and spiritual prosperity. Your direction will become so much clearer to you. You will have energy to burn as all superfluous actions are dropped. You will leave far less emotional and mental debris floating around. You will have time to live, breathe, celebrate and connect.

It can be a difficult concept to believe that spirit can help you create a thriving business, but look at it this way; it is the universe that birthed you and knows you better than anyone else. It is spirit that planted the seeds of your dreams and desires in you. It knows exactly what you want and what you need to fulfil it. It sees the whole of the universe, and what's going on in it, at any given moment. It knows when opportunities are ripe and when foundations need to be set. It knows what people, opportunities and circumstances are true and which ones are false. It knows the best people to help you along and when they'll be in your local café. Spirit knows how to synchronise everything you need and deliver that information perfectly to you as long as you drop in to pick up the guidance. The more often you tune in and fulfil your promise through daily action, the more effectively the universe can act on your behalf. It sets an incredible stage for you to be seen and heard at the deepest level. There is nothing the universe does not have a solution for.

The more you think of it, the more you'll realise you are totally crazy trying to work this out from the mind, or on your own. And the problem is many modern marketing techniques will consistently try to pull you away from your innate soul knowing and the wisdom of the universe. They increase a sense of competition, comparison and separation between yourself and others. These techniques have you believe you better hurry, you'll only succeed if you do this and so on. They are geared towards scarcity, doubt and fear, and worst of all they want you to join in the language and the illusion. You are not just shoved out in the cold and abandoned to your life at the mercy of an unfeeling world. Most of us live our normal human days and tap into spirit when there is a problem, or you need to get clarity on a direction, or are in distress over something. When all the while there is this incredible pool of information sitting at your feet. More than that; there is an incredible pool of love at your feet, and all around you. You are not seen as the poor cousin of a struggling world. You are seen as an abundant child of the infinite. Nothing is above you or beyond you. So step in, take part, and assume your natural loving state in the flow of flawless, glorious co-creation. And watch your life become magical, mysterious and limitless in the true sense of the word.

Ask Yourself

Do you believe the universe is here to love, support and guide you?
   What would you love to co-create today?
   Can you trust the universe to follow through and help you?
   Can you ignore the wants of the ego and listen to the needs of the soul?
   Can you see your life as a partnership with spirit?
   Can you disengage from fear and reconnect with your soul work?

Try This

Each day wake up with a smile; take three deep breaths into your heart, infusing each breath with the energy of joy. Place your feet upon the earth, stretch, wriggle and come alive in your body. Go into your meditation room or space; light candles, put on soft music, and set a beautiful scene. Come into the divine pulse meditation, feeling the presence of spirit in and around you. Ask what it is that spirit requires you to do today. Sit and wait for a feeling sensation, direction or a visual indicator. It may be to speak with more love, it may be to call someone, it may be to create the course you have been putting off, it may be to let go of something or someone, it may be to put your prices up, or book a holiday, or enrol in a new course. Whatever you are asked to do, fully embrace and execute it. Check in with your body first to make sure this is coming from soul or spirit, and not the mind. If you feel tense or uncomfortable, it is a request from the mind. Sit a little longer and see if there is another message. If it feels light, easy and freeing, it is a request from the soul or spirit. The more you practice this the more easily you will be able to feel that difference. Your life's purpose is broken down into small commitments made every single day that you either fulfil or do not. Make it your direct intention to fulfil each daily promise to the best of your ability.

It's never too late to tap into the flow of the universe again.

At midday ask yourself, how is my vibration? Consciously raise your vibration by going back into meditation, taking a few deep breaths of love and joy, feeling your heart expand, tapping into your soul or getting out in nature. Check in with your intention from the morning and ask if you are willingly involving yourself and making progress here. In the evening look back on your day and observe all that happened, large and small. Breathe in three deep breaths of thankfulness for the guidance you received and the courage to follow through. Again feel the invisible hands that guide your course forward in the easiest way possible. Know who walks beside you easing your way. If the guidance you received will take a while to execute, please still make sure you start every day by tapping in so you gain clearer instructions on the details, and so your mind or ego does not hijack the natural evolution.

Put your palm in the palm of the universe and know that what you want is exactly what spirit wants for you too.

Receiving

'You must have a capacity to receive or even omnipotence can't give.'
- C. S. Lewis

You can put all your best work out there, but you need to be open to receive to reap the benefits of your labour physically, mentally, emotionally, spiritually and financially. The ability to receive is very much founded in your primary relationships with your mother and father. When you are asking the universe or spirit for help it is easy to transpose your early experiences of receiving onto what the answer will be. In one sense we see spirit or the universe as a benefactor that either grants or denies our wishes. If your mother and father separated when you were young and were constantly fighting over bills, you may believe whatever you want from the universe will be given grudgingly, or not at all. If there was a free flow of money you may find things come to you easily because you trust in the abundance around you.

Your early experiences may have offered you false ideas about what you were worthy of receiving. In order to rewire these ideas, it is necessary to both examine the past and ask yourself what a limitless and radiant divine mother and father would have done differently. Beyond that you may ask yourself how a limitless, radiant child of the universe might receive. The divine father's role is to protect, guide, offer stability, resources, pathways, opportunity and so on. The divine mother's role is to nourish, nurture, impart wisdom, care, intuitive skills, comfort, creativity and so on. The balance of spirit and business in this book is very much about that balance of the divine feminine and masculine at play. One is nothing without the other, and in many ways they weave through together. Independent but tightly woven, co creative and supportive as all good partnerships should be.

When you allow the mother and father energies to flow through you, when you cease to view them with the masks of your own mother and father, a new relationship with the divine can begin. You can believe that the divine masculine energy is an incredibly strong and loving constant support in your life. You can feel the divine mother present to teach you all she knows, to love and to guide you. This new vision is born from the capacity to forgive both your parents and yourself. You know at the deepest level this is not who your earth parents are either, but to hold on to your old perceptions of them will always taint your vision of the divine mother and father a little too. Forgiveness is key. Come to it in your own time and as best you can.

Even if you see spirit or the universe energetically or as light, this work will still help. Above all remember that you are not separate from this energy. The more you can see yourself as a divine child of the universe, or better still as the light itself, the less separation there will be from who you are and what you want. You are your soul work, your purpose, and your mission. All you need to do is get as close as possible to who you are in essence, to who you are energetically, then commit to being that in human form. Then receiving is not so much asking, waiting and hoping, but simply being.

Ask Yourself

What were the positive and negative qualities of your mother and father? How has this altered your perception about the amount of love, money and support you are able to receive?

What kind of relationship do you wish you had with your mother and your father? Know that this is totally achievable, ready and waiting for you with the divine mother, father or universe today.

How can you remove the false labels or negative human qualities you have attached to spirit?

Try This

Start talking to the divine mother, father, spirit or universe every day. Build a relationship. Speak of your worries, fears and needs. Tell them what you want and what you need. Ask for guidance, support and a deeper relationship.

You will also have an internalised mother and father energy at play in your psyche, so take some time to examine where you may have internalised old habits and patterns of your parents like driving yourself too hard, not allowing yourself adequate time to rest or not supporting yourself. See what negative patterns of behaviour you are reliving and reinforcing here. Then vow to do the opposite. For instance if you are driving yourself too hard, bring in the positive masculine energy of structure to ensure more breaks are scheduled and the feminine energy of nurture to ensure you spend that time nourishing yourself. Continue to internalise and build the masculine and feminine energies and values that will love and support you.

List all the highest qualities that you admire and wish to be present for you. Do you want unconditional love, support and understanding? See the universe or spirit as your own personal support team. Know that they have your back in all aspects of your life, work and relationships. There is nothing they would not do to help you. Really feel that in your body and begin to feel a sense of lightness that comes with knowing you are never alone. Ask the universe to send their best spiritual helpers to love and support you, the highest quality information to guide, support and comfort you.

Meet spirit halfway by dropping that ego and letting in help. Create a ritual to release all old past grievances with your mother, father or spirit. Start to see the world with new eyes. You are no beggar. Living and receiving fully is your divine birthright, and only a heartbeat away.

Open your heart, mind and spirit fully to the belief that you are an abundant child of the universe. This opens the channels for deeper wealth both within you and for those whom you are here to serve.

See yourself as vibrant life force energy that is at one with the energy of the universe, and simply allow the universe to vibrate through you and fulfil all your hopes and dreams. Receive with the heart and soul.

Choose to receive by owning who you are.

Finding Your Voice

'Be a voice, not an echo.'
- Albert Einstein

As a wellbeing practitioner, teacher, healer, or leader, you need to find the courage to speak your unique wisdom, no matter the response. This is often scary, but well worth it. Make no mistake, I often ask myself are people going to understand me, will they get what I am trying to say, know who I really am, like me, celebrate me, and recognise me? Will they know I am genuine and soul driven? But all these questions are from the ego and pale in comparison to the one true question which is; will I speak my truth? For myself and for the millions of people I will help? Or will I stay silent, dance around topics and skirt around the edges, until I'm no good to anyone and no longer recognise who I am, or who I wanted to be? In the telling of your truth, you get closer and closer to who you are in essence. Your words get deeper and clearer. There are people waiting for you and they'll recognise your voice when they hear it, make no mistake about that. Your voice is your power and your truth, never forget that. Be gentle on yourself, but honest to the bone.

In order for people to know you, you have to reveal yourself heart and soul; to uncover your authentic voice and set it free. Now I am not talking about selling your soul, or your private relationship between yourself and spirit. I'm all for having strong healthy boundaries between yourself and your audience, to cultivate respect and independence. What I am talking about is taking your deepest truths as a teacher, leader or healer out into the world; putting the essence of your work into every class, workshop, consultation, blog, inspirational quote, retreat or social media post. We are being asked by the universe to go deeper, to take things further, to expand to our fullest capacity. To release the inauthentic, come out from behind generalities, and to say openly, honestly and courageously this is who I am and what I do. This is my gift and this is where I can take you with it.

I love that there are so many wellbeing practitioners out there now. Firstly because the world needs it, and secondly because it means if you really want to be seen you need to step out from the shadows, and stop hiding in the queue. If you want to stand out, you need to step forward. The universe is asking you to commit to your soul work, to show your hand. It is no longer enough to list the features and benefits of your practice alone. Your work is to take someone deeply into an experience of themselves. It is the difference between holding up a stick and saying 'look at the bumps and edges on this stick', and handing someone a stick and saying 'hold this stick, it has great power.' It is about taking them into a feeling experience, an awakening, an understanding of their own potential.

People cannot touch the power of your work unless you reveal it to them. Think of every contact with your clients as opportunity to do just that. Connect. Tell people what you believe in, what you're driven by, who you are, why you love your work, what you know for sure, where you can take them. Let your words make them *feel*, take them deeply into the heart, make it raw and authentic and powerful. Release the fear of being outcast or ridiculed and be honest. Be brave. Make it sweet, powerful and inspirational rather than full of old story. People are looking for the experience that takes them deep into their soul; searching, yearning and longing for the authentic experience, the deepest work. They are reaching for what is just right for them, and they won't know it until they hear your words, your voice, and your truth. Don't hold back, don't avoid, and don't hesitate. It's time….

Ask Yourself

What is your deepest work all about? What experience are you offering?
  What are you creating, what is your gift, what's really on the menu?
  What do you think this world is craving?

What do you believe in, how do you want people to feel when they come to you?

If you are having trouble finding your voice, ask yourself what is it I am not seeing, saying or doing?

What am I afraid of?

Am I being honest and open about who I am?

Why am I here? Am I holding back on my deepest work?

Am I stifling my true voice?

What would you like to see more of in the world?

Try This

Do a bit of soul-searching; make sure you're on track and on purpose. Challenge yourself to go deeper. There's nothing worse than waking up in ten years and realising you've been investing in the wrong place. What do you want to be known for above all else?

Look back over your social media or website content. Is the feel or energy consistent? Are the wording, the energy of the pictures, the links, and the shares all sending out the same message? Is it you? Where are the inconsistencies, and how do you want to be seen instead?

List all the qualities you want to radiate out into the world.

How will you feel when you find your authentic voice?

Understand that social media has given you an incredible opportunity to exercise your voice. The more you practice the better you'll become at it. Though it may be awkward to find your way, it is hands down a million times better than a load of shares, clichés, advertising and prescribed diatribe.

For one full week once a day, post your deepest stuff on Facebook (no shares, no advertising); just your voice, your help, your knowledge, your advice. Pretend this is the last chance you will ever have to say what you need to.

Imagine you had the opportunity to help a young woman or man express him or herself in the world. What advice would you give them on how to best be heard?

Go back over your blogs, newsletters and social media posts from the last six months. Write down similar themes you keep sending out. Is this what you meant to say or can you take things deeper? What do you cringe at, and what do you love? Is there another message you're holding back on, and how can you coax that into the light?

Be brave and speak up. It's fine for your first attempts to be a bit clunky. Keep trying; go deeper, get to know yourself, and have some in-depth conversations with your soul sisters and brothers.

Think of the energy of the words you are putting out there and the tone you use and ask yourself if it is soulful. How do you want people to *feel* when they hear you?

Being Soul Driven

'Do not let your fire go out, spark by irreplaceable spark. The world you desire can be won. It exists, it is real, it is possible, it is yours.'
- Ayn Rand

There are two ways of getting your spiritual business off the ground. One of them is all about coming from the outside in. That means looking for a target market, creating a customer avatar, seeing gaps in the marketplace, creating a voice to suit your customers and so on. The other way is from the inside out. To allow your career to emerge as a calling from the depths of your soul, utterly aligned with your purpose and intrinsically linked to who you are in essence. As you are born you arrive with a blueprint of your purpose, a built-in navigation system to get you there, and a world that offers every conceivable means of bringing your dream to fruition. When you align yourself with your deepest purpose, the whole universe unravels at your feet. It forms an organic evolution, where everything just clicks. You see the universe as your benefactor, you are paid for what you do best, love most and value intrinsically. Every fibre of your being lives and breathes joy because you are on track and on purpose. The perfect clients come to you because you are clear on who you are, and what you specialise in. You don't have to *look* for a gap in the market because this is a perfectly ordered universe, and you know because it is your purpose, it naturally fills a unique piece of the puzzle and you can't help but succeed. Your tribe is just waiting for you to emerge and become visible.

Think of how careers operate from a wider universal perspective. There is no job any better or worse than the other. Everyone has a perfectly delegated role that offers them the delicious experience of playing to their strengths and being utterly, truly who they are. The trouble starts when the mind or ego gets involved and the wrong jobs go to the wrong people. When we perceive one job as more valued than another. This can happen just as easily in the world of wellness. You might step into the corporate field with the promise of more recognition and pay, when what you really yearn for is to work with seniors. The notion that financial reward or success can only be achieved in certain areas is a total illusion. You will always experience more financial, mental and emotional success where your heart lies. Who's to say the government won't ask you to roll out a national wellbeing program for seniors that turns out to be both lucrative and heart fulfilling? Things come back into sync when you readjust, realign, retune and start to move forward with courage toward your dreams. Don't give your true work up before you start with presumptions, blocks and judgements. Give yourself a chance.

It's nice to be loved in general, but it's vital to be loved for who you really are, at a soul level. It is the fear of rejection of your deepest nature that can block your self-expression. What if you reveal yourself utterly, totally and deeply? What if you stand there naked to the bone and you are laughed at, criticised or judged? From the ego's perspective this is the worst possible outcome. Hard as it is, you need to learn to carry on despite any criticism or judgement from others, because unfortunately it will happen for reasons you really don't need to worry about. But here's the kicker; people will criticise you *no matter what you do*, even if you're supremely successful in the egoic world or you give up your dreams to keep the peace. There will always be something for people to criticise, and you can't abandon your soul to soothe the fears of others. This is what silenced you when you were young and exploring your purpose. What made you contract when you could have sworn the universe was a glorious place, before someone told you otherwise. What made you cautious and wary and willing to sacrifice anything to belong; including stifling your voice, your heart and your soul.

From the soul perspective revealing yourself is the best possible outcome, because then it can really begin the work it is here for. Today more than ever we need to help create a supportive culture where people who speak up and step forward are celebrated. Where courage is applauded and the authentic voice is encouraged. To allow others their dharma even if it makes things awkward or uncomfortable for you or if it is not your way. Spirit wants you to get out there and share what you love. It's counting on it. Forget what you think people want to hear. Start speaking from the heart and soul; from the inside out. Rediscover yourself. Let go of preconceived ideas of what will bring you success and start listening to your true purpose. It's right there waiting in the silence.

Ask Yourself

Where am I holding back from my true purpose?
   What would I really, really, really love to do?
   How can I reconnect to my soul purpose?
   How can I forgive myself for wrong turns and start again?
   How can I face criticism or judgement from others and not shrink back?
   Where can I create or join a community that celebrates courage in me and others?

Try This

If you are struggling to find your soul purpose or reconnect, do something about it today. Go on retreat, meditate, see a kinesiologist, coach, healer or reader.

When you are communicating or thinking of a new course or direction, ask yourself, is this my soul's voice or my ego's voice? Is this really who I want to be?

What programs would you create if you were courageous? Brainstorm some ideas from deep within your heart and soul and refuse to contract when you feel a familiar prick of fear.

Meditate daily to make sure you are connecting from the inside out. Know that all the information and direction you receive here fits a unique piece in the universal plan that you are being asked to fulfil. It can't fail. Be sure to test any information by feeling it in the body to make sure it's not the ego voice stepping in to steer you off course.

How many people would miss out if you decided not to speak up or follow through with your true soul work? Really acknowledge that by listening to the naysayers, and abandoning your dream, you are closing doors on people who need your assistance.

Practice discerning your soul's voice from your ego's voice. When you are facing decisions or choosing your direction, ask yourself what would my soul do here?

See yourself as a courageous leader; someone who steps forward with courage, determination and drive to make this world a better place, someone who lights the way for others. Live it, breathe it, and believe it.

Authenticity and Integrity

'This above all; to thine own self be true. Then must it follow as the night the day, thou canst not then be false to any man.'
- Shakespeare

Integrity is about more than just a moral code or list of ethics, it is about being whole or undivided. When you live from integrity everything you do, say and feel is intrinsically woven with the same energy. The best thing you can do for your soul, your success and your happiness is to ensure that everything you do is grounded in integrity. Follow only those actions, and make only those commitments that are integral to who you are in essence. There is nothing worse than feeling that your work is off centre. Or waking up in twenty years' time and realising that you never tried that one thing you always wanted to do.

Authenticity is about being totally genuine in who you are and what you stand for, right down to the bones of your business. Being truly, wholly, intrinsically authentic comes from deep down in your soul. It is basically the physical manifestation of who you are in essence. People can feel that, they flock to it, and they stay. It can never be copied or manufactured or mimicked. It's real, genuine and authentic or it's not. Your authentic spirit should be reflected in every aspect of your practice; from who you are in your business, to what venues you use, to your communication, to your digital marketing, to your aesthetics, to how your clients feel after visiting you and what they say about you. You are creating a vision and bringing it to life with every brushstroke. It is above all about knowing your self well and promoting that with consistency, consistency, consistency. People trust you when you are in integrity. They know that what they see is what they get. That you will do what you say and say what you do. That you are an expert in your field, and that all your time and energy goes into what you know and love. From this place you radiate your truth from every pore.

Authenticity relies on your willingness to extend and deepen yourself. You can do this in a variety of ways like reading industry articles, magazines, further study, conferences, TED talks, group chats, experimenting with styles and customer feedback. But the most important of all is a regular daily practice where you go deep into your own soul to see what it is you are made of. Trust that above all else. That is your point of difference. It can be hard to stand in your real raw truth without any mask. It takes courage to be totally vulnerable, asking to be celebrated for who you are, in a world that is so addicted to criticism and judgement. When all of us come into authentic alignment, we will create the integrity in the industry we wish to be proud of. Look at your whole business over the last few years and ask yourself how much of it was utterly in alignment, and how much of it was outside the whole, driven by some external need or fear. Being in integrity is about creating a life and business you can be proud of. A life that is whole, real, complete and true to your soul.

Think of it like this; when you look up into the night sky you see a wonderful array of stars scattered across the galaxy, and together they create a glorious vision, each a vital part of the whole picture. Now if a whole load of those stars decided to jump on a few select bandwagons, we'd end up with huge misshapen clusters of stars with big gaps in between. We can't see the beauty of any of those stars individually and are more likely to focus our gaze elsewhere, looking for a clear vision. Make sense? When each star is shining powerfully in its own essence, they create a beautiful whole landscape with joyous intricacies that everyone can admire. And I don't know about you, but I love to lie back and stare at the stars for hours. If you are feeling a little competitive you can think of this analogy too. No one is less than or better than, but everyone is unique. If you try to follow, copy or imitate others, you will never truly be seen. If your clients turn their attention to another star, know that new clients will also be turning their gaze toward you in a beautiful ebb and flow. There is no such thing as grab and hold in the universe. So authenticity is about being prepared to hold your essence, stand alongside others and shine your light proud and strong, no matter what changes around you.

It is the little things that permeate everything you do that infuse your practice with love. These include things your clients can see and the things they can't. The unique authentic spirit of your business is the essence of your point of difference. These little touches never disappear if the going gets tough. Getting really clear on your path is about making a promise to your clients that you intend to fulfil. So what are you offering; the most comprehensive yoga teacher training program available, the most transformative healing experience, the deepest bodywork session, the most compassionate counselling service, the most sensual dance class or something else that is utterly, uniquely you? If you are a multimodality practitioner it is imperative that you choose one promise that covers everything you do or you'll confuse people. Authenticity is about making a commitment. When you make a promise you put your integrity on the line and then a funny thing happens….you stand by your word and elevate your practice. Keep it clear, clean and true. Never, ever be afraid to make a promise that is faithful to your heart. If it is genuine, you are utterly, totally capable of seeing it through.

Ask Yourself

What are the three most authentic businesses you know? What do you love about them? What stands out to you? How do they make you feel? What makes them different to others in their field?

What is authentic about you? What are your best skills and qualities?

Is everything you do in integrity, or an integrated part of your whole vision?

What can you release from your business that is no longer in integrity with who you are?

When you are about to start a new program, product or service do you check if it is in integrity, or a valid part of the whole?

How can you contribute to the integrity of our industry by staying focussed and on purpose?

Can you remove your judgements about others' integrity or alignment and focus solely on your own?

Try This

Visit three different massage therapists, yoga teachers or meditation classes. What are the points of difference in each? What stood out to you the most? What was the tone, mood, instruction and atmosphere like? Would you return? Why or why not?

Experiment; offer a few select friends, family members or colleagues a free treatment session trialling a new technique you are using and see if it works by asking for feedback.

Your most authentic work will feel incredibly uplifting to you, so make a list of all the aspects of your business you love and adore, and all the aspects that tire you or leave you feeling flat. Do you need to remove, tweak or replace some practices or modems that no longer serve your authentic self-expression? Remember pruning makes the tree grow stronger, and flower more beautifully.

How does your business look, smell and feel to your clients? What qualities and unique aspects do you hope they sense here? Brainstorm your unique points of difference; what is distinctive about what you offer, what do you love to share, what quirky or joyous bits and pieces resonate clearly with who you are? What do you stand for?

Name twenty tangible things that people can experience from coming into contact with your business that stay with them long after the session. Eg a warm welcome, a warm goodbye, a cosy room, soft candles, a regular newsletter, a glass of water with lemon and mint, daily wisdom via social media, a birthday bonus, an amazing listener, practices, podcasts or info sheets to take home and so on.

Sit back and examine your business over the last five years, and ask yourself what has been in integrity (part of the sacred whole) and what has not. Then look at any patterns or fears that trigger you stepping out of integrity.

Take a look at your five year vision. Ask yourself if everything you have planned in is line with who you are or if some aspects are out of integrity.

If you're unsure as to whether something belongs in your plan, remember to take it back to the body and check in. Take each piece of the vision, close your eyes and see how it feels in the body. A sense of lightness, openness, ease or relief means you are on track and in alignment, while discomfort and tension signal something is wrong, you may need to throw something out or make small adjustments.

Look at the identity you are sending out there. Is it clear? If not strip everything right back to the essence of your work. Yes, it is scary, but this is where true success begins.

Creativity and Innovation

'When we all think alike, then no one is thinking'
Walter Lippmann

Creative fire or inspiration does not take root in a barren, cleaned-up, shiny template. It is birthed in the wild heart and soul. By breaking out, breaking free, and giving the heart free reign. Authentic creativity is about being bold, courageous, and innovative in your choices. By giving yourself permission to do that thing you've been thinking of for some time now, but were too scared to try for fear you would be judged. Every choice you make should be made from the inside out, not the outside in. Not from what you think might succeed or look good, draw attention or accolades, but from the deepest recesses of your heart and soul. No plans at all should be made without first consulting spirit. You need to release all the distractions from the mental realm to find the sacred tribe you were born to lead. Don't be distracted, save all your energy for your true work.

Marketing is a vital vehicle to get your true work out to your tribe, but it is essential that the work is fully formed before you even *think* about what programs to use to deliver it. Anything that is created purely from the world of form is by its very nature unlikely to last. If you are creating from spirit with the signature of the eternal upon it, your marketing will thrive and grow from the inside out. You will be far more successful than you ever anticipated, and you will love your life every minute of every day. The heart and soul love creativity, they live and breathe it, so there's no such thing as someone who isn't creative. Try tuning in to your spirit for inspiration and you'll find it has a wealth of ideas for you to pursue that are utterly aligned with your soul work. Remember it is better to have fewer programs that are rich and deep, than a mindless variety that gives you little scope or time to be innovative or creative.

Being innovative is about finding your way *through* to a new way of doing things. Rather than saying you can't, ask yourself how you could do things differently. You need to persevere, move past obstacles, and be prepared to take risks and make mistakes. Innovation is about being an industry leader, being prepared to stand up for who you are in essence, and what you believe in from the core of your soul. It requires the curiosity of a child, and a willingness to let go of all presumption, self-criticism and doubt. It's about stretching the boundaries, being open to new possibilities, and blending different permutations and combinations until you find something that is innovative, creative and breathtaking. Then have the determination to complete it, the courage to stand by it and the perseverance to give it an honourable form.

Innovation alone is not enough; you can't simply rely on great creative ideas alone, they must be supported by impeccable business practices, products and services. Let's take Lululemon as a case study. After years of buying masculine or sporty style yoga gear from huge sports stores with little soul or atmosphere, along comes Lululemon. Their women's range is feminine, stylish and comfortable. I can wear them to a community class or a corporate gig with equal confidence. Their materials are high quality and they last. Not only that, but they have great customer service and product knowledge. They write your name on the change room door and introduce themselves to personalise the experience. They also have yoga classes in store, a running club, a great blog and a list of yoga festivals and retreats. Lululemon has built a creative *culture* around what they do that embraces their clients. They have a strong feeling of connection and authenticity that is tied to their brand, and that's something you just don't get at a large sports store trying to cater to everyone.

Creativity has nothing to do with mimicry or conformity. The truth is despite the promises there is absolutely no program out there, no special technique or school or webinar alone that will make you a success. It's up to you and the fire in your heart, soul and spirit. That is where the life-giving power flows from; ceaseless, bountiful, beautiful, innovative and creative. All you need do is tap into it, stand by it with courage and conviction, and follow through on what needs to be done to bring your full blossoming to life.

Ask Yourself

Take a step back and ask yourself if you are comfortable in your heart, body and soul with all the practices you are using even if you think at a mental level that's what you need to do to succeed.

If you were not a teacher or coach, but a mentor or spiritual guide, how would you do things differently?

How can you use modern marketing techniques without getting lost in the crowd or succumbing to less than, inauthentic or unethical practices?

How can you create some innovative, creative programs that are intrinsically linked to your heart and soul?

Can you bring some sweetness and authenticity back into your work?

When was the last time you saw something so innovative it took your breath away?

Try This

Take a full week off all social media (yes, even scheduling posts) and get back to your heart and soul. Strip everything right back, spend some time in meditation and get back to what your core purpose is really all about.

Try some creative exercises to stir your ideas to life. Try drawing, writing, painting, dancing or sculpting. You don't have to be good, the idea is to play and stimulate the creative force without thinking, judging or analysing.

Take a look at your programs, products and services and ask yourself how innovative or creative they are. Name three things you can do to bring more life force or creative energy into the picture to make it an *experience* for your clients

Creativity is often intrinsically tied to the six senses. How can you use sight, sound, scents, touch, taste and intuition in your services to deepen and enrich your clients' experience?

How can you add ritual to your programs, products and services to create an innovative experience?

Make a promise to yourself to use only those platforms, systems and services that support your soul work.

What are the maddest things you could do now to be a bit different in your business? Brainstorm the wackiest things you can think of, let your imagination run riot, get right out there. Then choose a few that you'd love to use, refine, ground and align them.

Create some amazing ideas for gift packs or giveaways at your next conference or retreat. What speaks wholly of who you are?

Use soulful, authentic language to let people know who you are from the depths of your being. Try to stay away from typical sales or scarcity language and tell the truth of who you are.

Be yourself, whether that is quirky, wild or gentle. Never be afraid to bring a bit of sweetness or softness into play. In a loud world a whisper can be incredibly enticing.

Permission and Sovereignty

'All you have been waiting for is your own permission.'
- Pat Rodegast

Let's get one thing straight. You don't need to ask permission from anyone to start your true work, use your most authentic voice or create an incredible new program. Absolutely no one has the right, the power, or the authority to stop your deepest work coming into fruition. This is such a huge issue I see with clients who are worried what their peers, community or former teachers will think of the direction they want to take. Approval is a huge thing for all of us. Fear of outcast is even bigger. No one wants to walk alone on this earth, but to walk with a group through conformity whilst feeling uncomfortable in your own skin is no fun either. The truth is that when you start your most authentic work, you will attract connections that are genuine, reliable and true. The vibrations of those connections are going to help you develop your work even more deeply, and encourage you onwards and upwards.

At some point you need to step out from under any authority and begin to develop sovereignty. Sovereignty is about owning your own power and capabilities. It is about taking your purpose seriously and answering the deepest call within your soul and from the soul of the universe. It is not about being swayed or manipulated by what makes others comfortable, but by following through on what you were born to do. I know many people say they don't know what their true purpose is, but in my experience that is not quite so. They either know and the ego pretends they don't know, or they don't want to know, even though it is perched right on top of their nose. Have you any idea of the energy it takes *not* to see or live your true purpose? Or the years wasted in explaining that you haven't stepped into your purpose because of all the times your voice was suppressed in the past? Even if that stuff is true, is it relevant right now, here today? Instead of confirming your voicelessness with old stories, can you use that energy to ensure your voice is heard from this moment forward? Your authentic voice does take time to develop, but you can start today, so what are you waiting for?

You can blame anyone you like, but if you are not living to the full edges of your being today as an adult, you need to take full responsibility, push through the old stuff and make some changes. Give yourself permission. Free yourself. Look at what is possible right now. Take a few risks and start pushing your boundaries and breaking through your internalised thoughts of what is right, wrong and permissible. The highest mentorship of all comes from your soul or spirit. To rely on the outside influence of others too heavily can lead you off in all manner of directions that betrays your own soul. For every suggestion that is made, or advice that is given, check in with your own body, mind and soul. Ask yourself, does this feel true to me? Will it take me closer to my purpose or further from it? Perhaps it is time for you to lift your game and become a mentor to the younger practitioners coming up behind you. If so, how will you be sure to guide them from a place of truth? How can you encourage them to own their own sovereignty, and are you comfortable to teach them to trust their own soul voice above yours? Are you happy to help them develop their own insights rather than just dispense advice?

It is vital for your sense of love, peace, freedom and joy, that you give yourself permission to be exactly who you are in essence. It is a basic human right, not a privilege for a select few. The more people right now who can become more intrinsically connected to their heart and soul, the greater the gifts to all of us as a community. If you can develop that sense of sovereignty within yourself, you will never feel alone or unguided. Like anything it needs to be tended, felt and developed over time. Start to develop that connection today, give yourself permission to follow through and you will truly unleash your full potential. The whole of the universe is behind you.

Ask Yourself

What scares you about bringing the full power of your work to fruition?

What do you really, really, really want to say?

Who do you worry about losing if you become your true self? Will that really happen or is it just your fear talking?

When will you give yourself permission to be fully who you are?

Can you develop your own voice from within?

Try This

Spend a day writing out the boldest plan for your future that you possibly can. I mean get totally out there, no holds barred. Make it as deep and extensive as you can. Keep going and going and going. Have fun with it. Ask yourself again and again – what else? How can I take this further, higher or deeper? What else, what more, what have I left out? It may even take you a weekend, or hey you might want to hire a cottage for a week, getaway and go totally nuts. Keep going until you are well and truly spent. The trick is to let this get as wild as you can without the restriction of form or function around it. Then sit back and enjoy the vision for at least a day without moving to change it. Sit in front of it and breathe it in. Take note of how you feel; excited, energised or even a bit naughty? Take note of your dreams and see how your vision is allowed to develop with full permission behind it. Part of this process is really honouring the needs of the heart and soul, so observe and enjoy the vision with the respect that space and time brings.

Once you have spent all the time you need absorbing your wildest vision, it is time to draw it into a form or vehicle that honours its essence. Take care here not to squish it back into a box, but create something innovative and exciting that elevates it to express its full radiance.

Go over everything you have written, and pull out the stuff that makes you feel totally amazing, free and engaged. That's your deepest work, and that's just the beginning. Once you give yourself permission, your true work will start flowing out of you like a fountain.

Shining Bright

'Courage starts with showing up and letting ourselves be seen.'
- Brene Brown

There are just three things we really want in life; to be seen, heard and understood. To be known at the deepest level, and to be celebrated and loved because of it. To be recognised as who you are in essence is to claim your divine birthright. There's something about that experience that gives you the confidence to shine even brighter. That raises your joy to a whole new level. Revealing yourself authentically to others sparks something eternal in you, creates a more profound experience for them, and allows you to blossom to new heights and greater depths. It allows your clients to see a new window into what is possible for them as your light sparks their own awakenings. You are a better healer, teacher, leader and guide because of your courage to throw caution to the wind, and stand in the absolute truth of who you are, and what you are here to achieve. Imagine a world where everyone lived from the depths of their soul. How differently would we treat ourselves, each other and the earth that cradles us on our journey? You don't need permission to be wholly, truly who you are. It is no more than a conscious choice, followed closely by courage, determination, love and devotion.

To the ego revealing your true self can be quite terrifying. Fear of being judged, ridiculed or criticised is strong. Yet sadly you will be judged by others throughout your life, no matter how small you try to play it. So why not throw caution to the wind and back your heart and soul? Once upon a time the wellbeing or healing industry was seen as alternative, hippy or kooky, but times have changed. For those of us who have been working arduously in wellbeing for many years, we have seen cosmic shifts in public perception, and we can be proud of the foundations our work has created. But many of us are still caught up in our early years or past lives that have seen us victimised or shamed for being who we are. It is high time to shake yourself out of these old patterns, raise your vision, and really breathe in what is possible today.

There are perfumes called 'intuition', corporate companies are hiring life coaches and equine therapists, schools are running meditation and mindfulness programs, business schools are talking about heart and soul. It is even becoming quite competitive amongst private schools and corporate companies to see who has the most creative personal development programs on the go! And I'm not just talking advertising agencies or traditionally creative companies; I am talking banks, law firms and large accountancy firms. Creativity and mindful leadership is the new black. Language has changed, and if anything, many spiritual leaders are falling behind this new wave of enlightenment, and allowing the commercial companies to pick up the baton and run past us. It is absolutely vital now that you own your power, stand up and assert your place as an authentic spiritual leader. The time for hiding is over. It is time to stand tall, shine bright and let any criticism wash over you without attachment. You learn only by practicing.

When I talk about shining bright, I'm not just talking about simply getting out there as a yoga teacher, naturopath or life coach. It is not about your chosen profession, but the message you intend to deliver through it that counts. There is plenty of opportunity to hide in a sea of practitioners. I am talking about stepping further forward and making a bold statement about who you are, what your soul calling is, and stepping into that fully, wholly and deeply. Even if you're scared, even if you think you may be judged by your peers, even if you think there isn't a market for it. Trust me, there is *always* a market for your soul work. If your business is struggling, don't think you're not succeeding because there are too many yoga teachers, naturopaths or life coaches out there already. Don't imagine you just need to buy the next high-end program that has all the answers. If you are not being seen it is because you are melting into the crowd, and not revealing your true self. I love this about the universe. It is perfect timing. The increase in practitioners means that you now have to step into a higher version of your work to be seen. I'm asking you to get right down to the nitty gritty of who you are and what your soul purpose is, then use the modem you are trained in to deliver that message loud and proud.

So what is it you are really, really here to teach? How can you release the full force of your soul into your work? How can your qualification become the perfect platform for what you really want to tell people? How can you step away from platitudes and diatribe and speak from your heart? How can you resist looking for gaps in the market and be guided by the wealth in your soul? How can you resist being pulled by an imaginary audience and instead create an authentic tribe from your true voice? When will you trust that what you really, really, really want to do is *exactly* what will create your success? Do you really believe spirit is guiding and protecting you or not? Once you get to your authentic work, can you go deeper still? Can you aim to be a trailblazer, so that young practitioners behind you can reach further still? Can you stand by your heart and soul with courage and conviction?

There are people who are going to try and interfere with this process. When you step into the full force of your being, it can rock the status quo for those around you, and challenge their own stuff. But let's get one thing straight; you answer to your soul and the universe, no one else. You need to ask yourself whether you can withstand criticism from a peer, a teacher, your partner or a dear friend, and stand firm. Because I'm sorry to say, but it will often be the people whose approval you want or need the most that will challenge you. Rather than shrink from this, try sitting down with the person and saying 'This is really important to me, it makes me feel happy and fulfilled and I would feel lost without it. I know it's hard for you to understand, but please have faith and trust in me, and if you can, help me and encourage me, it would mean so much to me. If you can't do that much, then please don't criticise. This is what I feel called to do.' Use your words, but make them really raw and honest so the person can see you are serious. Ask them how you could better support who they are too while you're at it.

Make sure your spiritual plans are grounded, make a plan and then work your butt off to fulfil your purpose, and show anyone watching that following your heart does lead to success. Not for your ego, but for what inspiration it might offer. Despite any external opposition, the truth is *you* are going to be the biggest influence on whether you achieve the depths of your work or not. Criticism from the outside is just a reflection of the self-doubt, fear or anxiety within yourself; so its time to feel the fear and do it anyway. Talk to yourself, have some kinesiology, keep up with your energetic practices for success, pray, and release all excuses and resistance.

Do whatever you need to do to follow through on your authentic work. Resist stepping back into the crowd with all your might. Don't dip your toe in once, say it didn't work and run away. Dedicate your life to your *true* work. Tell people who you are and what you do over and over again, in a thousand different ways on a thousand different days, and then some. These will be the leaders of the future. Let us as an industry provide a glorious symphony of beauty. Let us not hide one behind the other, but spread far and wide so our diversity and unity may be seen as a glorious expression of infinite possibilities.

Ask Yourself

Are you playing small so you won't be criticised?

Can you turn up the light on your work?

What fears arise when you imagine yourself shining tall and bright?

How can you honour the traditions of your training, whilst honouring the needs of your soul?

Can you ditch any old diatribe and start speaking from a soul space?

How can you better encourage fellow practitioners and let them know you see them?

How can you communicate who you are to others in language that is deep, clear and true?

Can you show courage and commitment to your path and keep going, no matter what?

Try This

Look back over your life from a bird's eye view, and see the major themes that have stood out for you. What do you think is absolutely crucial for people to know or experience in this life? What are the major gifts you have to offer?

List all the initial reasons you wanted to get into your training. What were the greatest gifts it bought you? Look back on old diaries or your life around that time. What shifted the most for you? What did you embody that you would love to bring to others?

How can you make your marketing a more true and authentic reflection of your deepest work?

Try working out the truth from the opposite angle. For instance if you are a massage therapist, what do you feel is missing from many massage therapists you have seen? List as many things as you can, and then list all the ways you could bring the opposite experience. Look through the positive changes you would like to bring and see if you see a theme in there.

Practice your language/copy skills by playing around with phrases and words that describe who you are and what you do in essence. Write as many phrases as you can, then look for common themes, and practice turning them into marketable sentences to sell what you do from a heart-centered space.

Every time you criticise another practitioner mentally or out loud, write it down. Ask yourself why you are doing this; are you feeling threatened, jealous, or competitive? What has triggered this criticism? Dig deep for an answer and you'll find a healing for yourself in it. Understand criticism is always an indicator something needs attention in yourself.

Perfection and Excellence

'Excellence is caring more than others think is wise, risking more than others think is safe, dreaming more than others think is practical and expecting more than others think is possible'
- Ronnie Oldham

To be a teacher or practitioner you don't have to be perfect. Perfection is an illusion that doesn't exist. Let that go straight away. You'll have your blissful days when you fully embody your teaching and wisdom, and your human days where the ego takes over and you stuff up. Welcome to the human experience. You are going to make mistakes with your business, marketing, clients, decisions and plans. Just do your very best and try not to beat yourself up when things go awry. Some people won't even try because they think they won't be good enough. If you are willing to give it a red hot go with the best of intentions that should be good enough for anyone, including your inner critic. It is okay to make mistakes as long as you learn from them. By the same token, don't berate yourself over every minor detail you missed in class or session, because over time that is going to wear you down, erode your confidence and stop you from delivering your deepest work.

Instead of striving for perfection, can you aim for excellence? Excellence is about providing the highest quality space, and the best quality products, programs or services that you can deliver in this moment. It is about stretching yourself from okay to even better. Look at every aspect of your business right now from your customer service to social media to value for money. Are you doing the very best you can, or can you raise the standard of your work three levels today, right now? Can you do less with excellence, as opposed to a lot averagely? The less you are juggling, the more time you have to take things to an incredibly professional and innovative space. The more you are juggling, the more you will be cutting corners and providing an average experience for your clients. Commit to your soul work and follow it through to an excellent standard.

In five years' time you are going to look back and cringe and say I can't believe I did that back then. That's totally fine, your work should always grow with you. As long as you make a start and do your very best you will become a master at what you do, and part of that apprenticeship is making mistakes you will learn from. No one escapes this, so don't think for a moment that those shiny people on social media who seem to do it all easily didn't make some serious blunders in their time. I know I have. Anyone out there who is incredibly successful could tell you some mistakes they made that would make your toes curl. If you don't make a start at all because you're holding out for perfection, you'll never reach your full potential. Be kind, be confident and encourage yourself along the way. Refuse to be sidetracked by a quest for perfection. Do your very best, commit to your growth, and rest well knowing that is by far enough by anyone's standards.

Ask Yourself

Can you go looking for your light, not your faults?

How can you be the very best version of yourself right here and now? Not the most perfect, just the very best.

What does excellence look like to you right now?

Can you stop comparing yourself to others?

What mistakes have you made recently and what have you learned from them?

How have your errors changed the way you run your business?

Can you begin without needing to be perfect?

What mistakes do you need to forgive yourself for?

Is your quest for perfection sabotaging your soul work?

Can you have a sense of humour about your blunders and stop taking it all so seriously?

Try This

Take each program, product or service and ask yourself how could I take this up three levels right now? This is not about complicating things; it is about the quality of the work, and whether you can take it deeper or higher.

Resist the tendency to want to give up when you make a mistake, or if things are not working out. Ask yourself how you can work your way through this error, and ask for help if you need it. Don't say I can't, say how can I? There is always a way through if you look hard enough. What are you not seeing or acknowledging? Who could you ask for help?

What does excellence mean to you? List all the qualities that you think create excellence in a business. Then ask yourself if these qualities are present in all aspects of your business, and make any changes necessary.

Excellence is achieved one step at a time, so resist the temptation to go at everything like a madman or woman. Walk on with determination, thoroughness and dedication.

Excellence is what makes you stand out from the crowd. It is not all about having the most schmick website in town. It is often the little things like excellent customer service, a few little bonuses full of wealth and depth, kindness, or the ability to listen well.

Leadership

'No man is great enough or wise enough for any of us to surrender our destiny to. The only way in which anyone can lead us is to restore to us the belief in our own guidance.'
- Henry Miller

Leadership is a huge responsibility that should not be taken lightly. It requires knowledge, maturity, consciousness and a great sense of humour. As a leader you need to rely not only on the knowledge you have learned from education and mentors, but the integration and development of your own life experiences and personal development practices. You must also be able to let go of the ego, and open to the divine knowledge of the universe. That way when clients ask you a question you can answer from the deepest place of integrity and intuition. I'm not talking psychic skills here (not that there's anything wrong with that), I'm talking universal wisdom. Learned knowledge will only get you so far, but if you tap into infinite knowledge, all wisdom is at your disposal.

Leadership is not just about personal power. It is about the ability to guide, lead and inspire others. It is about empowering people to remember their divinity. I firmly believe that as leaders we should grab the hand of those who are struggling and hoist them up onto the dance floor. It is my great wish that all of my students should surpass me in knowledge and wisdom. If we all keep moving higher in our aspirations, then imagine what we can do. It is never my desire to keep people underneath me, or hold them back. That would be my greatest shame. Leadership is not about persuading others to your point of view. It is about helping them find their own truth, whether it is aligned with yours or not. It is as much about letting them go, as it is about creating a space for them to come and learn. It is about service, not rescue. It is about creating other leaders, not disciples or followers.

Leadership is not a mask you put on, it is something you earn. Being a spiritual leader is no different to holding a place of responsibility in any other field. You need to be passionate, authentic, have great communication skills, create a positive vibe around yourself, and have confidence in what you are doing. You need to inspire others to action, be creative and whole hearted. It is above all else about being accountable. You don't need to be perfect to be a leader (sorry, that's not going to happen), but you do need to apply yourself to your craft, treat your material and your clients with the greatest respect and live your principles. A committed daily spiritual practice is absolutely essential, so you are as close to your own soul or higher self as possible. This ensures your instructions are coming from the soul, not the ego.

There will be times when you need to stand up for yourself and draw boundaries around your leadership if people are testing you. There are certainly times you will need to switch off, and allow yourself to be led or healed by other practitioners. Still more times when you need to remind yourself you are above all a man or a woman, and a soul simply doing your best. The very best leaders know how to be playful too, to get out in nature and run wild along the beach with the wind in their hair. Do the best you can for others, and then leave it up to them to complete their work. Your task is simply to ignite, facilitate, rouse and inspire. Don't take it to heart if those around you won't move forward. Always direct your energy to those who are ready, willing and able, lest they should miss out on your wealth of knowledge while you're busy trying to move a bunch of donkeys who won't budge. This is not about excluding anyone, you are simply opening your work to those who are committed, and others are free to step up into that space any time they are ready. With love, passion and devotion, simply do your best, and at the end of the day feel satisfied, take deep rest, let it all go and rest in the arms of those who love you.

Ask Yourself

What kind of leader do you want to be?
    What qualities do you want to embody?
    What do you want people to say about you?
    What do you admire in other leaders?
    What areas of your leadership do you need to work on?
    What are you most proud of in terms of your leadership skills?
    What are you really great at?

Try This

Write down the three best leaders you have known and what it is you admire most about them. How could you embody the qualities you admire whilst remaining inimitably yourself?

Write down the three worst leaders you have known and why they lost your respect. What lessons could you learn from them?

Never put another teacher, guide, healer, leader or reader up onto a pedestal. Nor let others do the same for you. It can be a bumpy drop from the top for everyone.

Teach your clients and students with humility. Always encourage self-sovereignty and self-empowerment. You don't need to create disciples to build a community. The new spiritual leadership of the future is all about powerful leaders coming together to bring light to the world.

Success

'If your definition of success has little or no measure of love in it,
it's time to get a new definition'
- Robert Holden

Let's face it, success is a pretty loaded word. We all want to be successful. To be seen, valued, recognised and heard. Soulful success is about learning who you really are, being totally, intensely at peace with that, and with buckets of courage, showing it freely in the world. However, sometimes the soul's version of success bumps up against the ego's ideas of external success and things start to go a bit haywire. Or on the other side perhaps you bump up against the judgement from your spiritual peers, where it may be seen as disingenuous to be successful, make money or stand tall. Actually you need not concern yourself with others' ideas and fears around your success. We are all doing our best, but understand that if others have a problem with what you do or how you do it, and you know you are acting in integrity with your soul, you must carry on regardless. Otherwise you are allowing the negative mindsets, blocks or egos of others to dictate to you. Take your guidance purely from your soul, spirit and guides.

If it is necessary for you to launch a huge marketing campaign, or speak to wide audiences in order to fulfil your dharma, you just go right ahead and do it. If it is essential to charge high-end prices in order to fulfil your promise, then do that too. Likewise if it is your purpose to work with refugees or create a not for profit organisation, go right ahead. True success is what is has always been; the capacity to express yourself fully from your heart and soul, to feel free to act in accordance to your purpose and to be answerable only to a higher force. Never forget it is also about being successful as a human as well;

showing kindness and love to others, the ability to find success in the moment, and breathing in the small delights that make up your world along the way. Success in relationships is vital for your comfort and support too. If you are successful in your career, but have neglected your friends and family along the way, really try to make an effort to get things on track there too. None of us was born to struggle alone.

Bring your awareness to how successful you *feel* as well, because awareness is full of the power and potential to make changes where necessary. Whether you feel authentically successful or not will also drastically affect your happiness deep down in your soul. To measure your success is a very personal thing; it can never be judged accurately by the external world, or measured up against others. It is about how you feel about your life, who you are and what you have achieved. Act on what makes you happy, cease to act on the things that do not; it is really that simple. Then your actions for success are simply an extension of who you are in essence, and who you want to be. The inner always reflects the outer. The beauty of the creative universe means that you can always choose again if you feel you have wandered off track.

To measure your success you need to know what you are aiming for, and how close you are to achieving that goal. You will always follow your gaze, so be sure that what you are looking at is what you really, really, really want. Think of your fundamental intention. What is your end goal? Is it to have fifty thousand likes on Facebook or is to change lives through your inspirational songs? Is it to run a six figure business or is it to create a program for empowering millions of young women? One part of the statement is driven by ego and one part is driven by spirit. Does this mean that if you follow your soul work you won't build fifty thousand likes or a six figure business? On the contrary you can do all that and more with your soul work at your centre. A focus on your soul work will ensure you concentrate on the content and quality of your programs and services, which in turn will give you a stronger brand, voice, following and income to fulfil your purpose. And to top it all off you will have the infinite energy and power of the universe behind you.

The integrity, depth and substance of your soul work are the most important factors in creating authentic success. It will magnetise your tribe towards you, fill your heart and soul with joy, and bring you physical, mental, emotional, spiritual and financial fulfilment. Full, hearty, soulful success can occur in a small grassroots community movement or a home-based business as completely as it can on an international stage. Never let your ego tell you otherwise. No dharma is greater or less than another. Success is about knowing who you really truly are, and having the courage to live and breathe only that. To stand tall and support yourself and your purpose at all times and under all circumstances. Is it easy? Not always, but that's usually when the ego is sticking its oar in. I can tell you it is supremely joyful for the most part. Success is about taking action, following through and fulfilling your promises. It is about being a living breathing spirit in motion. It is about being able to celebrate your small and large achievements because you did the work. It means lying in bed at the end of your day, or the end of your life if it comes to that, and being proud of who you are and what you achieved.

Ask Yourself

What character traits are essential for success and how could you cultivate these in yourself?
How do you see success?
Where can you be of most authentic service?
Do you *feel* successful, and what would make that shift for you right now?
Are you measuring your success by external means or internal feelings?
What areas are you most successful in?
Are you celebrating your wins and what you have achieved so far?
Who do you see as successful and why?
What choices and actions are hindering or helping your sense of success?

Try This

Stop thinking about how you want to look and start thinking about how you want to *feel* in your business; fulfilled, powerful, confident, nurtured, admired, respected, treasured, acknowledged, genuine, wise and so on. Then when you are making choices ask yourself does this choice make me feel this way, and make your decisions accordingly.

Try to detach from external ideas around success or comparing yourself to others. That is purely the urge of the ego.

Measure your success by how close you are to your soul work and adjust your direction accordingly.

It may be interesting to examine how you feel about running your own business; is there any family history or old ideas you have about success or failure in this domain? Squish some of those old stories around success, clear the blocks and pave your own way.

Refuse to buy into others' fears and ideas about what success should and shouldn't be, especially in the spiritual realm. Be really honest with yourself about what your purpose is, find a soulful community who supports you, and go ahead all guns blazing.

Choose ten main signs that would indicate success to you. Try to make them as soulful as you can. Get back to what it's all about for you.

Remember soulful does not mean you are giving up financial success; on the contrary it is the key to a thriving, radiant, sustainable business.

Money

'It's not about the money, money, money,
We don't need your money, money, money,
We just wanna make the world dance
Forget about the price tag.'
- Jessie J

Okay – here we go……..Actually you do need their money, money, money, and I'm pretty sure Jessie J has a lot of it. She didn't give the cash back and has a bit more than keys and guitars. And why shouldn't she? Didn't she work hard for her dreams? Doesn't she need that money to take her art out into the world, be generous to others, and live out her dharma? Actually the moral of the song is about the art of music being destroyed by money to the point where the essence, the fun, the integrity has been lost. She's putting a call out there; a bold courageous voice in the industry. Good for her. And in celebration of her courage, her artistry, her power, her commitment, I would gladly buy her songs, attend her concerts and go a bit wild on the dance floor in celebration of her message. Snoop Doggy Dog, not so much.

People invest in what they believe in – physically, mentally, emotionally, spiritually AND financially. Another coach once said to me that people will find the money if they really want it. It's true. I would rather buy an expensive pair of pants that were perfect than six pairs that were cheap and crappy. As the saying goes, if you buy cheap you pay twice. Boy have I learnt that one on my journey! You get what you pay for in more ways than one. Cheap clothing means someone out there is suffering; the environment from landfill, water loss, chemicals, overproduction, and workers in dangerous and exploitative conditions, and you as your bum hangs out of those pants!

Did you stop to think that by making your courses, classes, products or services too cheap, that people may actually believe it's not a valuable service? I have had a great many lessons in this. I know you want to be affordable for everyone. I went to primary school in a fairly poor area and was then catapulted against my will to a private girl's school in one of the richest suburbs in Melbourne. The yawning gap between those two worlds on the daily two-hour commute couldn't have been more obvious. So I hate the idea that some people have 'everything', and others have close to nothing. I hate the idea that I may exclude someone from my help because they can't afford it. But here is a tiny portion of the Greek tragedy that happened to me in the early days when I offered people a discount or made things too cheap. One yoga student asked if she could pay for the term in instalments and I said sure, presuming she was struggling. She made less than the bare minimum payment, and then announced she was off on holiday for a fortnight. I offered a client crying poor a free treatment which she raved about, and then went on to happily pay two other practitioners I knew for treatments. Another client told me grudgingly she could pay me the term fee if I was starving. These anecdotes are but a drop in the ocean of what I thought was generosity, integrity and fairness.

I had sucker written all over me, and I knew who picked up the pen. You teach people how to treat you. You teach them how to value your service – or not! My poverty consciousness led me to financial stress and credit card debt. My students were feeling calm and replenished, but I was leaking blood from all sides. I was surrogating for the perceived poverty of others and a rescue mentality, and I paid the price for those presumptions. I had to go back into retail work full time to pay off my debt, and keep building my business before and after hours, and on the weekends. I was bloody grateful for that job too, so I worked hard and took the sales up fifty thousand dollars from the previous manager in the first year. I was clever, great with people, creative and innovative. It restored my confidence. I was good at business, so why not my own? And then it hit me….I felt bad about taking money for something I loved, something which came naturally to me, that was spiritual, that helped people, which was a gift, which felt like it should be free. If it's this easy, if it feels so good, if it's everyone's birthright, if it doesn't seem like work at all, then isn't it wrong to take money for it?

I had made a basic mistake. I felt like I was selling spirituality to those who could afford it, and robbing those who couldn't of it. The idea terrified and horrified me. It was like I was potentially robbing someone of their divine right. Then I got over myself. I don't hold anyone's spirituality in the palm of my hand to give or snatch back willy nilly, nor do I want to. Each person has their own unique path to the sacred and the choice of where to find that. The truest connection is that very intimate and sacred relationship between the individual and spirit, where neither you, nor I, nor anyone else has any place to interfere or be. My prices will never, ever stop a soul from coming to meet their spirit. They can do that on their own in a million different ways, everyday. Spirituality isn't up for sale, but my skill set is. The hard work, the well-won lessons, the education, the experience, the blood, sweat and tears, my resilience, my soul work, my great big heart and my passion is worth something. More than something; it is immensely valuable. How could I create the best possible programs for you without any financial backing? How could I offer scholarships when my business can't afford them? How could I build my fabulous, unique conferences without a wealth of funds behind me? How could I get you the best speakers, resources and information? I couldn't, so I changed the way I perceived my value and worth, and abundance followed.

It's time to get professional, and change your prejudices about what financial success and having money means as a spiritual practitioner. The universe wants you, me and everyone else to be abundant. I know this because when I wasn't, I suffered physically, mentally, emotionally, spiritually and financially. I was wrung dry and I had nothing left to give. I was running on empty. When I decided to value myself and my god-given talents, everything changed and I had much more value to give to others. Turn your social conscience into a positive, not an excuse to hold you back. Nowadays I value my wisdom, my education, my boundaries, my experience and my deservedness – wholly, utterly and truly. And I balance that with free information available on my blog and social media, affordable books with a wealth of information, and I make random acts of generosity on my own terms. From a place of abundance I can give more and more. And guess what? I don't feel tired – I'm full of beans. My central nervous system is relaxed. I'm happy. I have no interest in confirming a poverty consciousness in others because I used to have a big one, and it started to heal the day someone said 'no you can't pay for that in instalments, you'll have to save up if you really want it'. And guess what? I did. I felt proud and capable and abundant. Not left out, not poor.

There is a long history of spiritual education, solace and refuge being free. It's still out there. But the priests, Buddhists, retreat centres, yogis and so on have wealthy benefactors who allow their wonderful work to continue. Your clients are your benefactors. They provide you with money so you can eat, sleep, train, rest, grow, build and keep doing your unique work. Yes, even so you can holiday and buy yourself something special. They are giving you thanks with funny old pieces of paper that say I see value in what you do, and I want your work to grow and blossom so that you, myself and others may prosper. So take that with a full heart and a clear conscience, and open up to receive more so you can empower your path. Honour money as a sacred gift by expanding beyond your wildest dreams, so your light may bring joy, healing, love and peace to others.

Ask Yourself

Are you valuing and honouring your work sufficiently?

Are you basing your prices on what you think someone will pay or are you basing them on the value of your work?

Are you using money as an excuse to self-sabotage?

Can you reconcile earning money with being a spiritual leader?

Try This

There will be people who will challenge you on this, so get a sentence ready. It may be your clients, colleagues, friends or family. So what will you say when someone says to you 'I hate the way spirituality has been commercialised' or 'Aren't you supposed to give that away for free?' or 'I would love the opportunity to learn with you but I just can't afford it.' Don't skirt this question. Come up with a truth that doesn't sound like a justification, a defence, or an accusation. A deep down in your bones reason why what you do is worth it.

Sit down and count up all the hours you have spent training, doing homework, reading and researching your craft. Count up all the hours of teaching or practice you have behind you. Count up all the money in expenses you have spent building your business. Count up all the money you have spent on education. Count up all the years of study, meditation and self-development you have done. Take note of the impeccable wisdom you have developed. Are you telling me all that time, energy, money and dedication are not worth something in return?

There is no need to follow what other practitioners are doing. Always go with what feels right in your bones. There is more on this in the business section on pricing.

Explore your money stuff. Go and see a good kinesiologist and sort out what is holding back your abundance, and ask to be aligned with abundance and success. Then action some steps to create abundance.

Be open to being rewarded for your work. It's not about greed, it's about feeling nurtured, recognised, seen, nourished and valued. It's about having enough money to be able to do the things in life you would love to do like travel, learn a language, have time for friends and family, and enjoy further education.

Remember how much money you have is not an indicator of your corruptibility or integrity.

Time and Patience

'Those who are certain of the outcome can afford to wait,
and wait without anxiety'
- A Course in Miracles

Some days I feel panicked 'by time' as I think many of us do. I am neglecting some aspects of my social media by spending more time writing this book because I want to have it out by March this year. Why? Honestly for no other reason than that was the time I chose. It won't matter if it's September or even next year (trying not to cringe here). I could say that spirit has urged me that it should be out by the end of this year, but is that really true or an illusion I have created to justify my choices? Really all spirit wants is for us to grow and keep moving forward, but equally to rest and be; to absorb the beautiful world and people around us. Perhaps it is the many years in my teens and twenties I spent immobilised by depression that urge me on so constantly now, as if I can make up for lost time. It is true I am passionate and driven to get as much of my knowledge out there as I can to help you. This is my purpose and I feel it so clearly. But there was nothing in the contract about putting myself under duress to do so. I am smart enough to know that if I slow down, I get more done. The clarity and quality of information is better. I am less likely to have to go over and edit it. I think we cultivate a need to get stuff done so we can list achievements off to ourselves or others to prove our worth. Wouldn't it be a better aim to cultivate character traits or spiritual connection than achievements? To take the time to be a better practitioner, a more accomplished artist, a more compassionate teacher. If you have your head down, buried in the list of things you have to do or would like to achieve, you may lose sight of the bigger picture and your original intent. Take a moment right now. In fact take ten minutes. Close your eyes, sit still, breathe and do absolutely nothing. Choose to create time and space. You're not too busy; you have all the time in the world.

In many ways we are scared of time. Not so much of it running out, although that's what we tell ourselves, but being in it doing nothing. What would that even mean? I once read a quote that said 'there are only two things we know for sure. We want to be happy, and we're going to die.' Time is associated with death, and maybe that's why we don't like to pause and stand back and see what we're doing with it, but time is also very much pulsing with life. When you do die, you won't be thinking I wish I had more Facebook likes or clients or worked harder. You'll be wishing you had spent more time with your husband, kids, friends or mum. Or that you had more laughs or walks on the beach or long leisurely lunches in the sun. Or that you had done your true work and not filled your time with meaningless side projects and distractions. Or that you lived your wellbeing advice. In the end all that matters is love and how much of it you were able to drink in. So yes, this book is about achieving things and getting things done, but only at a pace that feels right to your soul. That still allows you to feel the deep and wide expanse of time. It is not my wish to hurry you or push you on incessantly, but to provide the tools that save time and open space while you live your dreams. Come to it as and when you can. On the other side of the coin, know when it is time to stop procrastinating and step in with full power. That is utterly your choice. Am I an action woman? Absolutely, too much so sometimes, but there is nothing I love more than stillness, silence, space and time. It helps me breathe and do my work at a much more profound level.

You can't control time but you can certainly control your use of it. Ever heard of the 80/20 principle popularised by Richard Koch? It states that eighty percent of your results come from twenty percent of your effort. If you run a retail store eighty percent of your income will probably come from twenty percent of your customers. The 80/20 principle works through other aspects of your life as well; you probably only regularly call twenty percent of your contact numbers or see twenty percent of all of your friends, or get social media engagement from twenty percent of your followers. Ever heard the saying it's better to have two hundred loves than a thousand likes? That's the 80/20 principle at work. If a thousand people love you but they are not sharing or liking your stuff or booking into workshops, your beautiful information is being wasted. That's a lot of your time, heart, passion and energy being expended for minimal results. If you have two hundred people who love you, book into your workshops, and help share your purpose to heal others, you're getting great results. It doesn't mean you put in less effort, but that your effort is being rewarded with much less strain on your time.

So the idea is what if you did less to get more; more happiness, more time, more pleasure, more space and more money. What if you focussed all your passion, time and energy in that lucrative twenty percent, doing the things you loved and reaping better results? Instead of teaching twenty classes and getting five students in each, what if you taught four classes and with twenty-five students in each? Instead of running ten workshops a year and getting twenty people in each, what if you ran five workshops and got forty people in each? Less venue hire costs, less marketing, less prep time, more time to spend with friends and family. Actually people are more likely to commit to a workshop if they know it's not available all the time, otherwise the tendency can be 'oh I can do that anytime.' Rare jewels can attract more sparkle.

We presume technology is asking us to speed up, but it is also offering us opportunities to slow down and implement the 80/20 way. Try only engaging on the social media platforms that work for you personally, your niche and your business. Instead of being involved in ten Facebook groups that don't offer much value, how about five carefully chosen groups that do? Create boundaries around your online time so you can stay connected in the real world. Spend a decent amount of your time networking and building relationships in the real world so you don't lose the art of conversation. Resist the urge to be all over everything all the time, and instead be wholly immersed in what matters. Really matters. What's so hard about letting go? If you were going to live forever you could just waft around doing whatever. Time asks us to choose. In many ways it's about not being really greedy and wanting to grab everything. Don't let competition or fear rile you up so much that you feel you have to run to catch up, or you have to do everything perfectly or you have to stay ahead or keep up with others. The same thing goes for your niche. Instead of trying to be everything to everyone, leave some stuff for someone else for God's sake. It's not your role to teach everyone, sorry, but it's not. You may want to reach large numbers, sure, but not everyone.

Get friendly with time. Play around until you find that balance between not enough and too much. Try to resist the urge to fill created space with other stuff. Be a good example to others. Spend time with your family, friends and colleagues. Go on retreat, out for a walk, to a movie, or a girls' lunch. Busyness is overrated. I certainly don't want a wellbeing practitioner who's timeworn or out of balance setting to work on my body, mind and soul. You have plenty of time. You are bathed in it. So take a breath, sit back and make a connection. Ask time what gifts it has in store for you and how you can create the space to receive them. Work as hard as you can to fulfil your purpose, and balance that with time and space. If you *know* all is coming, then you must also know it will come in perfect time; you can afford to wait.

Ask Yourself

Where do you put yourself under time pressure?

How can you open up more time for yourself?

What are you hoping time will make of you?

Are you committed to culling what's not working so you can have time for what is?

Can you resist your ego and choose to delete irrelevant activities that are chewing up your precious time and space meant for your soul work, rest or relationships?

Do you believe you can do more potent work in less time?

Try This

You can create time by intentionally slowing down. The easiest way to do this is by awareness. Look at your hands, listen to your breath, notice the tops of the trees swaying in the breeze or feel the stillness in the air. Every day practice this to keep you 'in time' rather than overwhelmed by the idea of it.

Meditate every day without fail; twice if you can, even if it's only for a few minutes. Then slowly come back into your day, hold your meditation energy as long as you can and take a few quiet breaths. Meditation will always create more time for you.

Find a balance you can live with between doing too little and doing too much.

Understand that your purpose lies inside your body, not out of it, so the more time you take for stillness the more connected you are to your path, the closer you are to your dream.

Name five ways you could create more time today. Notice what fears arise in your body, mind and emotions when you try to cut back to grow.

Explore the concept of dancing with time. How together you and time can create the perfect journey for the expression of your craft.

If you feel you've been applying yourself for a long time and nothing is happening, don't lose heart. Ask yourself what the block is to receiving. Rather than just try to work harder and faster, ask yourself what you need to change to succeed.

Self-Sabotage

'Unless we learn to know ourselves, we run the danger of destroying ourselves.'
- Ja A. Jahannes

Okay, so you have a spirit and an ego, or the soul and the shadow. However you like to describe it, sooner or later you are going to try to sabotage your success (unless you're already enlightened, in which case well done and carry on). Each of us has three to four repeating patterns that run through our lives, and amongst those there is usually a real cracker that loves to keep popping up. You need to be absolutely, totally clear on when you are sabotaging your own path. Just how often or how destructively you sabotage yourself is totally up to you, and the strength of your spiritual practices. If you have really great self-awareness, and know your triggers and patterns, you should be able to avoid, diffuse or solve any problems fairly quickly. If you are in denial, unprepared to examine your own shortcomings or always ready to blame others, you could be in for a laborious ride.

Any self-awareness work to clear sabotages is best done with a sense of humour and clear intention. Like ripping off a bandaid painlessly, it's better to grab the tail end and rip it off quickly, than do it slowly prolonging the pain. There is no need to feel you are a bad person or not spiritual enough if you have run into some ego conflict, it is all part of the human condition. Nor is there any need to berate yourself, or extend the experience. See it, feel it, understand it and release it. It's that simple. Love yourself up after any big breakthroughs too. Have a sense of detachment and humour around it. Resolve issues as neatly and cleanly as possible so there is less debris floating around in the universe, and less on your future path.

Self-sabotage is solely the work of the ego and can show up in a million different ways. Here are just a few common ones I see in my clients; feeling everyone else out there is successful instead of you, not feeling you have the qualifications necessary for your soul work, constantly changing direction, isolating yourself from others, making other individuals or groups 'wrong', not completing the tasks you have set yourself, mimicking others instead of finding your own soul voice, believing you can only get clients through fear-based marketing, not believing in yourself, sabotaging yourself financially, not following through on plans, constantly studying new modems, thinking it's all been said before so why bother, or constantly holding back on what you really want to do. The list goes on and you may have a few little crackers of your own. Knowledge is power. Whatever you recognise you can change. With a lot of self-awareness, a big dollop of love and compassion, your soul will stay firmly in the driver's seat and your journey will continue to strengthen and grow.

Ask Yourself

What sabotaging patterns are you repeating that prevent you from doing your soul work?

How can you watch out for these patterns in the future?

What negative patterns have appeared in relationships with your colleagues, partners or industry peers and what was your role here?

Can you take full responsibility for the mistakes you have made, heal them and move on?

What are your greatest fears?

Are you ready to stop sabotaging and start thriving?

Try This

Know your sabotages inside and out. For instance if you tend to waste time, energy and money running off on crazy tangents, write down all the projects you did last year. Count how much time in hours, and money in dollars, you spent on each distraction. Yes this can make you cringe a little, but better to see it in black and white now and heal it, than to keep doing the same thing. Now think of your favourite work. What if the same amount of time, money or energy had gone into this? How much more specialised would you be? How much further along your path would you be? Or perhaps it just would have left time and money for a marketing plan, a new website or beautiful holiday.

Once you know your patterns, write a checklist of questions you can ask yourself so you know you're not repeating the same mistakes. Your checklist of questions might ask; is this project taking me closer to my soul work or further from it? Is this project just another waste of time and resources to sabotage my real work? How is this project going to enrich my life? Do I realistically have the money, time and energy to invest in this project? Will it leave me feeling depleted or fulfilled? Does it add to the clarity of my brand or dilute it? What will need to be put on the back burner for this project to go ahead?

Write down your major sabotaging patterns that have been with you through your life (there are usually three or four) and before you embark on any new project, relationship or job, ask yourself if this will support your soul or if it is a repeating pattern you can say no to. Let's say one major pattern is about wanting to please others to gain approval. This can manifest in an amazing variety of ways, so if you want to break the pattern, check in. If a local wellbeing practitioner asks you to collaborate, check in first with your sabotage list. Ask yourself would I be doing this just because I want to please her or gain approval from other practitioners in the area for collaborating? Or would I be doing this because we have a deep soul connection and my inner being leaps with joy at the thought? Trust me, one of those answers will keep you in a repeating pattern of self-sabotage and the other will open incredible pathways. Sometimes the answer is no. And when you say no to old patterns, new exciting ones show up. You should check in with your sabotage list before you embark on any new project, action or direction.

A lot of sabotage shows up in money areas so be willing to look at how you sabotage yourself financially. Money is great to look at because it is a quantifiable measuring tool. You often underestimate the time or energy you put into something, but money is there in black and white in your incomings, outgoings and bank balance, so it can give you a bit of a reality check. You can be sure if your money is being drained your energy is too.

Try heightening your self-awareness, tuning into your body, and guiding yourself gently away from sabotage with loving compassion and understanding.

Go and see your favourite practitioner to help you stop recurring sabotaging patterns.

When you see a pattern, sometimes clearing it energetically is easier than clearing it with mindset tools. Energetic practices tend to pull problems out by the roots. Ask that this pattern be cleared across all timelines and dimensions so you can move forward on your soul journey.

Competition

'Alone we can do so little. Together we can do so much.'
- Helen Keller

Okay so let's be honest here - have you ever felt a little competitive with your fellow practitioners? Ever seen something they were launching, and had a sinking or lurching feeling in your stomach because that's what you wanted to do? Or did it make you feel behind or 'less than' in what you wanted to achieve? Ever felt overwhelmed, intimidated or a little jealous of someone else's success? Does it seem like everyone else is incredibly successful online and you're not? Relax, its totally okay. It doesn't make you bad or less spiritual just because your ego got a little bit bent out of shape. You wouldn't be human if you didn't have the occasional bad thought or esteem collapse. I'm sure your spiritual ethics certainly don't include being competitive or jealous, but this doesn't make you a robot. If you're going to beat yourself up every time you have a bad thought, you're going to be pretty pulverised by the end of your years.

Before you rush to say there's no such thing as competition, actually it's more common than you think, and we need to talk about it rather than ignore it. And just in case you do feel like this one day, or are on the receiving end of someone else's envy, let's pause and see what's going on when competition arises. Actually I believe the universe is pretty clever with this stuff and they know how to trigger your ego and get you moving if needs be. So if you've been floundering or avoiding your purpose, spirit is not averse to putting someone with skills, expertise and drive in front of your face to rev you up. The question is how will you react? Will you use it to raise yourself to a new level of your own aspiration? Will you demonise that person, shrink back or become competitive? Or once you're over the initial cringe, will you take it with good humour, get focussed and crank it up a notch?

There is plenty room enough for everyone, and then some, because as you know this world and its people need a lot of healing. There are going to be more and more wellbeing practitioners out there because that is part of the divine evolution of this world. Let's celebrate that. Let's include everyone. If the idea of a whole load of new practitioners coming into the marketplace scares you, ask yourself why. Honestly. Explore the fears you have around that and heal them. Start getting excited about it. Start elevating and recommending other practitioners you align with wherever you can.

I also want to address here the competition or judgement between modems. We never elevate ourselves by belittling or denigrating someone or something else. People have the right to choose what modem suits them at what time and in what stage of their life. They may stick with one practice for life, or weave through a variety of practices that deepen their souls' journey. There is no wrong. Interfering with that or convincing others to switch to your modem can backfire in a million different ways. There is a great blessing in individuals being able to choose from a rich pool of healing arts out there in the world. Be enthusiastic if one of your clients is getting great results from a practice that wouldn't be your first choice. Celebrate their sovereignty. Challenge your presumptions by getting out of your box and trying different classes, healings and practices you may otherwise have dismissed. If your students ask you if you have heard of new wellbeing practices you can say yes, rather than stare at them with a blank face. What if these practices opened up new pathways for you personally, inspired your work, made new colleagues or created some great new friendships? The largest demographic in my early classes and consults was other wellbeing practitioners. And they are a delight to teach because they are ready, present and enthusiastic. They are dedicated to their own wellbeing and learning new tools for their clients.

One of my main purposes in *Spirit in Business* is to bring together wellbeing practitioners as a whole. Not yoga teachers in their pocket, and kinesiologists in theirs and massage therapists in theirs and so on. I'm all about creating one tribe. My vision is everyone together in one big juicy community of wellness; supporting, sharing, laughing, dancing and growing together. Sharing and learning across other modems and a healthy respect for your fellow practitioners can never dilute your practice or reputation, it can only enrich it.

Ask Yourself

If you have felt jealous of someone else's success, person or practice, it's time to ask yourself a few direct questions. What is it about this person that annoys me? Can I use what I don't like about that person to reinforce or elevate what is important to me? Is this a call to action from spirit for me to get moving? Are they really taking anything from you or simply showing you what you could achieve?

If you have been on the receiving end of competition or someone else's jealousy, take a look at the way you are communicating, behaving, engaging and promoting yourself. Don't just dismiss it out of hand. If you can't be mature enough to sit with it and examine it, there may be a lesson you're not willing to see. Look clearly at the situation at hand and what the person is saying about you. Is there any tiny seed of truth there you could gracefully learn and move on?

Ask yourself if you have been criticising someone else publicly or unnecessarily lately. If you don't criticise others, you won't open yourself to the energy of criticism. Try a little compassion and understanding, knowing we are all just doing our best.

If you come into conflict directly with another practitioner, deal with it straight away. Neither take too much blame, nor push too much onto the other person. Find a place of honesty and resolution you can both live with. You may never be friends or you may become great colleagues. Let it be what it is. If you feel you have expressed yourself honestly and done the best you could to resolve things and the other person is still combative or interested in getting into a drama, just let it go. Cease communication and move on. Sooner or later they will tire of you. Maintain your integrity at all times. Go to your healer or counsellor if this relates to an old issue of yours that still needs healing, whether you are the receiver or initiator of the conflict.

Try This

Never, ever, ever speak badly of another practitioner. It only reflects poorly on you. Don't criticise their training, their methods, their ethics or their personality. Let it go. You don't need to recommend them, but you don't need to demonise them either.

If someone is crossing boundaries be prepared to stand up for yourself quietly, calmly and clearly.

If you are feeling jealous or competitive with another practitioner try this Buddhist exercise for compassion. Say to yourself; just like me this person wants to be happy, just like me this person wants to succeed, just like me this person is doing their best, just like me this person has worries and concerns, just like me this person has a family, just like me this person is sometimes frightened and so on.

If you are feeling agitated by another practitioner, don't keep letting it build, clear the energy around it instead. First write down all the things that annoy you about that person and then turn the mirror on yourself. If you think their work is dry and boring, is your work dry and boring? If you feel their marketing is too over the top, ask yourself if yours is the same. If you feel they are talking about you behind your back, are you talking about them or others? If you feel they don't acknowledge you, are you acknowledging yourself? Any discord can contain great wisdom if you have the courage to look.

Use your self-awareness to explore where the lesson is for you. If you feel resentful of another woman shining bright and feel you are not being seen, does this remind you of an old memory; perhaps your sister standing out in the family, whilst you were ignored, or an old incident at school? In any circumstance examine your own psychology and see where old stories that need healing may have been stimulating your feelings of jealousy or hurt.

Go and try a different modem, or talk to a wellbeing teacher in a different field about what makes them tick. Get really interested in who they are and what they do. If you're impressed offer to have their cards at your business place. Tell them about yourself and why you love what you do. How does that feel?

Think about having a wellness day with a variety of practitioners each sharing their wisdom. Or go to a wellness expo and walk by all the stalls learning about different practices. Make listening to them rather than talking about yourself a priority. Get your head out of your bum and have a look around. You may be overwhelmed by the love, opportunities and friendships available.

Illusion

*'A great deal of intelligence can be invested in ignorance
when the need for illusion is deep'*
- Saul Bellow

Okay, this is a huge one. The spiritual world can sometimes be a hard place to navigate, because you must translate the world of the unseen to the seen, with integrity, vision and clarity. Throughout your career I can guarantee you that your ego is going to try and distract you from your soul work as often and as craftily as it possibly can. It will try to sabotage your projects, and when things fall apart it will say 'see, I told you this would never work, you're not good enough, it's too out there, you're not qualified enough' and so on. Every time something doesn't go according to plan your ego will use it as an opportunity to drag you away from your true work. So you need to be vigilant.

You must have your heart and soul driving your vehicle at all times, no matter how scary it gets. You must hold fast with determination, focus and grit to get your real work out there. The deep and joyful rewards that come from this are by far the best feeling in the world. Sometimes the ego will try and trap you into a narrow conservative box, sometimes it will convince you a totally 'out there' project is viable, and sometimes it will show you just the right (wrong) person you need to work with to succeed. I have seen some incredibly masterful practitioners be totally hoodwinked by the ego, so when it happens to you have a sense of humour, own it and make a mental note for the future to be more aware. The best way to remain soul driven is to create an incredibly strong, grounded daily practice for yourself, so you are very clear on discerning the soul's voice from the ego's voice.

The ego loves to either rush decisions, or delay decisions over a period of months or years, so that is an automatic red flag. The soul operates on right timing. You need to sit back, feel, assess and make a considered decision. The soul loves to look clearly, absorb, observe and then act. The ego doesn't like to look at things deeply and makes decisions on presumption rather than a mature assessment, or on the perceived rewards, rather than how it will make you *feel*. In order to stay focussed on your soul purpose and ensure you are making the right decisions to move forward, you should approach it in two ways. The first way is to go to spirit every day in meditation and ask for the next step forward. This is the blueprint of your soul's path that is revealed to you step by step, day by day, month by month, and year by year for the fulfilment of your dreams. It couldn't be easier. The second part is to go into that same meditative space when opportunities are offered to you, to make sure that they are in line with your soul purpose. It takes great courage to politely decline opportunities that are not in line with who you are, but trust me, all sorts of disasters occur when you take on jobs just for the hell of it. If someone is pressuring you for an answer, simply say 'wow, that sounds like a great opportunity, send me all the details and let me think about it, and I'll get back to you….tonight or tomorrow.' Make sure you give them a time frame out of professional courtesy.

Even for the most experienced practitioners, I would recommend taking time and going into a meditative space for every decision you are making on your path, because we are human and vulnerable and all it takes is a few bad nights' sleep, something on social media that triggers an old pattern, or a poor diet to disrupt your system and throw you off balance. If you have a decision to make and you sit in meditation, but find that your ego is interfering, or you are not sure if it is your spirit or your mind advising you, always check in with the body. When you visualise one option how does the body feel? Is it constricted, tense or heavy? Or does it feel light, bubbly and open? What is your belly doing? Does it feel nauseous or is it full of happy butterflies? Then consider the other option and do the same body check. You should spend at least five minutes focussing on one option, ten breaths coming back to neutral mind, then five minutes focussing on the other option. Flicking from one option to the other is the ego trying to sabotage you, so make sure you give each option full attention.

Sure you can apply a hit and miss attitude to projects, where some work and some don't, but you're kidding yourself if you think this is going to take you into your deepest work, build your reputation and create a thriving practice. With everything you could possibly need available at your fingertips, it begs the question why so many practitioners are floundering in a million different directions, trying to be everything to everyone. There is only one part of your consciousness that believes it can make better decisions than your soul, and that's the ego. So the question is; do you want to choose a life of joy and authentic success, or a life led by illusion? All we really want to see is your authentic, beautiful, exquisite soul shining in all its glory, so hold tight, hold fast and stay true.

Ask Yourself

For every new project you want to birth, person you want to work with or training you undertake, have you taken the time to sit and tune in to the heart, the soul and the body before making your decision?

Has it come from the inside out or outside in?

Do you like the sound of it (ego) or do you like the *feel* of it (soul)?

When you think of working with a particular person, forget the external, and ask yourself, how does your skin feel when you think of working with them?

Can you fine-tune your feeling sense around making decisions?

How much of your true work has been swept to the side by distractions?

Instead of changing things or introducing new projects, can you choose to go deeper?

Try This

Write down the three largest motivating factors for your great idea (be honest) and ask yourself if these are ego driven or soul driven.

Know your ego's patterns by looking back at times you have diverted from your true path; see what triggered it, what chaos ensued, and how you can have a warning bell for the future. This is great stuff, so don't avoid it; take a good, long, honest look now, to save yourself greater problems in the future.

If you are not prepared to take twenty minutes to sit down, meditate and really *feel* whether a decision or direction is right for you, I hate to tell you, but that is the ego at play. If the opportunity is truly wonderful, it should be really easy to look at deeply and explore thoroughly. It doesn't need to be perfect, but the essence needs to be there.

Use all your strength, might and determination to resist the distractions of the ego and be especially mindful that the ego also loves to dress up as the soul. If you are totally stumped, always check in with the body.

Write down a list of features for decisions that are soul-driven and decisions that are ego-driven, and what each looks like. For instance soul-driven decisions come from the inside and are feeling oriented, ego-driven decisions come from the outside and are focussed on how you will look. Soul-driven decisions feel beautiful, light and joyful in the body. Ego-driven decisions feel awkward, heavy or tense in the body. Soul-driven decisions create harmony. Ego-driven decisions create disruption. Soul-driven decisions are cohesive and add to the whole. Ego-driven decisions are distracting and move away from the whole. The soul looks at the long term, the ego looks at the short term. And so on. Write down as many differences as you can and then use that checklist to go over decisions you have made in the past, and see whether the soul or the ego was driving you. The more awareness you can gather here the better information you have for the future. Every time you need to make business decisions, get that list of features out and ask yourself whether your decision has all the features of the soul or the ego.

Have the courage to really look and see what is going on in your business overall. Do you see a soul-driven business or an ego-driven business or a bit of a mix? Name three pivotal things you can do to address any imbalances.

Know your ego patterns and name them. Do you come up with great ideas and then stop before you start? Are you attached to success above the soul of your work? List out every pattern you can see in your business and *act* on making changes. You can do all the mindset and self-awareness work you like, but it is action that will change the pattern.

Trust me, the soul is the best business partner you could ever have. It will bring you everything you need from an infinite source, including financial success, an impeccable reputation and deep joy.

The Wounded Healer

*'Sometimes in order to be happy in the present moment,
you have to be willing to give up all hope of a better past.'*
- Robert Holden

Most, if not all of us have come to the spiritual path through our own wounding. In healing yourself, you have discovered an innate capacity to heal others. You listen, you understand, and you offer compassion to others, because you too have felt the pain of loss, grief, sadness and anger. You feel an innate compulsion to act as a guide because others have guided you. You offer wisdom that you have found deep in your own soul from your experience, search and healing. All this is powerful stuff if you use it to bring light, self-awareness and navigation skills to others.

However, there is a time for tending your wounds and telling your stories, and a time for elevating your work and moving on. The role of the wounded healer is one you can become addicted to, and at times it may blind you to the work you have yet to do. There is a delicate balance between continuing to heal your own stuff, and not being branded or debilitated by it. Not avoiding higher work by licking your own wounds for so long you cause an infection. At some point you should show signs of immunity; less triggering, more wisdom. What is the role of a healer beyond the wounding? I hate to say this, but there are some practitioners out there who are too invested in their own pain, their clients' pain, and their role as healer of ills, rather than bringer of the light.

We are not just the healers of wounds; we are first and foremost the bringers of light and love. We need to embody that now for ourselves and those we serve. We need to evolve. To offer services that promote connection to love, light, and spiritual growth. To step forward and actively pursue our own soulful expansion instead of waiting for the next set of circumstances that drag us there. And we need to bring our clients along for the ride; to educate them to come to us not just in times of pain, but as an essential part of their spiritual growth, as an active participant, not a wounded victim. How different would that feel to you as a practitioner energetically, and how different would it feel to your clients?

Let's face it, deep down many of us believe life is full of pain and that we need to learn our lessons to evolve. What hope is there then for our clients? Can you live on earth as you would in spirit with peace, joy, love and humour? To step forward openly, joyfully and willingly to the next phase and take charge of your soul path. What would your life be like without pain? What would you do with your time? As Marianne Williamson said "it is our light, not our darkness we are most frightened of". I would take that further and say we are afraid of peace and quiet and time and love and stillness. Look carefully at your own life and see if this is true. Where have you complicated things? Knowing yourself as the ultimate creator means you can choose again. I believe you have barely begun to tap into your true power. It's high time to step beyond old labels and archetypes and see what you are truly capable of.

Perhaps the most terrifying life is the one of joy. It feels like an excruciatingly vulnerable and dangerous state to those of us who have been swiftly wounded in a state of pleasure. But you forget you are stronger now; that you have many tools to deal with any disappointment or shock. And those things are far less likely to knock on your door if you are committed to a daily practice of drawing in and being the light. No matter what you come across, it is ultimately unable to affect the soul when you are in a state of grace.

Ask Yourself

What presumptions or old spiritual ideologies are you carrying around that need to go?

What can you do today to create a higher and lighter vision of the earth, humanity, yourself and your spiritual path?

Can you see a future of working with light or pure vibrations with your clients?

Look back over perceived difficulties of your spiritual path and ask yourself honestly if there were warning signs, a lack of consciousness or connection at that time. Did the indications to proceed come from spirit or the ego reaction?

Try This

Take an inventory of your self-care, energy levels and behaviour. How do you see the idea of living in service?

Look at the ways you might be leaking energy in your business. Are you giving away too much or giving til you bleed? There are no heroics in this; it is dangerous, spiritually immature and damaging to yourself and your clients.

Can you change your mindset from your spiritual life being an arduous journey full of processing to an active, willing co-creation with the divine?

List all your presumptions about what the spiritual journey entails and ask yourself if these ideas are true or if they have come from the ego or an archaic version of spiritual service.

Overcoming Disappointment

'Sometimes not getting what you want is a wonderful stroke of luck.'
- The Dalai Lama

If things don't seem to be working for you, please don't give up. If your dreams are born from your true purpose, if they are aligned with your heart and soul, if they will bring deep joy to yourself and others, if they will spread light across the planet, they will come true. Why on earth would the universe not want to support that? Every manifestation molecule will conspire to bring your vision to life. Consider every setback a direct message sent to you from spirit to rethink, reassess and reconsider where you are heading. It is either a warning to examine what you are doing, where you are going and with whom, a reminder to become fully aligned with your true soul work, a resilience training exercise to see how determined you really are, or an opportunity to face some of your fears and blocks. Always, always, always examine the warning possibility first. It is much better to examine beforehand than repair the wounds in hindsight.

If things are not flowing smoothly

If things are not flowing, hold up there a minute and check in. For instance if you are opening a healing centre with another person or persons, but you are having trouble finding a great venue, or coming to an agreement over how much you want to spend on the lease, the program, or how many practitioners you want working there, it's time for a reassessment. Don't get so carried away with the idea that you forget to listen to your intuition. Meditate, feel it in your body, go with your gut, ask yourself if this is an early warning bell. Even if you have invested a lot so far, even if your partner still wants to go ahead. If it doesn't feel right, for the love of God please don't do it. If you do a thorough examination and your plan to go ahead still feels great, examine what details you are missing. Do you have adequate planning and finances in place, is your marketing plan sound, have you discussed what would happen if the partnership dissolved, and so on, and so forth. Perhaps it is simply a matter of right timing. Imagine if you signed one lease for three years, and two months later the perfect venue with better parking, signage and a gorgeous little garden popped up for less rent. Listen.

Not getting enough students or clients

If you are not getting the amount of clients you want ask yourself why not? Are you speaking from the heart, are you too focussed on marketing and technology and not focussed enough on content, is your branding clear or are you sending mixed messages? Are you expecting too much too soon? If it seems like everyone else is succeeding and you're not, know that a lot of the success you see online is an illusion. Anyone can buy fans for their page or create a schmick marketing look, but the truth is often very different. Social media is littered with promises for getting a load of clients, subscribers or money in a very short period of time. This is a fear-based hook people buy into, eager to succeed, and when you don't get the same results as it seems everyone else is getting, you can be left feeling insecure and alone. I can assure you if you are not getting all the clients you want; you are missing an important message from your soul about deepening your work. Perhaps you are simply not giving yourself enough time. Trust me, good things build over time, not in an instant. Longevity, faithful clients, an impeccable reputation and a long career take time. And you can't buy that. You wouldn't want to.

It takes hard work

Success comes from hard work, perseverance, dedication and devotion. There's no shortcut, and that's the truth. You don't give in when you make a mistake, and you sure as hell don't give in when the first thing goes wrong. It's about doing whatever it takes (ethically) to earn your place as a leader, teacher or healer. Marie Forleo worked for seven years as a waitress and bartender while trying to pay off old debts and get her life coaching business up and running. Mama Gena's School of Womanly Arts began with a few people in her living room and grew from there. There are thousands of stories like this all around the world every day. When I say work hard I mean it. That doesn't mean wearing yourself into the ground, but it does mean following through and being realistic about what it takes to build a thriving business. Here is just a portion of what I do every day, week or month of the year to make that happen; I write newsletters, a blog, a wellbeing column, network in wellness and business groups, study social media, further my business education, plan, deepen my personal practice, use energetic manifestation techniques, go to expos, talk around Australia and overseas, run workshops, create online programs, write books, engage in Facebook groups, speak at industry conferences, take consultations and so on. And I do this over and over and over again, with joy, because this is my soul purpose. Of course it depends on your business model; the larger platform your soul calls you to, the more work you will need to do to get there, but even a small community business model takes hard work and patience to succeed. This is why when you take someone else's stuff, or someone else takes your work, it will never sustain itself long term; because the integrity, the blood, sweat and tears isn't there to uphold it, and sooner or later, it shows. Your soul work will always be protected by the universe; your ego work however will be allowed to crumble to dust and the sooner the better.

Get a part-time job

You heard me. If you are new to the wellbeing industry or not making much money, there is no shame in getting yourself a part-time job to tide you over. If it's good enough for Marie Forleo it's good enough for you. It's not a mark of failure, it's a mature choice that shows you are serious about succeeding and are prepared to go the extra mile. Just make sure you have an exit plan, and don't get too comfy there or sabotage yourself by spending your wages on other stuff. Get your priorities clear; you are doing this to support your soul work. I often see practitioners putting themselves under a lot of financial pressure or debt trying to build a business with little or no capital. It can affect the way you market and feel energetically to your clients. Of course you have beautiful intentions, but if your focus shifts to needing clients because you're stressed about money, rather than creating a space to welcome them, it won't be as fulfilling for either of you. Having part-time work means you have money to pay the bills so you can focus on doing what you love. It will give you extra money for marketing, creating a website, advertising, and everything else you need to have in place to succeed. Build your business outside your work hours, then as your clients increase drop back on your part-time job and shift into your business full time.

Confidence

Whilst you may not begin with great confidence, you can certainly cultivate it. Confidence comes with experience, dedication to your daily practices and time. There will always be a part of you that may second guess your capabilities, compare yourself to others, or wonder what other people think of you, but this is all the realm of the ego. You have been given your gifts for a reason. You have come here with a purpose. You are utterly, totally capable of carrying out your soul purpose. There is endless help for you internally from your own soul, and externally from the universe at large. There is nothing you cannot be, do or have when you are on purpose, because you come from an infinite source. Never imagine your dreams are not coming true because you are not worthy of them. They may need attention, effort, willingness and time, but believe all good things are on their way.

Believe

Do you believe you are a spiritual leader, healer or teacher or not? Do you believe this is what you were born for? Do you know you have something to offer? Do you know you can change lives? If you believe all this, then let all the doubt go and keep moving forward; with gratitude and joy. Consider disappointments as your greatest messengers from spirit; to try harder, to look elsewhere, to wait, to change direction, to tie up loose ends or something else. Spirit does not meter out success to a chosen few, so if you are experiencing setbacks, something is not right in your world. Spend some time in introspection; ask yourself what if you tried that one thing you've wanted to do for ages, what could you blend to create the perfect mix or what is missing? Success takes courage, resilience and strength, and you have that in your makeup whether you care to recognise it or not. For the love of yourself, this planet and the tribe that is desperately trying to find you; persevere, persevere, and persevere. Rest when you need to, but never, ever give up.

Ask Yourself

Can you honestly say you have been doing all the work necessary to succeed?

Do you have a clear business and marketing plan?

Are you trying to do too much instead of one thing really well?

Is your disappointment at something not succeeding less to do with your not being worthy, and more to do with an early warning sign?

Are you in it for the long haul or the short term?

Whilst building confidence, can you fake it until you make it?

Do you need to get a part-time job to take the pressure off yourself, and your clients, whilst you build your practice?

What are three choices you could make today to support yourself in overcoming a disappointment?

Try This

Instead of saying 'I can't', practice saying 'how can I' to build your resilience and problem-solving skills.

Have you ever gone ahead with a project and then been disappointed? Were there any early warning signs you missed, and how can you be more aware of these in the future?

If things are not flowing well, sit down and examine your whole business. Write down any gaps you see or anything you feel ill at ease about.

Name ten things you can do this week to give your business a kick-start.

Write down all your very best qualities as fast as you can without censorship.

Write yourself a letter of encouragement when things are not going well. List all the reasons why you know that you are capable of moving through this and turning things around

Get down on your knees and pray to the universe, God, Goddess or spirit to please help you, show you clear signs and to fill you with the strength and resilience to fulfil your dharma. No request is left unanswered.

Divine Helpers

'If you knew who walked beside you at all times on this path that you have chosen, you could never experience fear or doubt again.'
- A Course in Miracles

As humans we favour the three dimensional physical world that we can see, hear, smell, touch and taste. It is in fact totally necessary to be grounded throughout your journey on earth. I'm sure we've all met kooky spiritual practitioners who are just off on another planet, and this can be both scary, and downright dangerous, to themselves and their clients. Never forget though, that at your heart you are a spiritual being, and that whilst you walk this earth you are surrounded by unseen helpers whose job it is to support, guide and advise you on your soul's path. Even the most spiritual practitioners can turn a blind eye to this guidance, I know I have, but life becomes so much easier when you accept a little help along the way. Let go of any fear that you will be forced to do something you don't want to, or are incapable of, and allow some love, help, support and guidance to sustain and nourish you on your journey.

There is no right or wrong way to connect with spirit. Some people are clairaudient and hear messages, some are clairvoyant and connect with visions, some are clairsentient and have a feeling sensation, and others are claircognizant and have a vast pool of knowledge without knowing why. There are a million ways to make spirit part of your life from meditating, to creating rituals, to walking out in nature, to sending out a prayer. You can ask for clarity or help with a new project. You can ask for assistance with finances, relationship problems or decorating your treatment room in a way that invites more clients. No problem is too big or too small for spirit to assist you.

Usually things will shift in very ordinary human ways, synchronicities will occur and openings or solutions will magically appear. Wait, listen and act when you are instructed. Instead of worrying that you haven't been heard, expect to be answered. There are specific angels, archangels, animal spirits and guides that can help you with particular areas. Or you can just put the word out for 'the technological angels' to help you when your computer melts down, or you need to understand some new technology, or the 'parking angels' to help you find a space right outside a venue. I also like to throw some light on the path ahead of time, so I will ask for smooth passage in my travels, and that I may speak deeply from the heart and soul to my audience.

You can also ask for clarity with your purpose, and don't be afraid to be very specific about what you need to know. If you have trouble hearing messages in meditation, ask that spirit put signs, songs, conversations, people or synchronicities right in front of you so you can't miss it. Don't try too hard, just take note of what is going on around you, or what songs are in your head. At the end of the day write a general summary in your diary and look for themes. For instance if you bumped into someone, what do they represent for you? Are they too hard on themselves, were they telling you about a great new class they are attending, or are they a fellow practitioner you might be able to go to for support? Go to spirit every day, not just in case of emergencies, but to remind you who you are in essence. In fact you will find much less drama, and much more time, energy and money to fulfil your purpose when you are deeply connected to spirit.

Direct your requests to the divine beings that resonate with you. I usually call upon Archangel Michael to help me with discernment, decisions, direction and protection. I call on Archangel Raphael to help me with my writing or any healing, Archangel Uriel to help me see things clearly or shine light on problems, Archangel Gabriel if I am giving a speech or need to hear or deliver a message, Archangels Chamuel and Sandalphon if I need help with my career or to guide my business coaching clients in their soul work. I will call on God, the universe or my Guardian Angel if I am feeling scared and alone. It doesn't matter who you call on as long as it resonates with you. Understand that calling on spirit is not about abdicating your power or going off into fantasy land. To me it is a very mature spiritual call that recognises I am a spirit in essence, and am calling upon my spiritual assistants to help me with my purpose. The ego believes it can do it all alone; the spirit invites assistance because it knows all things are connected.

It is vital that you have sovereignty over these interactions with spirit by checking in with the body to see if the message you received *feels* right to you. The unseen world and your mind can be full of illusion, so double checking is only the responsible thing to do, especially if the guidance doesn't quite feel right, or seems quite elaborate or ungrounded. Spirit really doesn't mind you doing this at all. Then when you are sure of the message, follow it through with all your might. Spiritual guidance is always grounded and can be very funny in its solutions, so expect to be amused. What you want deep in your heart and soul is exactly what spirit wants for you too, so the guidance you receive should never fill you with dread, or ask you to do anything that is outside of your of integrity. If you have doubts stop, wait, watch and listen. Chances are it's just your ego chiming in. The more often you connect, the better you'll get at knowing which voice is which. Asking for guidance is about surrendering the wants of the ego to follow the needs of the soul.

Touching base with spirit on a daily basis is like a homecoming for the soul. It is an acknowledgement that you are part of something bigger, and you are supported, loved and cherished on your journey. It is enough to light a candle, put on some soft music and lie in your meditation room for a while. Don't expect thunderclaps and spooky visitations; connecting with the divine is just like patting the seat beside you on the sofa, asking if there is anything you have missed that could make your life a little easier. In times of crisis call as loud as you can and the angels will be by your side before the final sentence is uttered.

Ask Yourself

When is the last time you asked spirit for help?

Are you trying to connect to spirit in ways that feel unnatural to you?

Can you believe that spirit is as present in nature, or on earth as it is in the heavens?

Are you a little fearful of what a spiritual connection could mean?

Do you believe you are alone, or can you feel support weaving its way through your life? Are you open to being supported and guided towards your happiest life?

Try This

Create a sacred daily ritual for connecting with spirit. Take some quiet time in your garden, looking for messages from the natural world, spend some time in your meditation room or practice reading your spirit cards without referring to the manual.

Try this daily mantra from *A Course in Miracles* 'Where would you have me go, what would you have me do, what would you have me say, and to whom?' Then watch for openings, synchronicities and signs.

Keeping a spiritual diary can be a great way of staying alert to guidance. Ask spirit a question and then for the next week keep a record of what happened to you each day. No need to go into minute detail, just close your eyes, run your mind over the day and ask what stood out to you. What conversations did you have and what impression did they leave you with? Where did you go and what did those places represent for you? Who did you see and what traits did those people have, what do they inspire in you or how do they annoy you? What did you want to do, but didn't manage and why? Try to keep the inquiries light and spacious and more about a feeling sense than a thinking exercise. Look for themes and obvious signs and see how they relate back to your question.

Humans build relationships on trust. How can you begin to trust spiritual guidance and divine help? If you feel you have been misguided in the past, look back and ask yourself honestly, was it spirit or your ego that misled you?

If you don't believe in spirit, that's fine, just begin to develop a relationship with the deepest part of your being, your higher mind, or body intuition for guidance.

Light

'There will always be a door to the light'
- Shiro Amano

You are light. The universe is made of light. When all things are empowered with light they become more illuminated, alive and vibrant. When you connect to the light you become living spirit in action. By consciously raising the level of light in your life and your business, you tap into a higher vision, a higher vibration, and release what is heavy, dense or not aligned with your soul. You can use light to heal, transform energy and direct your intentions out into the world from the highest place possible. If anything is troubling you, infuse it with light.

To work effectively with light you need to draw it in from the universe, build it up in your being and then send it out into the world. We often talk of sending love, which is a beautiful thing, but the word love can have strong attachments for people, especially if they have felt hurt by love in the past. It can be difficult to harness energy you have had trouble with, and old memories can interfere. Just as white light contains the full colour spectrum of a rainbow, energetically light contains all the highest qualities like love, peace, devotion, kindness, strength and service. You only have to draw in light to gather all the qualities you need. Light increases your vibration, changes your mindset, and opens your heart and soul to what is possible. It is the great transformer. Light knows no boundaries. It is either present or it is not, and as a light being you have an infinite capacity to draw light in where there is darkness, heaviness, confusion or uncertainty.

By creating a daily practice to increase the level of light in your being, you will change yourself physically, mentally, emotionally and spiritually. You will experience more physical vitality in every muscle, cell, bone and organ in your body. You will feel clear mentally when making decisions and choices. You will feel emotionally resilient, strong and joyful. Your spiritual vibration will increase and you'll feel more deeply connected to your purpose and the tribe you were sent to help. You will vibrate at a higher level energetically and draw people to you. Your vibration will have a dramatic impact on people in your presence, lending a new energy to your talks, classes or consultations. The flow of energy will be stronger and breakthroughs simpler and more profound. Your light brings light to the world around you.

Light helps resolve all problems and anxieties. You can draw in light in the present moment, send it ahead of time for a big event, or back to the past to heal any old wounds. Rather than trying to solve all problems, repeating patterns of behaviour or addictions, try sending light to them instead. Light takes the sting of shame out, and moves in only with the intention to heal. Make a daily practice of drawing light into your body and energetic being. You can't act unconsciously when your light is at full radiance. Light is the best guarantee you have of living joyfully and fulfilling your purpose. Embrace light and light will embrace you.

Ask Yourself

What people, places or circumstances make your light contract and why?
    Can you commit to a daily practice of bringing in the light?
    Can you see drawing in light as surrender in action?
    What aspects of your being, relationships or work could use a little light?

Try This

Create a daily practice of drawing in light. Sit in meditation, breathe deeply and allow your body to release on every exhale. On every inhale begin to breathe in light. You can draw this energy from above you, the earth, or the universe around you, whatever feels most natural to you. Keep letting go on every exhale and inviting more light on every inhale. Imagine light moving through you, filling every organ, cell, bone and muscle of your body. Feel the light becoming stronger and more radiant. Feel it moving from the confines of your body out into your energy field, then into the world around you. You may see it as rays extending out from the body like the sun, or a vibrant circle of energy around you, ever expanding. Really feel that vibration. Then send light out into the day ahead. Imagine yourself moving through your day surrounded by light. If you have some new technology to master, send light to yourself sitting at the computer. If you have a new workshop coming up, send light to that too. Light your life with whatever you need. Then slowly come back into the room feeling full of light, alive and fresh for the day ahead. You can pause in your day to breathe in more light if you feel your energy dwindling.

When trying to heal a situation we often look at it, try to see where it came from and use mindset or self-awareness techniques to heal it in the moment, only to have it arise again. So let's try using light instead. Isolate a repeating pattern in your life and send light to it. For instance if you are addicted to spending money on clothes, send light back in time to any memories you have where you bought clothes and felt guilty afterwards. Imagine the scene filling with light for as long as feels right, then move on to the next scene and so on. You may find yourself back at an early memory of where it all began. No need to get into the mind, just fill the scene with light, then the higher energies of whatever was needed in each scene can work their magic. When you feel you have done enough, fill your body with light in the here and now. You can try this for any addictions, repeating patterns of behaviour and it is especially powerful for old feelings of shame. Just one issue at a time please, as this is powerful work. Listen to your intuition about when you are ready for another clearing.

Use light to manifest your purpose by filling your vision and intentions with light at a very real level. Spend time sending your website and social media presence light. If you are running a retreat, seminar, workshop or webinar, send light to it ahead of time. Everyday before you see clients, send light to your day. Fill yourself, your workplace and your marketing with light. Infuse your daily spiritual practice with light. Anything you want to create, fill it with light. If you want to increase your numbers at your classes, imagine a huge gathering of people and send that vision light every day.

Use light to manifest your intentions. Whatever you wish to bring into the world, infuse it with light. This will also help you gain clarity, fresh insights and deeper material, so be sure you are listening to any inspiration and seeing synchronicity when it appears.

Fill your being with light and commit to radiating light out into the world from a higher source. This will raise your vibration, the vibration around you and make your work far more powerful, easy and beautiful. This is what attracts your tribe. The higher your vibration, the stronger your light, the more you'll achieve.

Grounding, Clearing and Protection

'I am a spiritual being, protected by angels, helped by guides, and infinitely loved and supported by the universe.'
- Sonia Choquette

Grounding, clearing and protection is a really important skill set to have when you are working in the spiritual realm, and with all manner of people in your business. This is not spooky stuff, just a few simple techniques to keep your spirit and energy bright and clear. Read through the techniques below and choose just one or two of each that work well for you. You may like to change these over time or experiment, but don't feel overwhelmed by the choice, just pick those that resonate. Use the grounding and protection techniques to create a lovely daily ritual to connect to spirit, your beautiful soul, remember who you are in essence, and appreciate this wonderful world you live in. Use whichever one speaks to you, or make up your own ritual. Get creative, add your own ideas, and make it a joy to look forward to every day.

Grounding is most needed at times when you are feeling a bit 'out there'. This may include dizziness, scatty thinking, inability to make decisions or stand still, and general ungrounded acting, thinking and being. You ground yourself so you can come back to centre, and choose to think and act from a balanced perspective. Being ungrounded on a regular basis can confuse the body, mind and emotions and let fear run away with you. You should always ground yourself before making decisions. Trust me; this will save you loads of time, money, energy and angst. Being grounded also helps you stand wholly in who you are. It is an essential technique to use before a talk, workshop or class to help you speak from the depths of your being and ground the energy of your work.

Clearing practices are for when you are feeling out of sorts on a more uncomfortable level. It often occurs after having been in a negative environment, or in negative company. You may feel as though you're not your usual self, have a headache, a hooded feeling around the eyes, muscular tension or just a general sensation of discomfort. Don't let this worry you; it could be something very simple that you can easily clear. Regular daily protection practices should avoid the need to clear too often.

Protection is a regular daily practice you use as a form of spiritual hygiene. Just as you shower and clean your teeth to cleanse the body, you can create a lovely daily protection practice to keep your energy light and clear. It keeps you in balance and protects you from being swayed by outside influences that surround you everyday. The universe is made up of energy of many different vibrations – some elevate you and some leave you feeling depleted. There's no need to be paranoid about it. Protection holds your vibration and ensures you are less likely to be knocked off balance. It does not close you off from others or stop you from interacting with the world around you on the contrary, it is about taking responsibility and making a conscious effort to keep your own energy clear for the good of both yourself and the whole.

Read through the following exercises and highlight which ones feel the easiest or most light to you, then integrate them into your tool kit for yourself and your clients.

Grounding Exercises

Take a walk in nature, feeling the soles of your feet deeply connected to the earth.

Sit or stand with your back to a tree. Feel the bark, trunk and stability of this beautiful creation that is wholly grounded.

Visualize your body as a tree with roots reaching deep into the earth through your feet.

Rub a small amount of sandalwood, rosemary or sage oil on your feet and at the back of the neck.

Visualise your feet in the earth packed with mud.

Play sport or physical exercise on a regular basis to keep you grounded in your body.

Use cross-crawl kinesiology technique where you touch opposite hands to knees as you 'march'. Any other right/left instructions are good too; right hand on left ear, left hand on right hip, right hand on right hip, left hand on right hip, etc. Please be mindful of mobility issues; you are not doing aerobics, just switching the right and left brain on so you become present and grounded.

Anything that brings you back to earth gently and surely – gardening, vacuuming, or cleaning the bathroom. Sometimes mundane human tasks can be a refreshing equaliser.

Have fun – try running on the beach with the kids, juggling, being silly, playing and laughing.

Get into your body, by really connecting with your muscles and bones. Do a gentle joint warmup from your ankles to your head. Start with pointing and flexing the feet and circling the ankles, then move through the joints, keeping your awareness on gentle fluid motion.

Try a Yin Yoga practice to feel deeply connected and supported by the earth.

Breathe deeply, preferably outside, to increase the oxygen and prana in the body, and bring yourself back down to earth. If you like you can imagine inhaling energy up from the centre of mother earth, through you and into the heavens. Then exhale, drawing the breath down from the heavens, through you, and deep into the earth.

Protection Exercises

Remember this is not about thinking things are going to get you or separating yourself from others; it is simply about taking responsibility for your spiritual health and wellbeing, and a lovely daily reminder that you are a spiritual being.

Visualize you are surrounded by a bubble of white or golden light. Feel this pure energy moving from the ground up, filling the bubble with beautiful energy and clearing and releasing any negativity along the way. Try the same practice by imagining you are sitting in a triangular prism like a teepee filled with white or golden light. Feel the energy rising in the space and clearing any negativity in or around you, which is then released through the top point. The idea is that throughout the day, you are surrounded by this energetic clarity, and anything of a lower vibration just bounces off.

Imagine a bright light at the centre of your heart and with a powerful burst feel light rays streaming out in all directions, dispersing any negativity, and then surround yourself with a bubble of golden white light.

You can visualise a vibrant colour around the body or aura – pale blue, pale pink, white or golden light are said to be the highest protection, but it is really what colour makes you feel best.

Open and clear the chakras one at a time in the morning from the root to the crown. You can find a basic map of the seven major chakras and their colours online. Chakra means wheel and the chakras are depicted as having energy drawing in and vibrating outwards as they turn. This visualisation doesn't work for me, so I usually imagine each chakra as a vibrant ball of energy instead. I breathe light into each chakra until its colour becomes more vibrant and clear. When I have cleared each chakra I surround the body with a ball of light as above. If you want an instant vibrational lift this is a great practice. You can close and clear the chakras one at a time at night too for a peaceful sleep. I usually imagine petals closing over the chakra to seal for the night and then the petals opening back up in the morning to clear and energise myself again.

Clearing Exercises

If you feel like you have picked up some negative energy, or are carrying a little around yourself from a negative mindset, try one of the following;

Smudge yourself, your house or your treatment room with a smudge stick or using high-grade essential oils of rosemary, frankincense or sage in an oil burner or atomiser

Place a little rosemary oil on the back of your neck or put a drop in the palms, rub together, inhale deeply three times. 'Wash' the aura over your face, head and the back of your neck by simply moving your palms through this area about two to three inches from your skin. Then move your hands through the aura of the entire body.

Have a salt bath with rosemary, frankincense, geranium, basil, lavender or sage.

Place a salt lamp in your treatment room to help clear any processing that goes on there.

Light a candle with a prayer and dedication to heal and clear the space.

Add plants and crystals to your home or practice, place lamps in dark corners, bring in beautiful pictures, statues, shells and anything else to change the energy in the home or workplace without overdoing it. Remember energy stagnates around too many things so keep the pathways clear, open and free from too much stuff. A few sacred things that speak to you are enough.

Clean your house from top to bottom, getting rid of clutter, dust and cobwebs

Rearrange your house or treatment room to shift up the energy in the room

Open up windows and doors, let some light and fresh air in.

Take a big long walk by the sea, swim or bathe in the salt water.

Tune in and ask what you need to do to clear the energy.

Call upon Archangel Michael to help clear and protect you from any negative energy.

If you feel the energy is quite strong, ask Archangel Michael and the Brothers and Sisters of Mercy to come and clear the energy in you, around you and in your car, home, or workplace.

Imagine a giant vacuum from spirit that comes and vacuums up any negative energy from all over, around and within your being. Then breathe in white or golden light on the in breath and exhale any negativity on the exhale. Continue until you feel a shift, and then surround the body with white or golden light.

One very important point is that it is easy to say you have picked up a negative energy from somewhere and someone, but this is only part of the story. The truth is that you can't pick up a negative energy unless you are open to it in some way. Perhaps you have not been doing your daily spiritual hygiene practices, have succumbed to the ego talk or negative thinking, or have been hanging out in low vibration places or partaking in low vibration activities. Once you have cleared yourself, take an honest, detached look at what you think may have invited this situation.

If you are sensitive to energy you will need to be sure you are keeping up your practices, but never have a victim consciousness around it. I once had a woman come to a workshop who said she was so sensitive to energy that she couldn't even go to the supermarket without picking up a negative energy. Now that is totally ridiculous, and frankly delusional. Set the intention that you are always picking up negative vibrations, and guess what? You will.

Also a special note for healers; there is no need to take on your clients' stuff to heal them. There is no need to surrogate or take on the energy yourself before it's cleared, or you are just double handling the energy and making yourself sick in the process. This is a very dangerous game. Spirit never intended for you to suffer for another to be cured. Just send that stuff straight up to the hands of spirit to release. You are a channel to bring the light down, so your client can be flushed and then spirit will simply scoop up the negative overflow released and clear it. Take a close look at any old patterns of surrogacy or co-dependence from your formative years if you are struggling with this.

Ritual

'Ritual is the passageway of the soul into the infinite'
- Algernon Blackwood

There's nothing I love more than a good ritual. If you are running retreats and workshops, a ritual element is an absolute must. Ritual turns your theories into practice. It creates a space of empowerment, surrender and intention. It will take your clients to new heights and new vibrations. Nothing creates breakthroughs like a great ritual. It calls on the magic of the universe to step in on your behalf and speed your progress. It can be playful, creative and incredibly powerful. There is no end to the amazing rituals you can create for yourself and your clients. A ritual is a prayer to the universe, a wish, a promise and a request for assistance all rolled into one.

Each ritual must have a beginning, middle and an end. It must have a contained area that acts as a vessel and holds the energy beautifully as you gather power. A ritual must be performed in an impeccable space, so be sure to choose the right venue and clear the energy of the space before you begin. You can do this by burning a smudge stick, using rosemary, frankincense or sage essential oil, using sacred symbols, calling in spirit or any other practices that work for you. Show respect to spirit and invite the light by creating beauty in the ritual environment. Light some candles, bring in crystals, flowers, plants or statues. Rituals performed out in nature have an extra special energy. Be sure to honour any cultural traditions, ask for permission and feel the land to be sure it is the right place for the ritual.

If you feel stuck and need some help with your purpose, a ritual is a fantastic practice. To perform a ritual by yourself, first think really clearly about your intention, meditate on it and ask yourself if this is what you really,

really want. The more ceremony and presence around a ritual, the more powerful it becomes as the universe sees you are serious about your intentions, so prepare yourself physically, mentally, emotionally and spiritually for your sacred ritual. Have a salt bath with rosemary oil or throw a few drops of rosemary oil at the base of your shower and breathe deeply. Wash your hair. Put some beautiful moisturiser on, or olive oil with a few drops of your favourite essential oil, and massage your skin. Wear a beautiful dress or outfit that you feel special in. Adorn yourself with jewellery, flowers in your hair or a beautiful scarf across your shoulders. Dress in a way that makes you *feel* like your beautiful, sacred spirit self.

Then slowly and mindfully create the space for your ritual. It is nice to have the space already set up, but please don't light your candles until you step in (safety first). Sit for a few moments in meditation and begin to quietly talk to the universe about how you feel, what you want to let go of, and what you would really love to bring into your life right now. You can ask for assistance, synchronicity, clarity, money, support, or whatever you need. This is a totally open space. Ask spirit to remove any old thoughts, patterns or beliefs that block your way. Write down any old ways of being or thinking that no longer serve you on a piece of paper. Take your time with this; you may be surprised with what comes up. Every time you think you are finished, wait a few moments more and see if anything else appears. When you're totally done burn the paper and be sure it has all gone up in flames. If you are performing the ritual indoors, leave a window open so the old can escape. Then sit quietly with eyes closed, visualising what you want to welcome in now. Feel this new positive intention in every cell in your body. When you feel it is time, give thanks for the support and close the circle mindfully and purposefully. Spend the rest of the evening or day quietly and mindfully. There are more auspicious times in the lunar calendar to create rituals, but if you really need some help, don't wait three weeks for the right time, spirit is always listening.

Big rituals shouldn't be performed *too* often. For every ritual you do, you will experience changes physically, mentally, emotionally and spiritually, and your system will need time to adjust. Let the dust settle and changes integrate before you go again. I would recommend a full ceremonial ritual once or twice a year, but always feel into the body and see when it feels right for you, checking in that your system won't feel overloaded. Smaller rituals like grounding, protection, clearing, self-love, setting intentions and so on can be performed on a daily, weekly or monthly basis.

To create a ritual for a group, set up the space with beauty, care and a clear intention. Make sure everyone is really clear on the intention and don't waver from the subject. It needs to be powerful, purposeful and clear. You are asking folks to commit to one thing, so don't take them to a space you haven't gained permission for. Make sure you check in with spirit beforehand and be sure that the intention for the group is aligned with what will be best for them, rather than what you think they need. Ask the group for their commitment to attend the ritual. Let this be a choice for them and don't attach to it. Whilst you may want everyone there, it really is a personal choice as to whether that person's system is ready for the huge shift that will follow. Keep it beautiful, sweet, powerful and protected, so clients feel safe in the space.

Ask everyone to shower and dress up. Before anyone arrives create a stunningly beautiful space, clear the energy, and call in spirit, the universe, angels, goddess, or whatever is appropriate. Set the tone so that everyone there feels like a loving and loved spirit in human clothing. Lead everyone into a beautiful circle that holds the space. Give them a flower, crystal or something to make them feel special. You may like to move through the circle, look each person in the eye, and place your hand on their heart or shoulder. To me silence in the opening can be very profound. Begin with a beautiful meditation to set the tone and bring everyone fully into their body, heart and soul. Speak gently, intentionally and powerfully. Let there be space and time, don't rush, be totally led by spirit on when to talk and when to remain silent so people have time to integrate. Have a fire or fireproof dish at the centre of the circle. You may have asked everyone earlier in the day to write down everything they wish to let go of that is holding them back, or you can get them to do it in the space of the ritual. Make sure the list is relevant to the theme of the ritual, retreat or workshop. So not just what is holding them back in general, but what is holding them back from creating abundance or feeling beautiful, or living their dream or whatever the focus is. That way it will be a lot more powerful, and energise the whole experience astronomically. Invite them when they feel ready to move forward and release their list to the fire and spirit, then come back to their spaces and sit quietly for a while. Ask them to imagine, visualise or pretend they are living the opposite of what they have released. How would it feel for them to receive abundance, embody their beauty or step onto the path of their true calling? Let them sit in this energy, asking them to really feel and absorb that positive energy in every cell in their body. Ask them to lie back in Shavasana, arms slightly out from the body, palms turned to the ceiling in a gesture of surrender and receptivity. Let them feel the pulse of new life right throughout their body. Provide blankets or mats if they are outside. You will need to sit up and watch over them. If you are doing this in the daytime by the sea, a beautiful swim afterwards is a lovely refresher.

Make sure you are fully grounded throughout the process, as the energy is going to feel pretty strong. Try as much as possible to let the group, earth or spirit hold the energy. You are a channel for the ritual, but it will be too strong for your energetic body to hold everything, and this can stop or limit the flow through to everyone. Let it go, let it flow and ground into the earth. Let the ritual create its own energy pattern for release and healing. This is just one example, but the possibilities are endless. Remember to keep it simple, powerful and clear. Too much going on will bring people into their heads and out of their hearts and souls. If you have never performed rituals before you are going to *love* it. If you're a little nervous, try practicing on a few willing friends and getting their feedback.

Ritual brings the sacred to everyday life and reminds you that you are indeed spirit inside a human body. By bringing your full intention and awareness to bathing, eating, cooking or moving, anything can become a ritual of beauty and love. Small everyday rituals are more subtle, but no less powerful in their own way. They bring the sacred to life simply, powerfully and sweetly, and change you vastly over time.

Ask Yourself

Are you sure what you are asking for is what you really, really, really want?

Is the space for the ritual safe, beautiful and comfortable for yourself and your clients?

How can you bring more ritual to your work?

How can you fill your daily life with small rituals that invoke respect, love, devotion, appreciation and abundance?

Try This

If you are running a retreat where there is a labyrinth, this is also a beautiful subtle way of performing a ritual. You can create as much ceremony as you like around it. Clients can walk into the centre, thinking about everything they would like to release, sit at the centre for a while consciously letting go, then journey back out, inviting the new when they are ready.

A walking ritual is also powerful when you need to process or release. You could walk out to a certain point releasing something specific, and then walk back welcoming new energy to empower your intentions.

The possibilities are endless and only limited to your creativity. List three ritual processes that appeal to you, then fine-tune them, beautify them and try out the one that appeals most.

If you perform a large ritual at the beginning of each year, record it and look back at the end of the year to see the shifts you have made and how powerfully the intention, commitment and devotion around your ritual has empowered your life.

Get your retreat attendees to write a letter to themselves in the days following the ritual, then post it out to them in thirty days to see what a difference that ritual has made to their life.

Self-Care

'There are days I drop words of comfort on myself like falling leaves, and remember that it is enough to be taken care of by myself.'
- Brian Andreas

You know you need to look after yourself, right? Clients flock to a healthy, radiant practitioner who teaches what she or he preaches. It is amazing the amount of wellbeing practitioners out there who are just not looking after themselves. Part of creating a healthy, thriving business is creating a healthy, thriving you. The universe will not send you clients when you are running yourself into the ground. Potential customers also pick up when your energy is flat or out of balance, and there is the danger of passing on negative energy to them, which I know you would never intend to do. It is essential first and foremost for your own wellbeing that you schedule a daily program of self-care. I guarantee you that when you are vibrating at your peak, your manifestation practices will operate at a whole new level of power and attraction. It will help you manage any anxiety about your business and well, you just need to love yourself, okay?

Daily Practice

A daily practice is like a spa for your soul. It doesn't have to be complex and roll on for hours. Nor does it have to be part of someone else's prescribed medicine. Create your own unique daily ritual that centres, clears and nourishes your soul. It may be a walk in nature, dance, yoga or lying on your treatment table with a rose quartz crystal at your heart. Whatever you choose, I would thoroughly advise ten to twenty minutes meditation at the end.

Meditation is the space in which all guidance is received and all knowledge is opened up for you. It is where you receive guidance for yourself and your work, and it can make a huge difference to the way you move forward, and the level of support you feel. For best results I would suggest an opening practice for the beginning of the day and a closing practice to clear, release and centre for a restful night's sleep. By all means add a lunchtime practice too if you like; the more connected you feel to spirit throughout the day, the closer you will feel to living with purpose. This daily focus ensures that your life is full of positive intention and self-care. It is a clear indicator to yourself that you are worthy of your own care and attention.

Holiday or Retreat

You need a minimum of two weeks' holiday a year. There are so many cheap holiday packages and flights around these days that there is no excuse. You can also go on a very basic yoga retreat, but if you need a bit of luxury and pampering, own it. It is not true that you can't afford the time or money to have a holiday. That is a total fabrication of your mind. Get a part-time job if you need to, block out the time at the beginning of the year, put money aside and do it. If you are choosing a wellness retreat, make sure it feels nourishing and nurturing to you, and is not just for extra learning credits. The last thing you want to do is to go away for a break and come back feeling like you've been in your head the whole time. Take the time to wind down before you go too. Also set aside time for a weekend spiritual retreat every now and again, so you can immerse yourself in the spiritual life away from the distractions of the modern world. I recommend Brahma Kumaris for a simple break away. I don't necessarily align with everything they believe, but they are an incredible organisation that totally radiate love and live their talk.

You may find it challenging, but take yourself off all technology, business, marketing and social media for the duration of your break and get back into your body. You need to let go of this idea of urgency or push, or that you will miss out if you are not available to clients 24/7. Your identity should be firmly rooted internally; you don't disappear because you're not on Facebook. Trust that your tribe will be waiting for you when you return, and will be extra excited to hear new ideas and fresh inspiration from a well-rested spiritual leader. A little unavailability can do wonders for your popularity.

Nurture

I would recommend a nurture treatment such as a massage or healing once every two to three months. There is something very beautiful about allowing someone else to tend to you, especially when you care for others. Even if you don't think you need it, I guarantee you'll come out feeling a million times better than you went in. Remember healing treatments are not just for healing wounds or blocks, they are an essential opportunity to heighten your connection to spirit and your soul. Look for a lovely practitioner and space where you feel cared for and nurtured. You could choose a spa, but never underestimate the incredible home-based practitioners who are highly talented, intuitive, qualified and experienced. In between sessions create some simple nurture experiences at home. Have a lovely bath with salts and essential oils, set some time aside for inspirational reading, wandering through markets or spend a day at the local beach or forest. Make a list of everything that makes you feel nourished.

Positive Growth

I thoroughly recommend finding a good kinesiologist, coach, healer or practitioner of your choice to aid you in the fulfilment of your dreams, or help you through any crisis when you have a meltdown. You were not meant to walk through this world alone, and employing someone to help you along the way only makes sense. You can use this practitioner to stay on track, overcome any mindset issues that may be holding you back and cheer you on when you are feeling despondent. There is no shame in chucking a wobbly every now and again. It can be tough to navigate the world between being human and fulfilling your spiritual purpose. Rather than suffering in silence, swallow your pride and reach out for help. On most occasions you'll come out of your funk faster and wiser than if you tried to navigate your way through on your own. Do your homework and find a high-calibre practitioner who takes confidentiality seriously, will allow you to maintain sovereignty in your quest for help, get who you are and what you're trying to achieve.

Physical Fitness

There is a direct correlation between your physical health and your mental, emotional and spiritual health. It doesn't matter what shape or size you are, but part of being spiritually healthy is the free flow of energy throughout your body, and a physical practice must be part of your regular weekly routine. It will ground those who work in the more spiritual realms, clear the mind for those in more mental realms and energise those who spend too much time sitting at the computer or consulting. There is a movement form for everybody including tai chi, walking, qigong, yoga, Nia, dance, Pilates, or even boxing. Choosing a movement form that you love and brings you joy will ensure you follow through. Buy in bulk so you are committed to attending class. Even if you are a physical fitness teacher it is still imperative that you attend another class, because as you know the experience of receiving is totally different to the experience of teaching. Just choose a gentle class to balance up if you feel you are at your physical limits. The stronger you feel physically, the more energy you will have to complete your purpose, and we are so lucky to have an amazing array of spiritually based physical practices these days that there is something for everyone. More on the importance of this in the next chapter.

Fun

Part of self-care is getting out in the real world and having fun. Visit a gallery, have lunch with friends, go surfing, walk on the beach, learn Spanish, go to a cooking class, read, take up archery, or do any crazy hobby you love just for the hell of it. Do something that has absolutely nothing to do with your business and you'll come back fresh, alive and invigorated.

Ask Yourself

Are you getting the food, sleep, rest, water, nourishment and support you need to be as well as you can be?

When was the last time you had a holiday?

How often do you book yourself a massage or healing?

Does your daily practice need some refreshing?

When was the last time you sought out professional help with your direction?

Are you sacrificing your own health and wellbeing to service your clients?

How much physical movement are you doing?

How much fun are you having?

Try This

Take each category above (daily practice, holidays or breaks, nurture, professional development, physical fitness and fun) and rate your self-care on a scale of one to ten in each of these categories. Then ask yourself what is one thing you can do today to make a difference. For instance you might organise a night out with the girls, block time in your calendar for a holiday, sign up for a term of exercise, or book a massage. Ask yourself how taking notice of your needs and caring for yourself makes you feel.

Do some research; find a great holiday site, massage therapist, kinesiologist, coach or fitness class so you have details on tap for when you need them.

Create some self-care cards for yourself with specific actions listed on each card like; have a massage, go to yoga, buy yourself some flowers, make a hearty soup, go out to dinner, have a hot bath, go for a walk in nature, list ten beautiful things about yourself and so on. Try to create at least fifty options of self-care that feel good to you. Some that are free and some that require time or money. If you are feeling depleted, or out of balance, choose a card and follow through.

Commit by buying classes in bulk, booking appointments every couple of months and paying for holidays. That way you have something to look forward to and feel supported and nourished while you commit to your work. Trust the money will always be there.

Please take your self-care seriously. I have seen so many practitioners on burnout and even with serious physical ramifications of their choices to put others before themselves, or saying yes when they really should have said no. Don't put yourself through this when it is largely avoidable. Shower the same love and care on yourself as you would on a sweet, precious client. It can only do wonders for your spirit and your business.

Get out there and have some fun. Run amok with the humans. 'Get your halo dirty', as Danielle La Porte would say. Play with your kids, have mad sex with your partner and live the full breadth of your experience as it was meant to be lived. Get your fingers into the earth, your feet in the water, laugh and dance. The world is at your disposal.

Physical Vitality

'We need places to scream and run wild as well as places to be quiet.'
- Marty Rubin

In order to perform at your highest spiritual level, physical vitality is essential. Now that is not a statement about weight or age or shape. It is about creating a clear flow of energy in the body so that the spirit may flow through easily. This can be done with gentler practices of tai chi or qi gong as easily as it can be done with dynamic yoga, aerobics or dance. Physical vitality has absolutely nothing to do with punishing the body through exercise. On the contrary, if you are engaged in punishing physical routines you need to step back and look at your level of self-care and self-love. Ask yourself why you are driving yourself so hard. If more energetic practices fill you with joy, passion and drive, if they make your soul come alive, then by all means, immerse yourself. The trick is to find which physical practices are best suited to your being; that feed you on a physical, mental, emotional and spiritual level. If slow or deeply meditative yoga drives you crazy, try Bikram or Ashtanga yoga. If Ashtanga yoga is too strong for you and what you need is stillness, try Hatha or Yin yoga. You really should exercise in the way that is most supportive to your spirit and most calming to your ego.

A physical practice is a very powerful way to transmute energy, increase the level of prana in your body and clear the channels for spiritual connection. If you imagine that spiritual energy or prana is constantly moving through the body via the oxygen in your lungs, blood, muscles, organs and cells, then you want to create the clearest pathways possible. If your system is full of kinks or stagnant energy, that will go on to affect you on every level. Eat the highest quality food you can find, breathe deeply, move often, and sleep adequately, and you will be well on the way to incredible physical vitality that enlivens the spirit.

A physical practice gives you an opportunity to work with energy at a physical level that can be incredibly therapeutic too. I once had a boxing session on building personal strength and power when I was having trouble setting boundaries. It created incredible shifts for me. When I was feeling jittery from the energy of the book, I would take a long run in nature to ground myself and burn off some energy. In Nia dance each class is set with a focus and intention that you deliberately step into, becoming a powerful force for manifestation moving through the body. Right now every day, I am dancing the energy of my purpose into being.

Remember too that the subtle energies of the body are influenced by physical movement. Pilates has a strong core focus, so you are working very much on the three base chakras. This is a fantastic physical practice for helping you become grounded in who you are, reconnecting to your sensual power and gaining self-confidence and self-esteem. Think not only of what you are receiving physically, but what you are receiving energetically as well. Belly dancing may connect you to your sensuality, boxing may help you with your personal power, tai chi may help you to slow down and so on. Think about what you're really looking for and find a movement practice you love, so you're more likely to stick with it.

At the end of every physical practice, slow down with some stretches, allow the breath to lengthen and finish with a meditation. Lie back in Shavasana; arms slightly out from the body, palms turned to the ceiling, ankles slightly wider than hip width apart. Feel the physical vitality moving through your body. Feel the life force energy creating new pathways, helping you to open, receive and grow. Trust your physical body. Love it, nourish and nurture it. Movement is healing. The right physical practice will always remind you that you are stronger than you think, and create robust energy and stamina to take your spirit work out into the world.

Ask Yourself

What do you need the most right now from a physical practice?

How much vitality do you feel in your physical body right now and what could you do to increase that?

How does a physical practice help you feel stronger, more confident and connected to your body?

Can you see your body as a sacred vehicle for your soul?

Try This

Before you choose a physical practice, try to think of it more from the perspective of what qualities you would like to generate, or what energy you need, and which practice offers these.

List all the practices you ever wanted to try and get out there and give it a crack; from belly dancing to acroyoga to surfing. It may be wacky, wild, wonderful or conservative and it really doesn't matter. Just ground yourself by getting back into your body and connecting with your vitality. Getting physical should be fun too.

Put intention into whatever practice you choose. Go to yoga intending to find stillness, dance intending to release or Pilates intending to build your internal strength. Whatever you want to manifest or release, bring it to your physical practice. Where your attention goes, energy will follow. It doesn't have to be serious; you can just go to simply be as well.

Find the practice that resonates with you. If something is no longer working for you, go out there and try something different. Don't stop moving. Walk, run, breathe, stretch, dance or pump iron. It really doesn't matter as long as you are conscious about it.

Learn to love the vitality in your body and see what a difference it makes to your spirit. Try to get out in nature too for an extra boost.

Living Spirit

'Travel light, live light, spread the light, be the light.'
- Yogi Bhajan

Here's a funny thing, but whatever you move towards, moves towards you. Whatever you focus on, invest in or indulge in becomes charged magnetically. The busier your life, the harder it is to see this at work, but if you take a step back, it's really quite spooky to see what extent the power of attraction is at work in your daily life. Every action you take, every choice you make is like rubbing a magic genie lamp and saying, 'I'll have more of this please, universe'. If you're rubbing the lamp in all the right times and places that's fantastic, but if what keeps popping into your awareness and life is less than you deserve, it may be time for a rethink.

Now you may be purer than the driven snow, in which case move on, but if you have some old habits that need tending it's time to take a look. Ever noticed how when you buy that gorgeous dress you just have to have new shoes to go with it, or when you work yourself into the ground other things just keep piling up on your desk, or when you feel competitive with one practitioner several practitioners start pushing your buttons, or when you skip meditation one day, the next day seems easier to miss as well? Of course many addictions and choices are tied to self-worth, but what makes them so hard to break free of is the charge that gets magnetised every time you act.

Kundalini yoga guru Yogi Bhajan says 'Don't solve your problems, dissolve your problems so that they should not recur again.' The greatest cure for any addictions or unconscious choices is to actively pursue the sattvic life. Sattva means purity in the yogic tradition and is all about creating a life with as much clarity and purity as possible, so you can support and increase your spiritual growth. It's not a judgement call; it's a beautiful, simple, loving way of living. I'm not talking hardcore religion or fanaticism here, but simply the intention to make the choices that offer you the greatest chance of clarity, peace and success in your life.

In the modern world with a family, business, social life and all the distractions that come with it, this can be a challenge, but all the more reason to create a space for consciousness. The idea is when you introduce high-vibration practices to your day the lower vibrations eventually melt away. Often when trying to make changes we work on clearing the negative behaviour, without giving enough attention to building the light at the same time. So whilst you still should try to cut back on any unconscious behaviour, thinking, relationships and actions, you also place the emphasis on increasing light-filled practices such as meditation, exercise, clean pure food, breathwork and the daily practices of your tradition. You can spend loads of time and effort removing 'the bad', but the truth is by increasing the light and higher vibration choices, a lot of the old stuff will just fall away.

Invest in the light. The more you can commit yourself to your spirit life, the easier everything will become; the clearer your purpose, your vision and your life. Accumulations in the body and mind from unsattvic choices create confusion, diversions and stagnant energy. Sattvic choices create incredible light that can dissolve all obstacles on your path. The more sattvic your choices, the clearer your space becomes physically, mentally, emotionally and spiritually. What if you were to commit to being the living light? It is amazing how many spiritual leaders dismiss this out of hand because it's unrealistic. What if you were the light in your family, community, or workplace? How would that feel to yourself and others? The truth is beyond all our goals and intentions, beyond all form and function, being the living spirit is our one true purpose. As a spiritual leader embodying the light you can create incredible shifts in yourself, your environment, your teachings and the world.

Ask Yourself

If every single person on this planet were living spirit right now how different would things be?

For every action forward ask yourself is this a higher choice?

Instead of battling against addictions or distractions, can you try to dissolve them by making different choices that raise your level of consciousness?

What aspects of your life, business, communication or relationships require more light?

Can you take responsibility for the level of light in your life and increase it today?

Try This

Get away to a traditional ashram style retreat and experience life the sattvic way, with no distractions, social media, television or rush. Talk to people, meditate, and absorb the prana of wonderful food, fresh air and sacred company.

Break your life into different sections of leisure, relationships, work, money, health & fitness, physical environment, romance and personal growth/spirituality. In each section ask yourself how much consciousness is present on a scale of one to ten. Then in each section ask yourself one thing you could do to increase the level of consciousness in that area. For instance in money you may choose to start saving a little more, giving something to charity, or increasing your level of maturity and responsibility around money. For your physical environment you may need to add more plants to your space, have a big cleanout or consider moving. Small changes in each area can make a huge difference, and you can make a note in your diary at the end of each month to run through these sections again, see how you're doing. Examine the impact of each choice and explore some new changes you could make.

Small changes are usually more sustainable unless you really feel you need to do something radical.

Make meditation a non-negotiable part of your daily routine. It is the fastest, most direct route to a higher vibration and greater light.

Create a weekly schedule of physical activity that could lift your vibration.

It could be as simple as walking on the beach, out in nature, or whatever leaves you feeling energised and clearer.

Make every choice, every movement, every word a higher choice. If you slip up, just choose again. It is time to embody living spirit in its truest sense.

Honouring Yourself

'When you put your house in order you put your affairs and past in order too.'
- Marie Kondo

On holidays recently I bought a really beautiful book called *The Life Changing Magic of Tidying Up* by Marie Kondo. Marie Kondo recommends that you put every single piece of clothing in the house onto the floor with the idea that you are going to throw everything out. Then you pick up each garment one at a time, hold it, touch it, and connect. If it sparks a sense of joy in you, you can keep it, folded beautifully in your wardrobe. Each garment is treated with respect and love for the joy it brings you. As I went through this process it was alarming how little of what I had was sparking joy in me. Was I going to be left in the nude? Actually the whole experience was very liberating. When I cleared all the superfluous, all I could see was beauty…the really special things. And I noticed something else. I wasn't really wearing the stuff I loved. I was saving it. And then I thought about all the beautiful organic veggies in my fridge that I wasn't eating, because I was saving them (although of course they don't keep so I was throwing them out each week). I was waiting to experience, wear, eat, and feel the very best I could. I was holding back on enjoying things that made me feel beautiful, loved and cared for.

Then I looked at my office space and realised my bookshelves are filled with books I've long outgrown, and my favourite books were buried in the milieu. What would it be like for me to eat, wear, read, and look at nothing but the very best? To keep just a few deeply treasured things. I felt like a huge weight had lifted from me. Of course you need to invest in those things that bring you joy, but to fill your life only with those things? The possibilities were endless and rebounded through my business, life and relationship with myself. Years ago when I read affirmations about surrounding yourself with the very best, I thought it meant the very best you could afford. Buying the best labels, the latest fashion would send you a message of self-love and abundance. But actually it's all about what is exquisitely joyful to you. It's about authenticity and what feels like a gathering of treasures to your heart and soul. I get so excited about a posy of flowers beside my laptop I can't tell you. If I add a candle, a shell and feather I'm virtually apoplectic. Seeing that out of the corner of my eye as I write reminds me I am above all a soul. I am fulfilling my purpose to serve others with love, and that I intend to treat myself with love along the way. That's a whole load of affirmation, recognition and joy for a few simple, beautiful things.

Furthermore this realisation gave me permission to move away from groups I no longer resonated with, and increase time with those whom I did. I could give up the clients who were dragging their heels and focus more on those who were 110% invested. This freed up an incredible amount of my life force energy. I also proceeded to fill my life with simple pleasures and meaningful rituals. Although I was always very particular about setting a beautiful environment for my clients, I had neglected myself. So I began to play lovely music in my office, buy beautiful little flower posies, have tea ceremonies on my verandah, light gorgeous candles by my computer, and fill the room with essential oils. The change was simple, remarkable and uplifting. I realised I am worthy of beauty while I work and serve. More than that, it is essential to replenishing my life force.

One of the major things I insist on with my clients is to clear out all the superfluous stuff in their business so people can see who they really are. So they can live their most authentic work. It is so liberating, although I understand very scary. Some clients strip it all back, go into fear, and then gather anything they can to cover their nakedness. More still thrive here. But it takes determination, honesty and above all else courage. If you can hold firm, radiating only the absolute truth of who you are, sit and bask in the absolute pleasure of it, you are made. You deserve nothing but the very best and most authentic beauty to surround you. Once you start clearing out the superfluous, what is left may just take your breath away.

Ask Yourself

Where are you resisting filling your days with beauty?
What would honouring yourself with beautiful things mean to you?
Can you move past what 'looks good' to what feels good?
What is intrinsically beautiful to you?
How can you surround yourself with the beauty and care you lavish on your clients?
How would it feel to have a life filled with beauty?

Try This

You deserve to have a life filled with joy. Grab yourself a copy of Marie Kondo's book and start clearing out your wardrobes, your cupboard and those notes from that personal development course back in 1984.

Be willing to clear space, to see the beauty that was there all along.

Write a list of things that feel like treasures to you and fill your home and your life with them. Simple things like a collection of shells, feathers or crystals. Beautiful sacred books or a leather-bound journal. Arrange freshly picked flowers, candles or essential oils. Try a luxe organic moisturiser, raw food cooking classes, a beautiful meal out with friends or whatever sings to you. Try something that has never even occurred to you before, but other folks do all the time.

Be sparing with the placement of sacred objects and don't overcrowd them, so each treasure has its own stage and you can glimpse them easily as you move through the house.

Look at your business and ask yourself where the beauty of your authentic work is being hidden amongst the fillers.

Meditation and Visualisation

'Meditation makes the entire central nervous system go into a field of coherence.'
- Deepak Chopra

Meditation is an essential part of any successful wellbeing business. It will help you personally with self confidence, deepening your intuitive wisdom and staying centered and calm whilst building your business. When you are tapped into universal wisdom, everything is at your disposal. There is nothing that cannot be answered or resolved here. Meditation is a very high vibration space; it carries the energy of pure potentiality and the seeds of manifestation. It is the rich soil in which you can plant your dreams. Meditation is the direct path to your soul, spirit and the soul of the universe. It helps you receive messages and guidance from the divine, clarify your purpose, clear your mind and make better decisions. It is an absolutely crucial element of both your soul's journey and a vibrant healthy business. Meditation will help you uncover your true purpose, and become a living spiritual force for awakening on this planet. It will help you lead from the heart and soul and open you up to incredible opportunities.

Traditionally meditation is pure stillness or 'being consciousness bliss' as they say in yoga, where you simply merge with the divine and all that is. It is the opportunity for a moment to return to the source, merge with its light and return refreshed. It elevates your vibration and burns away all that is less than, distracting or worrying you. Stillness meditation is a beautiful experience where the mind and questioning stop and you almost receive on a visceral level. I am not a traditionalist who would say stillness meditation is the only way, but I would encourage you in whatever meditation style you practice, to leave a little room for pure stillness in there. Many people need a gentle lead in to stillness and I love to use the beautiful music of Deva Premal, a gently guided body relaxation or a breathwork focus to help. Our lives operate at such a busy pace and are filled with so many distractions that some days it can be hard, or damn near impossible to drop right in to meditation, even for spiritual folks.

Remember there is no such thing as a good meditation or bad meditation, there is just meditation. Keep going to your meditation space even, or especially, if you are not in the mood. You must understand your ego will fight against meditation and being guided, as it wants to always be in control and meditation threatens its grip on you. The trick is even on bad days, or when you are angry with spirit, go to that meditation space to receive. That is spiritual maturity. A regular meditation practice will make you a much better teacher, healer, leader or practitioner. It will help you to listen deeply, embody stillness and communicate with a rich vibration that alters people's lives for the better. You'll cease to teach by rote and begin to talk with a voice filled with deeper wisdom. Your material will become more profound and authentic and you'll be intrinsically connected to your soul's voice.

You can keep your meditation as simple as you like, the trick is to find the style that works for you. If you are very Pitta (intellectual, direct, sharp witted, able to concentrate, good decision maker) you may find Buddhist-style meditation better for you. If you have a vivid imagination, try to stay away from journey meditations or you'll be leaping over mountains and flying on unicorns before you know it, and although this may be fun at one level it can actually agitate your mind and spirit. At the end of your meditation you should feel calm, clear and centered, so choose whichever style takes you there; experiment.

Visualisation isn't meditation per say, but it is an incredibly powerful tool to help heal your body, focus on your business vision or a specific goal. Visualisation isn't a mad kaleidoscope from an unbridled imagination. It is about being wholly focussed on your vision and every day at the end of your meditation, when your vibration is high, focussing on that vision until it becomes a reality. It takes discipline and effort. You hold the vision and infuse it with as much love, joy and energy as you can in the moment. It is a super clear message to the universe that yes; this is what I need help with. I have absolutely no doubt that with daily focus, and *action* on your behalf, your dream will become a reality. It has certainly been a driving force in my success.

Let's get one thing straight; spirit will never, ever ask you to do something that feels wrong to you. We really need to let go of that idea that we need to sacrifice ourselves to be on the spiritual path. There are sacrifices to be made, but they are sacrifices *towards* your happiness, not away from it. Sacrifices like writing your book when you really want to go out shopping for clothes. Or not going to that party because you have a talk to give the next day. Or giving up your Sunday to have a stall at a Wellbeing Expo when you want to lie in bed and read. The incredible joy you feel at the end of your book, talk or expo well outweighs the sacrifice. The truth is there are sacrifices in every job, so we really need to get off the cross there.

The more time you spend in meditation, the more attuned you will become in your daily life. You will notice that directions and decisions become so much clearer. I was very remiss in my meditation for many years, and I can tell you that I could have saved years in blood, sweat, tears and turmoil if I had only gone to this sweet, soft, gentle space more often. There is no need to be scared to go within, there is nothing bad there, only the deepest, sweetest part of your being waiting to reach out to you, and an infinite universe wanting to pour its many blessings on your path.

Ask Yourself

How is your meditation practice?
   Are you resistant to meditating and why?
   What are you visualising every day to make your dreams a reality?
   Can you commit to making meditation a regular part of your day?

Try This

There are loads of meditation books, apps and courses out there (many of them free) so if meditation training wasn't a part of your education curriculum, try a few styles until you come upon one that works for you.

Once you have found your style, try an app like habit seed which helps you set an intention, and then asks you every day if you have followed through.

Traditionally you would meditate sitting up to stay relaxed and alert with the spine tall. You can sit cross legged, on a meditation stool or in a chair. As I say I am not a traditionalist so if you feel you can let go more lying down, then go for it. Lie back in Shavasana, which means lying out flat with your arms slightly out from the body, palms turned towards the ceiling in a gesture of surrender. Ankles are slightly wider than hip width apart, allowing the hips, pelvis and lower back to open and release. If you have any lower back problems, you can use a bolster or rolled-up towels under your knees, so your back feels supported. You can use an eye pillow and a blanket too if you like. If you are working on your self-care I thoroughly recommend adding these small touches of self-love.

It is ideal to meditate twenty minutes morning and night, but you can start with just ten breaths and work your way in. You have been listening to your breath since the day you were born and it carries a unique signature that is incredibly soothing to you. Find a quiet space and begin by bringing your awareness to your breath as it enters and leaves the body. If you are lying down, on every exhale allow the body to release, on every exhale simply sink further into the floor. Over time you will find you naturally sit for longer and go in deeper. This is a good starting point if you feel scared of meditation for any reason.

Traditionally you would meditate in silence, but I like the mantras of Deva Premal. Mantras carry a specific vibration that can help attune you to the heart and soul, and because they are sung in Sanskrit the mind doesn't tend to attach to the words. Aad Guray, a mantra to open and protect the heart, is my favourite. Simply sit or lie down, focus on your breath and allow the mantra to wash over you.

If you really struggle to let go at all, I fully recommend doing some yoga first to step into the body and calm the mind. Despite the incredibly physical focus on yoga these days, the yoga poses were only ever invented to aid meditation, so you'll find it a lot easier to meditate after a few yoga stretches. If you are joining a class, call to make sure they have meditation at the end, or you can try a virtual class at home and finish with your own meditation.

If you are feeling anxious you could start with a simple yoga nidra. Lie out flat and connect to your breath. Slowly bring your awareness to each part of the body, breathing in and then letting go, starting at the feet and moving to the top of your head. For instance bring your awareness to your feet, your ankles, your calves, your knees and so on as you move up the body. Take your time, allow each part to relax and fall into the floor, before you move on to the next. Try two to three breaths at each point. Bringing your awareness to the body is grounding and calming to the central nervous system. Try a few yoga nidra apps or videos from You Tube to get you started if you like.

Be mindful that when you are lying down for meditation, you may well nod off to sleep, so be sure you're not going to be late for work! If you need to pay attention or find the answer to something a seated meditation is often best, as you'll remain more alert and relaxed at the same time.

The Sweet Spirit

*'As we become purer channels of light,
we develop an appetite for the sweetness that is possible in this world.
A miracle worker is not geared to fighting the world that is,
but toward creating the world that could be.'*
- Marianne Williamson

Never underestimate the power of sweetness. When I come across a business filled with sweetness and generosity I am hooked. It is the small things that bless us in life, and it is certainly so in business too. Never feel that because you are a sweet spirit or soft spoken that you will not be heard. There are many ways of finding your voice amongst the fray. The older I get the more I appreciate a sweet, honest voice. Sometimes it is the quiet voice spoken with softness and stillness that touches our hearts most deeply. If you are an extrovert challenge yourself to find a quiet voice within as well. If you are leading people to their truth there can be great power in creating space, softness and sweetness to calm their spirit and encourage their deepest selves to emerge. Look at Mahatma Ghandi or Mother Teresa or the Dalai Lama as sweet spirits that stayed dedicated to peace and love. When the Dalai Lama talks slowly and softly, people lean in to listen.

If you are a sweet spirit and a little sensitive, just be mindful that it is important to offer the gifts of your heart and soul in a place where they will be valued and appreciated. I remember once making a beautiful wild bouquet of herbs from our garden to take to a local café. There was more than my husband and I could eat, so I gathered a big bunch of dill, coriander, basil, rosemary, chives, lemon verbena, mint and oregano and tied it together with kitchen twine. It looked so beautiful and smelt so gorgeous I was really excited to share it, but as I gave it to the café owner she couldn't have cared less. She said 'we've got most of that stuff' and literally tossed it over her shoulder to the counter, where it hit the bench and fell onto the floor! I was so shocked I just left, but I wished I'd taken my beautiful gift back with me. Needless to say I never went there again.

It is easy in these circumstances to withdraw, but I would encourage you not to withhold your treasures or change who you are for the sake of a few. It would be a great tragedy for others to miss out because you have been hurt. You may even go on to help others who are sensitive create healthy boundaries for themselves. Never be shy or embarrassed about your sweetness, keep giving from your heart, and find the best way you can do this that supports, nourishes and protects you. It may be through artwork, writing, small groups, nourishing skincare or meditation classes. Go with your nature and keep building your inner strength.

That doesn't mean playing small, but if you want to go onto bigger stages I would really recommend starting small and building up, not because I don't think you're capable, but because you need to build your risk muscles. Whilst many folks would see me as very strong and capable, I have managed my sensitive spirit by generating a strong internal guardian that is right on point when it comes to letting me know who and what to steer towards and away from, when to rest and retreat and when to put myself out there. For the most part I listen keenly to that voice and take it seriously. I never do anything that doesn't feel right to me, no matter what external pressure I feel under.

You need to keep your central nervous system healthy, so always ask yourself honestly is that what I would really, really love to do? Is that what I am called to, or am I choosing it because I think I should be able to? The incredible beauty of this universe is that you have a nature that suits your soul purpose. Do what feels right to you. That may mean quietly working behind the scenes, quietly working up on stage, or anything in between. Sweetness is a quality that is greatly needed on this planet; in fact I would encourage anyone to drop out of their ego and into the exquisite sweetness of their spirit. This is the place from which no wars could ever be fought, no friction ever started, no competition ever begun. It is a place of deep love and generosity in which to bathe our spirits at every opportunity.

Ask Yourself

Are you living in line with your sweet nature?

Do you see your sweet nature as a blessing or a burden?

What avenues could you pursue which would allow you to express your sweetness without feeling stressed or anxious?

Are there some ways I could build my inner strength so I don't feel scared about expressing my true nature?

What could I change about where I live, work or socialise that would allow me to feel safer expressing my true nature?

Can I challenge myself to stay in my sweetness when circumstances challenge me?

Try This

Never change your behaviour or hold your sweetness back because you have been hurt in the past.

Your sweetness offers you great opportunity to create an incredible healing space for others, so use it to your advantage and create beautiful, unique, precious moments for your clients.

Sweetness always creates more sweetness by opening others to the opportunities vulnerability offers, so remind yourself of the gift your sweetness brings.

If someone can't accept your sweetness, remember it is all about what they are capable of accepting, and not about the quality of your offering.

Offer sweetness in spaces, places and with people who will honour it and create boundaries around those who won't.

Never be pressured into doing something or joining someone that doesn't honour who you are in essence. Look for the tribe that resonate with you and will listen to you however softly you speak.

Generosity and the Giving Heart

"When you enchant people your goal is not to make money from them or to get them to do what you want, but to fill them with great delight."
- Guy Kawasaki

Generosity starts with the quality of the products or services you offer your clients. The quality of information, the amount of work you put in, the value of the material you use, the time taken and the thought put into how to help them. You can also add beautiful gifts that enhance your clients' experiences, add value and show you appreciate them. Your special additions should be sustainable, and speak uniquely of you. Gifts don't have to be expensive or over the top; often small, thoughtful or homemade things given with great love leave a resounding impact. Make it relevant to what you are teaching, supportive to their learning, and from the heart. Let your clients feel they are cherished and valued. So what about a lovely tomato plant at the end of your wholefoods cooking lesson, a personally tailored oil from your aromatherapy day, a crystal to finish a healing workshop, a follow up free e-book from a training session or a simple letter of encouragement and acknowledgement to attendees. Let them know you are grateful for their presence in supporting your dream. There's no need to be ingratiating, but let them know they are deeply appreciated, and not just part of a gravy train.

At my book launch for *The Art of Joy* each of my gift bags contained a handmade teabag from the mint in my garden, an aromatherapy candle for limitless possibilities, a handwritten original affirmation card, a lemongrass foot soak and instructions for 'a moment of peace'. So my clients could take a moment at home, make a cup of tea, light the candle, soak their feet, read their inspiration card and get their copy of *The Art of Joy* out in the perfect space to soak up its wisdom. Now there is a sensory memory of relaxation attached to reading my book, so I hope that every time they feel out of balance or in need of some peace, their first thought is to pick up my book for healing and joy. I gave a few clients extras to take home for their young daughters, and they all lined up in a row for their relaxation experience.

You will need to ensure you are not over-giving to win favour, nor burning up your profits in the process, but a small act of authentic generosity leaves a resounding impact in the heart and mind of your tribe. And that little act of love is what it's all about.

Ask Yourself

Who can you help out?
What can you give with no expectation of return?
Who was generous with you in your early days and how did it feel?
How can you be more generous towards yourself by integrating your favourite work, time to rest, the ability to receive?

Try This

Write a list of twenty possible gift items you could offer your clients as a reward for their support. Sweet, handmade, small and loving is best. You can rotate them over time so if the same people are coming to your workshops they are getting a different takeaway each time, or you can tweak or update current offers. Keep adding to this list every time you get a bit of inspiration and you will never run out of ideas for a little added bonus when needed. It may be a crystal, a mini e-course, a discount on your coaching package, a lovely organic skincare sample. Remember to keep it in line with your business and brand. There are a lot of giveaways at the moment to get people to sign up to mailing lists, which is fine. Just don't forget a good dollop of quality and love in the offering. It's not just to build your list, it's to give with the fullness of your heart and the generosity of your soul.

Ask aligned businesses if they would like to contribute something to your goody bag at a conference or workshop. Be picky; for example you wouldn't want a can of cola, but a herbal tea sample could go down well. Small quality contributions are best. A few discount vouchers and a few products. You don't want to offer your clients a bag full of fliers. Let contributors know how your target audience aligns with theirs and it's a win-win. Be clear and acknowledge contributions from others in your gift bags.

Remember you need to choose gifts that are sustainable; if what you choose eats away all your profits, it becomes a little more ingratiating than gifting. I know it is so much fun to give things away, but if you are carrying the costs for expensive extras, you might need to look at your self-worth issues.

Remember that a gift can never replace high-quality products and services; it is simply a little icing on the top.

Appreciation

'Let gratitude be the pillow upon which you kneel to say your nightly prayers, and let faith be the bridge you build to welcome in the good.'
- Maya Angelou

I'm ashamed to say appreciation hasn't always been my forte. Sure, I've jumped for joy when fantastic opportunities have come my way, or something I have strived for has come through, or when I've reached huge milestones. But as far as the daily appreciation of the million things that love and support my journey, the truth is in my hurry to 'get things done' I have been quite remiss. I know a little more appreciation would have eased my journey. Appreciation is an acknowledgement to the universe that you know a thousand unseen hands are at your side, working on your behalf to help you fulfil your dreams. Appreciation helps break down the walls that make you feel overwhelmed, lost or alone. It is about accepting the help that is offered to you in the form of guidance, financial support, love and encouragement. It's about taking a little input from the universal wisdom that has just a touch more knowledge and experience than you. It is about opening; to receive, to serve and to connect.

The truth is to really connect to appreciation in its purest form you need to throw over its ugly cousin resentment. Those midnight laments of why isn't this working for me, why can't I get this, why does it seem like everyone is succeeding but me? Never be afraid to go there. Even though it is all about ego, at its heart this is born from a sense of pain, hurt, separation or unworthiness. Have some compassion. It's hard to appreciate when you feel less than, abandoned or alone, so you need to work through your stuff to get to the other side. What are you not allowing? Why are you looking for your power in the external world? Why do you believe your access to all things is restricted? When you really truly feel that your abundance and wealth comes from the inside, and can never be withheld from you, new doors open and the light comes on. You can begin to take responsibility for what has and hasn't happened for you in the external world, and make changes accordingly. You are not an empty shell waiting to be filled when and if someone or something out there deems it appropriate. You are no beggar. You are a child of the universe; rich, capable and free to choose. This knowledge is liberating; if all power comes from within, then you can create, accept and welcome whatever it is you truly love.

If you are spirit, if you are God or Goddess or universal energy, nothing is unavailable or outside of you. Ask yourself how you would act and feel if you were spirit. Chances are you would sit back in your body and your heart and smile. You would gently cast your eye over all opportunities in front of you, and with a relaxed and deeply humble gratitude, you would say 'oh look at this beautiful experience, yes I would love to do that', and then you would simply gather it in your arms with love and kiss it all over, accept it and go ahead. It really is that simple.

Appreciation paves the road to co-creation with spirit. It makes your world gentler, more loving and more connected. You begin to see breathtaking beauty in every corner; from people, to places, to your glorious self. It is like lifting the veil. You give thanks, you expect success, and your power of attraction is automatically elevated. You recognise beautiful opportunities and gravitate to the right people and places. Above all else you learn to appreciate yourself, your unique skills, talents and abilities. This in turn radiates a new energy out to your audience and the cycle of appreciation continues.

Ask Yourself

Can you learn to trust that the universe will be there to help you?

How can you create a daily appreciation ritual that reaffirms your place as a walking spirit in the universe?

Are you afraid that if you appreciate what you have now things won't get any better?

How is resentment or disappointment getting in your way of feeling appreciative?

Even if you wish you had more clients, how can you better appreciate the ones you have?

What are you thankful for?

Can you be grateful without being ingratiating?

How would it feel if you were pure spirit, God, Goddess, or universal energy simply moving through form?

Try This

Write down all the resentments you feel about your life or where you are at right now. Let it get as ugly as you like; the more childish, petulant or 'ungrateful' the better. Have a tantrum if you like. Chuck a good old-fashioned wobbly. Go to town. This isn't going to work unless you are totally thorough in your resentments first, so don't try to be too nice and spiritual about it. Then when you are utterly, totally done, challenge those resentments. For each one ask yourself, is this really true? Could there be another reason why this hasn't worked out, and if so, what is it? Take responsibility. Look for all the evidence that shows you are succeeding, make lists of all your breakthroughs big and small. Get really excited when someone likes your Facebook post or joins your mailing list. Do a little dance every time a client books in. Take each tiny, medium and large win as though you have won the lottery and expect the next success any moment.

Look back on the more difficult lessons in your life and ask yourself what you can appreciate out of the lessons learned. This helps you take responsibility for your part, ensures you won't repeat the same mistakes in the future and helps you become a wise advisor to others in the same circumstances.

Take some time daily to really tune in and appreciate yourself. What do you love about yourself? What skills have you used in your business this week to make someone's life better? What have you overcome that may have been difficult for you? You don't have to wait until you're perfect to appreciate yourself. Small, regular acknowledgements make for great confidence.

Look at areas of your business where you are not feeling appreciative. Perhaps you feel technophobia; maybe you don't feel you have enough clients or are clever enough to run your own business. List anywhere where you see gaps and rather than feeling overwhelmed, challenge them by appreciating what you do know, your determination to succeed, how you have overcome obstacles in the past. Chart a way through and appreciate your own ingenuity. Have faith and know *everyone* doubts themselves, even the most successful, prominent, spiritual leaders of our age. It's nothing to worry about; it just requires a shift in thinking.

Make your own markers for success and appreciate them fully. Don't compare the beginning of your journey to the middle of someone else's, or your bad day to someone else's good day, or your first attempt with their last. Resentment slows you down and if you really thought about it, maybe you don't really want what they're having after all.

Create a daily practice for appreciation. You may lie in bed at night listing everything you're grateful for (a lovely way to go to sleep), keep an appreciation diary, or light a candle and say a prayer of thanks. There are a million ways you could show your appreciation so go ahead; be creative, make it a beautiful ritual in your every day and just watch the shift it creates in your world.

Sit in meditation and feel yourself as God, Goddess, universal life force energy or pure spirit. Don't think about what you want to ask for, think about what you'll *choose* with deep gratitude, love and appreciation.

The Essential Bridge between Spirit and Business

'Your problem is you are too busy holding onto your unworthiness.'
- Ram Dass

Self-love is the bridge that leads to success, helps you believe in yourself, gives you permission to take your gift out into the world, and builds your integrity. It helps you move with faith, trust and confidence in the direction of your dreams. If you feel worthy all things open up for you. If you feel unworthy the energy becomes stagnant, blocked or circular. So it is vital that you identify where any unworthiness sits in your body, mind, soul or energy field and rectify it immediately. This will increase the energy flow that builds, sustains and nourishes your purpose. Make it your first priority. Given the abundant energy of the universe, all things should produce results given the right focus and intention. If you are investing time, energy and money in an authentic project and it is not coming to fruition, you need to know why. What is blocking you receiving at this level? What is stopping your spirit or soul from blossoming out into the world? What is preventing the delivery of your purpose? Where is there a gap between your spirit and your business?

Here's the thing; you can be really fantastic at knowing your soul and your work, be deeply dedicated to your spirit and your craft, have impeccable integrity, talent and vision, and still not be receiving. Why? Because you are operating as an island, and fulfilling your purpose is about laying down the planks and building a bridge to take your work into the world. And here's where things get complicated. You ask yourself am I worthy of holding, delivering and transporting this sacred message? Who am I to get this out there? Why do I have to be seen? Can't I do it from the back room? Or wait here quietly in my yoga studio until someone shows up? Well, no because it is your responsibility to step forward and say exactly who you are. To open your heart and your palms, and offer the gift that was entrusted to you with all your being. There is one bridge that you must cross in order to succeed in your calling, and it has three planks; self-love, self-worth and self-trust. You can have all the best marketing programs and sales funnels in the world, but if these are not present, you won't get the results promised. If you are having any trouble at all translating your soul purpose into a healthy thriving business, you can be guaranteed there is a lack in one of these three areas. You can come up with every reason in the world, but I guarantee you when you look at it, it will be one of these three. And it's high time to repair that bridge so that the soul has a clear journey forward.

Self-Love

When you love yourself enough you will believe in yourself wholeheartedly and you won't be frightened of what others might say. You will treat yourself with love, devotion and respect. You will be kind, rather than critical, optimistic rather than cynical, and open rather than judgemental. You will find the courage to be exactly who you are, without excuses. You will reveal yourself at the deepest level and blossom from that truth. You will set aside time to fulfil your dharma and do the work needed. You will nourish your body, mind and spirit to sustain you on your journey. You will fill your life with high-vibration people, places and practices that support you at every level. You will sit in the absolute glory of your spirit and feel deep gratitude at the opportunity to serve. You will treat yourself kindly and patiently along the way. You will teach others from the space of deep love and devotion. You will know that who you are is enough, and then some. You will take the time to really get to know yourself. You will immerse yourself in the blessings of spirit through a nourishing daily practice. You will be ready, willing and committed to spending time alone to deepen your craft. You will return to the touchstone of your inner light whenever you feel troubled. The level of radiant love in your being will increase your magnetism, drawing others to you from a deep heart space. You will step forward to be seen and heard with love, faith, confidence and ease.

Self-Worth

When you see yourself as worthy you will totally accept the majesty of your being, and your role as a force for divine light in the world. You will fully embody and embrace your calling. When you feel worthy you will create healthy boundaries in your business and with your clients. You will open wide to receive abundance on all levels, including financially. When you feel worthy money will not be seen as a burden, but a sacred gift. When you feel worthy you will not be embarrassed to succeed. You will embrace your role as leader, healer, visionary and teacher. When you feel worthy you will have no need to copy others or follow a prescribed way of acting or being. You will receive invitations from higher places and accept with grace. When you feel worthy you will be proud to be a driving force for love in the world. When you feel worthy you will feel the living spirit moving through you.

Self-Trust

When you trust yourself enough, you will follow your own judgment or inner illumination. When you trust yourself enough you will no longer doubt or question yourself. When you trust yourself enough you will never undermine yourself by questioning your decisions, integrity or vision. When you trust your knowledge you will embody your teachings. When you trust your authority you will lead without ego. When you trust yourself enough you won't need permission, approval or direction from anyone. You will merge your soul with the divine soul. You will listen to the callings of your soul across time, trust the guidance you receive and your capacity to follow through. You will rest, breathe and *know*. Self-trust is about inner strength, resilience and an unwavering sense of faith in yourself and your spirit. You will trust the soul of the universe, that blesses you with its sacred assignment, and you'll trust yourself to get it done with joy and ease.

Ask Yourself

Of the three planks which do you struggle with the most; self-love, self-worth or self-trust?

What can you do to move forward everyday and build your sense of self-worth, self-trust and self-love?

Can you see that it is vital you step forward to remove any blockages around these in order to fulfil your purpose?

How can you convince yourself you are loved, you are worthy and you are to be trusted?

Try This

Write down all the difficulties you are experiencing in getting your purpose thriving out in the world. Make it a long list if you like, you might as well see all the illusions you are living under! Then take each one at a time and ask yourself is this an issue of self-love, self-trust or self-worth? Take a note of which one comes up the most often. For each issue ask yourself how you can resolve or heal it. Pick one large or three small steps for each that you can action to heal and clear the energy.

It doesn't have to be complicated. If you need to work on your self-love you could simply place a rose quartz crystal on your heart every night before you fall asleep. Or you could ask the angel of self-love to help you, or you could start buying yourself a bunch of flowers every week, or have a massage every ten weeks and so on. The essential part is to keep that promise once you make it to yourself.

Identify the ways in which you send yourself messages that you are not lovable, worthy or trustworthy and get determined to eradicate these behaviours from your life.

Treat yourself as the most precious being that ever walked the planet. Be gentle, kind, loving and respectful towards yourself in every moment. If you are experiencing anxiety or tension, pause and choose again.

Take that self-love, self-trust and self-worth into the sacred bones of your business.

One Tribe

'We are only as strong as we are united, as weak as we are divided.'
- J.K. Rowling

A pivotal part of my purpose is to bring all wellbeing practitioners together, regardless of lineage, modem or training. To leave all judgement at the door and foster diversity, love, inclusion and mutual respect. There is so much division at the moment between modems, and even within them, when our capacity to work together and support each other could bring so much to us all. I'll never forget when I completed my yoga teacher training and excited to connect with other teachers, I met a frosty reception. From yoga retreats to classes to yoga magazines, much of what I saw and heard was filled with judgement, prejudice and narrow-mindedness from style to style. Each proclaimed to be the best, the original and the only. It caused me to withdraw from the yoga community for a long time. Let's make no mistake, where judgement and criticism rule, the ego is at play. What you don't like or appreciate isn't wrong, it's just wrong for you. Where we isolate ourselves from what others might teach us, we perish. When we are not prepared to sit at another's table, taste their food, and hear their wisdom, we can have no insight into their culture. Judgement, prejudice and assumption have no place in the spiritual realm.

Imagine if we all came together like different tribes to share our wisdom, our breakthroughs and our innovations. What if we looked upon each other with the eyes of love? What if we assumed the best instead of the worst? What if we honoured the traditions and cultures of another tribe without moving to change or fix them, even if they weren't for us? Where we are not sharing, we are not learning. Where we are not connecting, we are not growing. Let's break down walls and look with love and anticipation to a future where all wellbeing practitioners come together in a space of community, connection, optimism and hope for a beautiful experience of light and devotion. Let no one be outcast.

Ask Yourself

Would you be willing to release assumptions about what other tribes could and couldn't offer you, and listen instead?

How open is your spirit of adventure?

Would you consider yourself narrow or open-minded?

Is it possible that a particular training is not as insufficient as you have presumed?

How would it feel to come together as an industry to teach and learn from each other?

What if we could all help free each other?

Try This

Spirit in Business runs a conference once a year where wellbeing men and women from many different modalities, cultures and countries come together to listen and learn. We have the very best speakers, a vast variety of wellbeing experiences to try and incredible healers, teachers and leaders to learn from. It is all about attaining excellence in wellbeing, and feeling the incredible love, connection and energy that comes from impeccable spiritual leaders in one place. You can just imagine the incredible changes that happen for you personally and professionally here. Sign up to our newsletter at www.spiritinbiz.com.au to get notifications of our next event.

Every month, or at least once a year, try something different to get out of your box. Attend a new training, go to a networking event with other wellbeing practitioners, go to an expo and see what's new and innovative in your industry.

What complementary therapy that you have tried recently could you recommend to others?

How can you cross-refer with other practitioners?

Are there any projects you have coming up that would benefit from introducing other practitioners to your mix?

How well-known or regarded are you by other practitioners in your area? Have you made the effort to go and introduce yourself and create connections?

Release the illusion of competition and the 'other' and start thinking about authentic connections.

It's Not All Rainbows and Angels

"You need a work bone not just a wish bone"
- Clarissa Pinkola Estes

Those folks you see out there who are successful; who are at the forefront, who are all over social media, who give TED talks and write in magazines, and teach internationally, and pull the big numbers - they have worked their butts off. Day in, day out over a period of five, ten, twenty years or more. When they didn't understand something they found out how to do it. When they went through a tough time they cried, got angry, got frustrated, balanced back up and started again. Sound exhausting? Not really, not if you LOVE what you do. Not if you're driven by an inner fire. Not if you live and breathe your passion. Not if you're dedicated and determined and brave. Not if your heart is huge and your passion is strong and you're a warrior. Not if you're ready to jump on that horse and ride it. What's exhausting is the bullshit you give in to that holds you back. Not the forward movement.

Every vocation has its challenges. Imagine being a doctor or lawyer or truck driver or builder or police officer or a pilot. Imagine all the things that could go wrong in those vocations. What a nightmare. But they deal with it because that is what they love (hopefully) and they are prepared to work through the challenges for the privilege. I can deal with the challenges in my work and so can you. You know you can. At moments it might not feel like it, but would you rather have to face the problems of a truck driver with a blown tire in the middle of the night in the outback? Or a police officer facing a life-threatening situation? All of a sudden getting your head around social media doesn't seem so bad, does it? I don't believe in the saviour complex that says that soulful practitioners sacrifice their lives for others. I'd rather spend a lifetime investing in something I love, than be bored to tears with something I don't. I take full responsibility for doing this because it feeds me – it fills me up. I'll spend my last breath doing it – I never want to retire because this work is my lifeblood. That's not a sacrifice, it's a choice. It's a privilege and one I don't want to waste.

So you need to choose the size of your vision; from the heart, not the ego, and there is a lot more on this in the business model section of the book. If you have a big vision, know that you're going to have to work for it. That means putting in the hours, marketing, networking, sending applications, putting together packages, a million and one things that will need your attention. You'll need the drive, the energy and the passion to do it. I had a lovely client come to me and say, 'I just don't want to be out there doing public speaking and being all over the world. I want to stay at home with my kids and make beautiful food, work locally and build a healthier community.' Wow! What a vision. It sounded totally beautiful to me. While I'm out there speaking and travelling, this beautiful woman is at home building strength and health in her self, her house and in her community. I almost wanted to drop everything and do the same. But of course that's not my path. No vision is more or less than the other. I am all about helping practitioners achieve their authentic vision, whether it's huge and out there, intrinsic and local or anywhere in between. As long as that vision is pure and true.

It does annoy me when practitioners are resentful of others' success or expect all the work to be done for them. If you want it – get on board with it. Go out and get your hands dirty. Don't sit back and complain that things are not happening. Ask yourself why. Be honest. Have you really been doing all you can? Are you in it for the long haul or just the accolades? Don't say you can't, ask yourself what will it take? There is no place for resentment in what you do and your clients can feel it. If you want a small joyful practice that fits in around your lifestyle, then really immerse yourself in that and own it. Don't let the ego compare your work with others, or drag you away from your soul work. Who do you think supports the leaders who go out onto a large stage? Who helps them work through their fears, keep their immune systems healthy and their central nervous system calm? It is the yoga teachers, healers, and naturopaths in local communities at home or abroad. Who is the greater? Do your soul's work, wherever, however or whatever that might be and you'll live a totally happy, joyful, fulfilling life.

If you want to be out there, know that there's a lot of work to be done and some of that work is the boring nitty gritty stuff, but on the whole it should feel inspiring, exciting and energising. I'm all for play and rest and fun, but work isn't a dirty word. Energy in equals energy out. Give it time. That means head down, bum up and work it.

Ask Yourself

What will it take to get you to where you want to go, and are you prepared to do the work necessary to get there?

How resistant are you to making a concrete plan and getting it done?

Is your criticism or judgement of others' success a way of avoiding your own work, or not acknowledging your own mindset around success?

Can you celebrate what others have achieved and take pride in your own craft?

Can you see it is the value in your work, not the size or shape that matters?

Try This

Take a good look at what you need to do in your business to give it an injection of energy. Think of one specific goal; for instance, to get ten more students in your Pilates class by next term. Then brainstorm all the ways you could do this. List at least fifty ways and get specific. For instance; taking fliers around to all the local cafes, offering a promotion where current students can offer a friend a free trial class, getting a stall at a wellbeing market, having an editorial in the local paper and so on and so on. Then set a precise time in your week where you will move through this list and complete the actions required. Either you want the students or you don't. Once you reach those targets set some new ones. Keep the awareness of how much love and light you'll be able to spread front and centre. You will feel fearful of some of these ways, and you'll either do it anyway or you won't.

Before Dr Ajit from the Australasian Institute of Ayurvedic Studies came to Australia, he was a Panchakarma specialist, lecturer at several Ayurvedic colleges in India and was employed by the Indian Government as an Ayurvedic Medical Officer. When he arrived in New Zealand in 1996, passionate about bringing Ayurveda to the western world, he literally stood on a street corner himself handing out fliers to people. It takes humility, passion and dedication to get your soul work out there. Give it your best shot and the universe will shower you with synchronicities and help. Show your hand, your heart and your intentions. Take it back to the love, ignore the ego and never ever forget why you're doing the work in the first place. And that leads us right into the business end, so it's time for action stations...

Business

The woods are lovely, dark and deep.
But I have promises to keep,
and miles to go before I sleep.

Robert Frost

Marketing

*'If you have something to offer in this blessing and disaster
called human life, then for heaven's sake contribute.'*
- Unknown

Things have changed quite a lot in the world of wellbeing. Ten years ago many of our practices were still on the fringe of society. Now there's a veritable explosion in the wellbeing audience. So what does all this mean for you? It means you are at the leading edge of a boom industry, and it's time to get jiggy with it. Can marketing be unethical? Yes, absolutely. Marketing is a specific plan to build your brand and your business. Make that plan full of deceit, lies and manipulation, and hey presto you've got yourself an unethical plan. If you cringe at every word you write because it comes from a cookie cutter, hard sell script that doesn't sit well with you, you're not going to sell anything. You'll feel uncomfortable, inauthentic, and the universe will block the flow. Make that plan full of love, passion, devotion and authenticity and you've got yourself a beautiful heart-centered, ethical marketing plan you can be proud of. It is all about making choices about what is aligned with your spirit and your business, and what isn't. Prejudice and presumption about marketing is easy; the truth is the level of integrity in your business and marketing is totally up to you. But make no mistake, you need business and marketing skills to get your soul work out into the world, and not only is the universe behind you on this, they will help you in every way possible to get there. You were not sent here with an incredible gift simply to sit in a dark cupboard clutching it to your chest. If you have fears around sending your work out into the world, remember the skills in this book are there to guide, protect and support you.

So what is marketing and how can you use it ethically, powerfully and consistently to build an amazing business? Marketing isn't just about advertising your product or service. It includes; planning, getting clear on your audience, public relations, branding, customer service and support, sales, pricing, platforms, media and advertising. Sound complicated? Not really when you break it down. And we'll be doing just that in the following chapters. In its simplest form marketing is just a way of putting systems and structures around your business and your brand so you can get more results for your effort. You need to get what you do out there so you can help others in the most powerful way possible; and using marketing efficiently means greater results in less time. That means you get to reach more of your faithful customers and make deep and lasting connections. Does it take time and effort? Absolutely, but the clearer you are, and the more structure you have in place around it, the easier it will be.

Marketing is about letting your clients know what you have, how you can help them, giving them information on your products and services, offering easy pathways to purchase, and letting them know you appreciate them from the bottom of your heart. It is about relationship building above all else. If they trust you, value your services and have great experiences, they will tell all their friends, family and colleagues. Every step in the process should be seamless and welcoming. You can have the best marketing strategy in the world, but if your products are not up to scratch, it's too complicated to buy from you, or your clients have a bad experience, no marketing strategy can help you.

You need to understand your audience; who they are, what they want, what they need and how to let them know about the amazing programs, products and services you have to help them. Because after all that's what you're here for, right? That's your purpose, your gift, your passion, your spirit, your calling. Now I want to make a bit of a statement here about your audience. You cannot create them from the outside in, with fictitious customer avatars that have nothing to do with who you are. Your path needs to mean something to you, express the deepest part of your being and bring you a profound sense of joy. If you create a business purely from your head, chances are it's not going to work, or if it does, you won't feel fully satisfied. So instead of looking to the outside world, you're going to dive deep inside yourself and find out what your purpose is. Then you're going to integrate it into a sublime package that is all about your truth, your path and your wisdom. Then you're going to radiate who you are out into the world like a lighthouse burning out in all directions. And people are going to turn around and take notice and be utterly, soulfully drawn to you. You're not going to take a little light and run all over the clifftops in desperation hoping to find someone, anyone who needs your light. You are going to stand tall and proud and strong and centered in *who you are*. And with the full force of your being you are going to turn that light up until it is clear, pure and utterly, totally unmistakable. And people are going to run to you, and that's how you find your voice and your people authentically. Once you have a really clear understanding of who you are, you'll know just where to radiate your light.

Are there loads of wellbeing practitioners in the marketplace? Yes there are. Thank goodness because we need every one of them, and there are loads more coming. And before you have a panic, and start to feel competitive or overwhelmed or run off in a million different directions because you better hurry and get started. STOP. Take a breath. Centre yourself. There's no need to panic because the size of our audience has grown astronomically too, and there's plenty for everyone. And different people are aligned with different practitioners, so your prime job is to send out the signal that is uniquely you, so your tribe can find you. There is absolutely no one out there exactly like you, nor will there be in the history of the universe, so you can take your time to explore what it is you really have to offer from the deepest, richest part of your being. Every single practitioner has a unique offering based on who they are in essence, their path through life and their training. We need that diversity so that there is a wellbeing option for every unique being on this planet. I for one celebrate it.

So what is your unique path? What is your signature? What makes you different? You need to know yourself fully and deeply before you even think about marketing it out into the world. I know you have a great idea and probably want to go ahead all guns blazing, but please take the time to get super clear first. Marketing takes a lot of time, money, energy and effort, so don't waste it by putting something that isn't you out into the world. I promise you once you're clear on your purpose your marketing will be so much easier.

I know it can be a little difficult to sell yourself, especially in the wellbeing or spiritual realms. The truth is you need to sell as many of your products and services as possible so that you can make a difference in the world, and so you can earn enough money to continue to do so. Every day people spend millions of dollars on things that don't make them happy, so wouldn't it make sense to ask them to buy something that could change their life? As far as I know you are selling health, happiness, joy, love, healing, strength and wellbeing. You are trying to make someone's life better because you have the skills, knowledge and experience to do so. Every success you have is going to make the world better. Be PROUD of who you are. Feel confident in your product or service. If you believe in it why shouldn't others? People can take or leave what you offer, but it is your responsibility to your purpose to get your gift out there in the most clear, active, honest way possible. So that when they need you they can find you.

To do that you need clear marketing goals that will achieve specific targets. Having vague goals will bring vague results, and you really want to make the best use of your time, money and energy. A good guide is to say; I intend to do 'this', with 'that', by 'then'. You can check out the planning section for more help with goal setting. Always check in and make sure your marketing plan is relevant to your purpose, overall business goals and brand. Making your goals realistic is absolutely key to your success, and getting your head around new technology can take time. If you consistently set huge goals that you're having trouble achieving, it can lead to feeling overwhelmed, stressed and incapable. If you set clearly defined goals that are achievable, you can celebrate small wins and keep building your confidence. Break it down and take it step by step. You can always bring other goals forward if you are ahead.

Ethical marketing is about turning your heart and soul into a beautiful business package that invites and entices others, has a totally professional look and feel, and fills your being with delight. I am here to help, but this isn't going to work without your full commitment. The next chapters will offer step by step ways of getting out there so be sure to move through the exercises. It's time to do whatever you can to help in this world. What I need from you is courage, determination and dedication. And I know you can do it, because even though you may be scared, I'm pretty sure you ain't no chicken.

Ask Yourself

Do you have a clear, concise marketing plan?

What are your marketing goals over the next 12 months? What do you intend to achieve?

Are you super clear on who you are and what you have to offer?

What prejudices and presumptions do you have about marketing and are you ready to release them?

Are you standing fully in who you are, or are you projecting something you think people will want and constantly changing to try to fulfil that?

Try This

Create a marketing plan for your business that is SMART; specific, measurable, achievable, relevant and time framed. Then evaluate where you are getting the best results and why and where things are not working and why.

Once you fully understand your soul work, ask yourself who can I serve with my unique skills? Who needs this information the most? Who do I love to work with? Don't forget you have a say in this too. What qualities do you want your clients to have? I know I want clients who are ready, willing, committed, positive and passionate. They don't need to be perfect by any means, but a willingness to change and grow is a must.

Make it personal. There's no need to sell your soul, but by making a more personal connection with your clients, you'll create an amazing committed tribe.

What are you selling in essence? You may be offering yoga classes, but are you selling an experience of peace, love, confidence, strength, connection or self-esteem? The more connected you are with the essence of what you are offering, the more comfortable you will be in promoting it.

Write a list of all the presumptions you have about marketing and challenge them.

Ask yourself how you could market in a way that is ethical, beautiful, sustainable and joyful.

Whose marketing do you most admire and why? What stands out to you?

How can you connect and create a vibrant energetic flow of giving and receiving in your soul, your business and the world?

Your Niche

'May the long time sun shine upon you, all love surround you.
And the pure light within you, guide your way on.'
- Snatam Kaur

Okay so first things first; before you get all super excited about taking your message out into the world, let's take a moment to find out what that is. To you spiritual folks your niche is your heartland. It is the deepest essence of your work. It is what you love most. It is what you would do if you only dared. With a plethora of wellbeing practitioners out there, how can you stand out from the crowd? How can you explain what it is you do? How can you stay true to your core values and beliefs? What is unique about you? If you simply say you work in health and wellbeing, or teach yoga, there is no point of difference. You are left with a confused audience who will just pick randomly and perhaps wander from practitioner to practitioner until they find the one for them. It is vital to integrate your work with your unique message, a deeper calling. If I leave you with only one message from this book, let it be that.

Okay I know you may have already heard, learned and tried a load of marketing techniques around niche, but I want you to forget absolutely everything for the moment and come in with beginner's mind. Let's think a little laterally. Did you know that before it was hijacked for the marketing world, the term niche actually referred to evolutional biology? Bear with me on this analogy and we'll see how it can help you find your niche. In the natural world each organism has what is called a fundamental niche which contains the best circumstances and conditions for it to thrive. For example imagine a fish that needs particular water temperatures, food sources and levels of sunlight to survive. If the fish steps too far out of its fundamental niche, into colder water or less supportive nourishment, its chances of survival become weaker. In short the wider the organism steps away from their niche, the less likely it is to thrive, and the less likely it is to fulfil the unique role it has in the ecosystem. How well each individual job is done effects the survival of others around it too. Leave your job undone and you're actually affecting more than you know.

So what has all that got to do with you? Well, I hate to break it to you, but you're an animal baby. And you need to find the most supportive environment for you to thrive physically, mentally, emotionally, spiritually and financially. Think back to school biology, or look around you at the natural world. There are no two organisms the same. This planet is filled with weird and wonderful creatures of different shapes, sizes, colours and species that are specifically suited to a particular environment. What makes you think you'd be anything different? There is a place especially for you, where you will thrive, and we're going to uncover it. You need to find your fundamental niche, not just for you, but for the people who need your help and well....for the rest of us. Start moving into others' food sources or crashing around in their environment and the whole system becomes destabilised. Head off into a water temperature that's below your comfort zone and you'll end up feeling cold and alone. There is a whole chain reaction that is set off when you move away from your niche, heartland, soul or purpose; for yourself and for others. This isn't about confining you to a space to clip your gills. It is about finding you the exact place where you can breathe deeply, express yourself from the depths of your being and *thrive*. So before we look at where that might be for you, let's get past the excuses and resistance first and blow a few myths out of the water.

Being asked to commit to your niche may send you into a bit of a cold sweat. There are a load of excuses and fears around choosing to state clearly and openly who you are, what you do and what you represent. So here's a list you may be familiar with; a niche will trap me, I don't want to narrow down my field, there will be fewer customers there, there are loads of people doing it already, I want to keep it broad, I don't want to exclude people, I want to help everyone, I might lose my current clients, I'm scared, what if people don't like it, I'll earn more if I diversify, there's so much out there, everyone knows this stuff already and yada, yada, yada. But here's the thing; I have a sneaking suspicion that what stops you is less all this stuff, and more you just need to be brave.

So its time to break a few of those myths open, and look at the truth inside. Let's look at it as though you are the client. What if your dear friend had cancer (touch wood)? Would you send her to a naturopath that had many feathers to her bow or one who specialized in nutrition, recovery and support for cancer patients? What if your darling sister was pregnant after many attempts and you wanted to send her for a massage? Would you send her to a general massage therapist or one who specialized in pregnancy massage? Finding your niche is about doing the right thing by yourself, and your clients. You need to have the courage to let go of who your customers are not, to find who they are. So let's address some of those fears and presumptions around finding your niche, and what could happen if you gave yourself permission to release them.

A niche will trap me

If you are a bit of a freedom freak like me and you are worried a niche will trap or confine you, you're in for a treat. The rule is to make your niche specific and take it *deep*. As soon as you choose your niche and release distractions, you are going to see a whole new world open up to you. Then it will open up again and again, until you realize you are in a wonderland of opportunity. You will become *known* for your unique skills, the referrals will flood in, your knowledge will deepen and you will LOVE what you do because it's all you. Let me give you an example. Imagine you are a doula whose niche is teenage births. You may think that's a pretty narrow field but let's take it deep. You can offer assistance and support during the pregnancy, birth and post natal. You could offer support to the wider family. You can write blogs or a book on how to cope with a baby as a young mother. You could run support groups for young mums, breastfeeding workshops, post-natal depression, self-care and connection with bubs. You could talk about transition emotionally and physically. You could talk to teenagers in schools about pregnancy. You could speak about teenage motherhood at conferences, on television or radio. You could start a Facebook group or e-courses for young mums. You could apply for a grant to set up prevention, support or education programs for teenage pregnancy. The possibilities are endless. Can you see how this commitment could produce a rich and expansive career?

I don't want to narrow my field

Clear, specific marketing gives us as the consumer the right to choose. And that's only fair, isn't it? Trying to be everything to everyone is a little greedy, and a little dishonest. That kind of thinking comes from fear. I hate to break it to you but you can't be the best at everything. Specializing in your field makes you an expert in it. 'Wellness' is not a specialty; it is a huge, massive, growing field. And if you think you can run all over that field and catch the ball every time you're going to end up tired, confused and more than a little dizzy, and so are your clients; 'Hang on a minute, didn't she say she was that last week, and now she seems to be saying she's this?' Ever notice how in cricket the bowlers are usually really average batsmen and vice versa? It's because those bowlers have spent years perfecting their craft, the batsmen the same. They have specialized. Let go of the illusion of the all-rounder. You should always strive for mastery. Staying broad based makes you ever the apprentice; you'll know a bit about a lot of subjects, but you'll master nothing. As a client who would you want? I would choose the expert every time. And that's who I recommend. I never, ever refer to someone who wants to be a jack of all trades, because I know their knowledge won't be as deep as someone who specialises.

You may be worried there will be fewer customers by going niche. Actually there are a whole load of customers out there you are barely tapping into. More than you can possibly imagine. When you are clear on your niche they will finally see you, and they are the best kind of customers because they are loyal, they are true and they are great advocates for you. They will know exactly who you are and can communicate that to others easily and clearly, because you are clear. But just dabbling won't do it. You need to commit and follow through. A quick toe in the water and then a change of direction won't give you a clear identity. When clients come to find their authentic niche, I guide them deeply into a meditative space, connect to the soul and they come out excited, thrilled, full of possibility and absolute clarity. Then one of two things happen; either they follow through and send that niche out with fire, or they start backpedalling at the speed of light.

Don't hide it, leverage your niche

If you have a healthy café where your niche is not to have coffee, but to offer a wide variety of healthy alternatives, you don't stand at the counter and say meekly to everyone who asks sorry, 'we don't have coffee'. You put a HUGE sign out the front saying 'no coffee here, come inside and ask us why'. You put it out there, front and centre. You make it your *thing*. You leverage it in unique and beautiful ways. You have special evenings where customers can come and taste shot glasses of all your lovely hot beverages. You write articles for the local paper on the negative impact of caffeine and the incredible health benefits of your hot drinks. You give them cute and funky names. You create culture around it: you invite local wellbeing practitioners around to try them, you offer students from the local yoga studios a discount, you talk at the local wellbeing expo, you hold a 'caffeine free high tea' event, and you run a quirky social media campaign. That's what you call leveraging your niche.

I don't want to lose my clients

If you are worried choosing a niche will alienate customers you have now, think of it this way. Some clients will stick with you just because they love you, and there will be a transition period where some people drop off whilst you gather clients in your true direction. If you do this well it should not affect your financials, but you need to think long term too. This is about your heart and soul work and it shouldn't be left undone. You shouldn't be investing in anything now that you don't want to be doing in ten years' time. If you want to move into healing massage instead of remedial massage, switch your blog posts and social media from a muscular, physical focus to a nurturing, healing focus. You don't have to go over the top with it, just gently weave in extra articles over time on indigenous cultures and the healing power of massage, lovely warm pictures of massage and candles and so on. What you put out there is what you will attract, so no more posts on healing sports injuries, unless you want clients with sports injuries. Makes sense, right? Some clients may drop off, but new ones will come, and I guarantee some of your old customers will surprise you by saying, 'yes I really wanted to know more about that.' What if they are craving your authentic work but choose another massage therapist instead because what they really want is a healing massage and you're not offering it? Really you need to have more faith in your clients, and their capacity to grow and be open too.

I don't want to exclude people

If you don't want to exclude people, and want to help everyone, I hate to break it to you, but you are not the sole saviour of the universe. You don't need to hold and heal every single person that ever walked or will walk the earth. This is a dangerous state and comes very much from a rescuer archetype. It is not your job to rescue anyone and everyone, or to be personally responsible for their happiness; it is your job to *empower* the unique tribe of people you have been entrusted to help. By naming and owning your niche you free your clients to use your service, or find someone else who is best suited to them. If you love teaching gentle and restorative yoga, but decide you'd better expand your repertoire and teach gentle, athletic and hot yoga so no one 'misses out', you are cheating both yourself and your clients. You put yourself at a disadvantage because you have less time and energy to spend on becoming a master in what you truly love. If you stick with gentle and restorative yoga, you will learn more about it with each client, each workshop, and each article you read on the benefits. There is a great sense of relief and freedom that comes with making authentic choices. If you commit to your true love for gentle yoga a symphony of rewards follow. You will deepen your own home practice. You become recognised as an expert in your field and start talking at conferences and expos. You will start getting referrals from the local chiropractors, doctors and counsellors as your reputation builds. You attract people who are stressed, people with physical limitations and conditions and so on. You need to have the courage to hold on to who you are in essence, and trust there is a practitioner that will support others wanting a more physical style of yoga as well or better than you. Not because they are more intelligent or worthy, but because they live and breathe power yoga. Then you can send clients to them and vice versa.

I'll earn more if I diversify

I want to address the great diversity myth here because it's a crucial point I see all the time. Practitioners feel that the more they have to offer clients the more valuable they'll be. If you diversify your products and services *within* your niche you will capitalize on your market. If you diversify *outside* your niche, you're kidding yourself. It means more time, more marketing, more money, more effort, more explaining and more diluting of your energy and identity. This is a huge trap and is very much fear and ego driven. If you want to keep changing direction do some self-awareness work on why. Do you think you'll only be loved by making everyone happy, do you think who you really are isn't good enough or is it something else? Looking at this stuff honestly early on will clear the way for an amazing, joyful, peaceful life, so do the work. I say this from a space of deep love.

How could you diversify cleverly *within* your niche? Let's take naturopathy for mums and bubs as an example. You could have herbal remedies, teas, tisanes for pre/post-natal support. You could offer consultations for mums, talks in schools, kindergartens or child care centres, write a regular wellbeing column in a parenting magazine, create an e-course for a variety of different subjects all relating to mums and bubs, run nurturing getaway retreats and so on. Of course you don't need to do all those things, just choose the delivery method and platforms that best work for you and your clients (more on that later). Webinar recordings or podcasts mums can listen too whilst taking the pram out, or support groups they can take bubs to may be a great fit here. Everything you choose should reinforce who you are and support your clients. Do you think you could possibly run out of information or supportive advice on parenting or finding better ways to deliver it? I can't imagine how. People want to know what helps them specifically. Remember if you diversify into different specialties you are going to weaken your identity, your brand and your ability to be relied upon as an expert in your field. However if you diversify cleverly *within* your niche you reinforce your brand, specialty and reputation, and most importantly, you serve your clients to the best of your ability and do what you really, truly love.

It's all been done before

I'm over hearing there are loads of people doing it already or it's all been done before. Not your way it hasn't. There has never been another person in the history of the universe that has the same personality, training, skill set, life experience, communication skills or outlook as you. People are attracted to very different things. A few years ago I left a yoga retreat that was all discipline and hard edges. It was a difficult time and I needed some sweetness. So I left the retreat, hired a cabin by a lake just a few kilometres down the road and spent my time meditating, walking out in nature and cooking myself delicious food. It was just what I needed. Before I book into a retreat now I do a lot of research about who is running it, what their philosophy is and I check in to see if it feels good in my body. I have been to talks on mindfulness that were all theory and bored me out of my brain, and I have been to some that have engaged me at a deeply visceral level. If you keep it the same as every other teacher; mimicking, transcribing, or borrowing material, then yes, you're right, it has all been done before. But bring something unique and totally you and you're onto a winner.

People already know all this stuff

It's easy to make presumptions that everyone already knows about the information you have to offer. You love wellbeing. You probably surround yourself with people who are into wellbeing. You talk about it, read about it, watch talks on it; to you it's everywhere. You have a load of information in your head and you presume because it comes easy to you, everyone else knows and understands it too. In terms of the layman, however, you'd be surprised how many people have heard of different wellbeing modalities, but don't know exactly what they can do for them. Or they want someone to guide them through it. They can spend hours on the internet or reading books trying to understand it, piece it together, or see how it can work for them, wasting the precious little time they have, or they can come to your class, workshop or retreat and let your knowledge guide them through. You are the interpreter for them. You gather information, skills and tools and deliver it in a way they can understand, digest and experience. And chances are they want a support group, workshop or retreat where they can deepen their skills and lean into others for support. To your clients that's well worth paying for. It is hard to travel a spiritual journey alone. Everyone needs somewhere to belong and a tribe, teacher or guide to lead the way, so put your hand up and get busy with it.

Choose from the inside out, not the outside in

It's vital when you're deciding on your niche that you make the decision from the inside out, not the outside in. Get rock solid on your commitment to yourself, the universe and your path first so you won't be swayed. Some people won't like who you are or what you do, and that's okay. Yes, I know it can be hard to take sometimes, but you have to ask yourself if you would rather be honest or be false to win the approval of others. There are some folks out there who wouldn't be happy if you were a master at every craft. You need to learn to let that go, and not get involved in any kind of fear or distraction that will coax you from your truth. If you create an innovative new heart and soul class, will some people look at it and say my goodness that sounds amazing, sign me up? Yes they will. Will some others say that sounds a bit full on, I'd rather do aerobics? Yes they will. But you don't want those people and you know why; because you'll start to alter the class and change your language to accommodate them, and the people who really love your authentic work down to their bones will get annoyed because you're not delivering what you promised. The clients who didn't want it but you convinced to come in a different language will be annoyed because it doesn't feel like aerobics. And you won't feel right because you didn't get the chance to do your deepest work. And your inner saboteur will say, 'see what happens when you go deep'? And your soul will say that wasn't deep, that was fence sitting. Remember too, that most imagined disapproval in the outside world is really a reflection of your own doubts or lack of confidence, so be prepared to confront some of your fears, build a bit of risk muscle and make a commitment to step forward in spite of your ego. Be prepared to start with just a few people with your real work and be patient. I promise you if it's true, numbers will boom. Mama Gena started her school of womanly arts in her lounge room with just a few people, and look at her now. That didn't happen overnight. It took time, patience, courage, commitment, love and deep soul work.

So how can you find your niche?

So now let's look at ways to find your niche. There are several ways you might go about discovering your niche, but as far as I am concerned the first is always the best; go with your heart. Who are you? What do you believe in? If you had one breath left what would you tell people? What do you know for sure? If you saw someone in distress who needed your help what would you say? What wisdom have you gathered over the years? What do you think is the best way to create a healthy, happy life? What does the world need more of? You can build products and services around it later, but let's get clear on your message first. You know the answers to these questions. Be honest, be brave and name it. Brainstorm with a pen and paper, talk out loud, keep searching, probing, exploring and going deeper. Do whatever it takes.

Come from the inside out, not the outside in. That means feel it in the heart, the soul and the body. Don't decide to work with seniors because you think there would be a big market in an aging population. Seniors deserve a teacher who is totally connected and passionate about them. Don't decide to become a coach because it is really trending right now, so were Lurex jumpsuits. If you're not called to it, don't do it. If you feel truly, deeply propelled by an inner calling, go ahead all guns blazing.

Look for clues. What makes you feel great, what do people often ask you for, what articles attract your attention, what leaders do you admire, what TED talks float your boat, what subjects fascinated you at college, what personal experiences have you had that you have gathered wisdom from, what do you think isn't being given enough attention in the media?

Let go of what you 'should' be doing. Be prepared to break away from the crowd, diatribe or opinions, both internal and external, about what you should be doing with your craft and start thinking about what is possible. Get creative. Be different. What if you mixed this with that? Whoever thought there would be nude yoga? Let's stop judging and start celebrating innovation in wellbeing.

Don't let finding your audience mean losing yourself. Let's get one thing straight. Niche and target market are two different things. Your niche is your specialty, and your target market is who you deliver it to. So your specialty may be mindfulness meditation and your target market may be teenagers. Always think of your niche or specialty first, before you even *think* about who you will deliver it to. Trying to choose your target market first is the fastest way to cut you off from your truth. When you are clear on your niche, your audience will become a no brainer. You can read more on your target market in a later chapter.

Develop your niche by intention. What do you want to achieve with your niche? It's essential to break it right down to the nitty gritty; health and wellbeing are just too broad. What are you offering your clients? Go beyond the modem to the message. What's *really* on the menu? Is it weight loss or is it body love? Is it coaching or helping people find purpose? Is it fitness or is it inner strength and confidence. Is it yoga or soul nurturing? Is it massage or sensual connection? What are you really offering? What qualities lie beneath what you are teaching? Brainstorm the qualities behind what you do. List as many crucial qualities as you can and you'll start talking about what you do and teaching in a different way.

Try one or more of the methods above that make the most sense to you in terms of trying to identify your niche. Play around, brainstorm, I know it's there. Actually you know exactly what your niche is already; the question is will you let it out? Stay out of the head and come into the body. Place one hand on the heart and one on the belly. Breathe deep and slow until you are centered. Feel the earth below you. Ground yourself. Try your niche on for size. How does it feel? If you feel energised, open and light you're there. If you feel irritated, uncomfortable or tense, you need to keep searching. When you find it sit with it. Let it flow into every cell in your body. Once you know your niche you can clarify it, deepen it and set up systems around it. You can create a great business name, by-line, innovative marketing, content, products and services that reinforce your brand at every turn. You can crank up your point of difference and create an experience that people talk about.

So how do you find your niche if you're trained in a lot of wellbeing modalities? Not everything you have ever learned needs to go into the brochure or on your website. In fact, please don't do that. It's overwhelming; remember if you confuse people you will lose people. They want to know what you're all about, what you represent, how you can help, who you are, why you're here. In one easy statement that makes a promise. At Spirit in Business® we provide the best business & marketing support available to wellbeing practitioners, in a language you can understand, because no one knows the wellbeing industry like we do. That is who we are and what we do. Clean, clear, powerful, simple. Nothing ever, ever goes to waste. So if you have studied a lot of modalities, let them sit neatly in behind who you are and what you do and radiate out at a deeper level.

If you have lots of modalities it is vital to choose a niche that encompasses who you are intrinsically. You are selling a feel, energy, an emotion. The truth of who you are. This is your point of difference. If you have a wellbeing practice that provides a wide variety of therapies, you need a name and a by-line that describes what you do as a whole. Yes you may have many ways for your client to experience this in your practice, but it is all tied to one central theme. For example you may have a wellbeing centre called "Inner Bliss".

At Inner Bliss you may offer massage, meditation classes, wellness seminars, yoga and so on. But the central intention is to offer people tools for inner bliss. Your niche is inner bliss through wellness therapies, as opposed to simply listing modems that make you the same as every other centre around. Then you can write a blog on inner bliss, Facebook posts on inner bliss, Instagram pics that promote inner bliss, a little e-book on inner bliss and so on. At your centre you want the oils, the lighting, your language, your practitioners, in fact everything you do to promote inner bliss. It's no good to just slap a name on a healing centre and then just throw a load of practitioners together without a centralised theme. You want to hand pick a team that are devoted to helping people find inner bliss.

Be brave, go deep, tell the truth and hold fast. It will take a while and you'll need some balls. Those clients who absolutely love the truth and authenticity of your deepest work are going to go out there and talk about you. And you are going to reiterate your niche; who you are and what you do over and over again through your marketing, social media, products and services. You are going to sell your point of difference loud and proud, and create innovative programs around it. You are going to stop being distracted by every shiny thing that walks past and commit to your *real* work. You and your brand are going to grow strong and true. Most importantly you will feel alive, connected, energized and totally authentic in your heart and soul. And that is a life to be proud of.

Ask Yourself

Do you have the courage to stand in your true soul calling no matter what?

Are you prepared to stand in your truth when tested?

What could you eradicate from your business today to bring you closer to your niche or heartland?

What do you really, really, really want to do?

Can you resist straying into someone else's work out of fear, competition or illusion and dig right into your own?

Try This

Write down all the excuses you use to avoid committing to a niche. Fast as you can without thinking now, get them out and get them gone.

Brainstorm all the qualities that sit behind what you do. What do you offer your clients, or what do you want to give them above all else?

Once you have found your niche create a mind map for your social media, blog, products and programs that are all directly related to your niche, brand and identity. You can read more about mind maps later.

If you are struggling to find your niche enrol in one of our niche workshops and let's get you sorted. There is only one thing worse than not knowing your niche today, and that is not knowing what your niche is in five years' time. Everything stems from this one crucial point, so get super clear and feel everything else open up.

Brand

'When the personality meets the soul you create authentic power.'
- Gary Zukav

A brand is a unique name, personality or image that surrounds who you are and what you do. In a spiritual sense it is how the essence of your soul radiates out into the world. It's about the energy of your business. Where niche talks about your specialty or purpose, your brand is about how your personality or style differs from other practitioners. For instance, imagine there are two teachers whose niche is soul coaching. One teacher's brand or business personality may be peaceful, mature and traditional, whereas another's may be fun, quirky and modern. It is yet another way to give your clients a clearer vision of who you are so they can make the best choice for what they need. Again this personality should be genuine and come from the inside out, not the outside in. When you align your soul with your personality, it becomes a powerful force in the world because it comes from a totally authentic alignment and is infused with your life force energy. In turn that attracts the tribe you were born to lead.

The most important factors for clients to get to know, like and trust your brand are clarity, transparency and consistency. You want to reinforce who you are and what you represent at every opportunity with absolute honesty and impeccability. For years I tried to be that serious traditional yoga teacher when actually I am very quirky and love to bring humour to my work. The more permission you give yourself to be who you really are, the stronger your brand will become. If you are a quiet teacher or an introvert, own it and be that, because goodness knows we need some quieter people in this world.

Your brand reputation builds over time through your marketing and your customer's experience. A consistent positive experience creates brand loyalty and trust, so your clients continue to return to you, rather than choose someone else. This is not about competition for its own sake, but about securing a fantastic reputation in your industry for being wholly truly you. Brand is both an intangible and tangible asset from the image to the experience. Your clients hold your brand, so you need to be really sure that what you promise is what you deliver. You can promise people the sun, moon and stars but if what is promised in the brochure isn't what is felt in the experience, your brand and reputation is in trouble. So how will you express the unique essence of your brand? How can you be sure your clients are aware of the unique features and benefits you offer? By keeping things super clear and simple. If you are sending your customers different messages all the time in a world of information overload, you'll lose them. People want simple, clear choices. If they are happy with what is promised, feel connected to your brand, feel heard and understood, they will become a loyal customer and will be thrilled to recommend you. They don't need to keep looking, they feel positive shifts and that's one less thing that they have to worry about in their busy life. So who are you and what is your promise?

Be Unique

When you label yourself clearly your tribe can find you. When is the last time you gathered a bunch of massage brochures or wellbeing business cards together? Notice anything different or is the message (and often the picture) always the same? Offer people a choice of black and white and that choice is easy. Offer them a million shades of grey and that choice becomes overwhelming. They will walk away, dabble with different practitioners or stumble upon you if they are lucky. What if someone out there really needed you, but couldn't find you? Your brand needs to stand out as something unique and innovative that works. That brings pleasure, joy, peace and ease to peoples' lives. You need to find out who you really are and tell people only that over and over again in creative and engaging ways. You can do a whole heap of things averagely, or one thing amazingly well. You have to have the courage to let go of what isn't you, to embody what is. Similarly you have to have the courage to let go of who your clients are not, to welcome who they are. Forget the idea of getting everyone to love your brand because not everyone will. If you change your language, information and plan to chase a few people who are never going to like you anyway, you are wasting your time. And more importantly you'll lose your faithful followers. So who are you? What are the core values of your brand, what are you here to solve, how are you going to serve others, what are you promising to deliver, what is your vision and your purpose, and how can you translate that into a marketable brand simply and effectively?

Personality

Your brand should have a unique personality that is instantly recognizable from its imagery, name, feel and tone. From the visual appearance of your logo, to your treatment room, videos, social media, website, products, services, customer service, events and so on. This is why it is really important to get to the heart of your brand first. You need to LOVE it. You need to live and breathe it, because that's exactly what you are going to invest in, sustain and develop long term. You need to connect authentically. You are talking to people, your beloved clients, so resist the temptation to become robotic when talking about yourself and your business. Authentic brand identity should be present in your marketing, your business and you. And you can't fake that. You wouldn't want to. Your brand needs to be utterly and totally trustworthy.

Think of the emotions you wish to evoke or create with your brand. For example your business may be warm, welcoming and trustworthy. It may be passionate, joyful and professional. It may be innovative, authentic and playful. These personality traits allow clients to get a feel for your brand. This increases the awareness, growth and popularity of your brand as something they can trust, connect with, and tell their friends about. It is something that exists in your customers' mind or perception, but at the same time it feels very tangible to them, because they can go out and *experience* it too. If the felt experience is the same as what is promised, it builds your brand awareness and popularity. A good brand evokes emotion, connection and trust with its audience by adhering to its values at all times. Eckhart Tolle tells a story in his teacher series of ringing up a famous wellbeing author and hearing screaming in the background. Deeply concerned, he said to the receptionist 'My God, what's happening, is everything alright?' To which she replied 'Oh it's always like that here, I just can't stand it anymore.' Every aspect of your business needs to live and breathe your brand to keep your image and reputation intact, because you know how energy filters through, right? Do whatever personal and professional work you need to keep things clean and clear. You need to embody your truth, not just give it lip service.

Engage the Senses

Your brand should engage the senses in a pleasurable way. Clients need to taste, look, touch, smell and hear your devotion to what you represent. If you are a massage practitioner and your brand personality is warm, nurturing and inviting, offering clients into a cold, clinical room isn't going to cut it, nor are cold fingers and a brusque stroke. Welcome them into a warm space with candles, soft lighting, scented oils, cosy towels and gentle music and you're right on track. If you are a yoga or meditation teacher who specializes in stress and anxiety relief, but arrive late to class, talk excessively and generally agitate the vata energy in your students, you may see numbers diminish. Create a still space for students to enter, keep your voice soft and soothing, offer nurturing blankets and scented eye pillows, and your students will feel safe enough to let go.

Now this may seem like a no brainer, but if you think back on some experiences that you have had yourself I'm sure you'll come up with a few hair-raising examples. So what is your brand personality and how does it come out in everything you do?

Consistency, Consistency, Consistency

Your clients are placing their trust in you and that is a sacred thing, especially when it comes to their physical, mental, emotional and spiritual wellbeing.

They are not just buying a fridge here. They want and expect what they have been promised. They want to feel safe, valued and rewarded. Consistency in your brand is essential. Ever been to a restaurant that promotes itself as offering fresh, innovative, healthy food only to find that means a wilted lettuce leaf on the side of a greasy hamburger? Or hired a venue to find the light, modern airy photos on the website were in reality dusty and dark? Or expected excellent retail customer service to find no one greeted you, asked if you needed help, or even bothered to lift their eyes from the magazine they were reading? Or recommended a spa to a friend to find out they were treated in a careless slapdash manner, when they were in need of some serious nurturing and love? How did that make you feel? Chances are you felt angry, embarrassed, deceived, and disregarded. Certainly not valued or respected. Certainly not loved and cherished. Changes in values that can be felt by your customers may have a lasting impact on your brand. Any employees need to have a clear understanding of the values that are important to your brand, and a willingness to uphold and promote those values at all times. If you do run into a damage control issue with your brand, address it immediately with maturity, courtesy and professionalism. Apologize, make amends, and take responsibility. A problem handled well can make for great PR and a fiercely loyal customer in the future. Plus, it's the right thing to do. Your brand promise needs to be fulfilled in all aspects of your customer service, marketing, social media, products and services. Keep your promise to your clients and they will keep their promise to you.

Brand Collaboration

Brand collaboration is a wonderful thing when done correctly. If you are thinking of aligning with someone else, you need to sit down together and have a really good look at how your brands do or don't intersect. Examine your values, how you like to work and how you might deal with any problems that arise. If reliability is huge for you, but your potential partner has a problem with punctuality, cue flashing red light. Just because you love someone it doesn't mean they'll make the perfect business partner. There is a lot to be said for having professional colleagues in their own separate businesses wholeheartedly supporting each other through cross referral, moral support or think tanks. Partnerships with totally aligned practitioners or industries can help you extend your reach, promote you as an expert and open new professional opportunities. It gives you the chance to showcase your products and services to a wider market, and extend your contacts. If partners are well regarded in your industry, then certainly a connection with them can offer your brand additional influence in the marketplace. Think not just of what you will get, but what you can give. Make sure that any collaboration is in line with your niche and brand. For instance if you are running a nourish retreat and teach gentle yoga, you could partner with a nourishing healthy chef, and aromatherapy massage therapist. There is no point offering to speak at a conference or partner with someone who has a wide audience just for what you can get. If you are not aligned their audience probably won't connect with the authentic you, and you won't want to change your identity just to fit in or you'll dilute your brand.

Personal or Business Branding

For many well-known people their name is their brand like Oprah Winfrey, Marie Forleo or Eckhart Tolle. It's totally up to you, but if you intend to be a speaker, media personality, author or coach then using your own name may work best. If you have a healing centre, massage college or wellbeing travel service a business name may be better. There are no absolutes but think of a name that will serve you long term, because you don't want to have to start from scratch all over again. When I went to Louise Hay's writer's workshop they suggested using your name for your website/ brand as if you changed what you were doing as your career developed, you wouldn't need to change all the branding as well. If you do choose to go with a business name buy the domain for your own name as well if it's available, just in case you want to switch to that later on. You can get it to point at your business website in the meantime. You may promote your name as the face behind the business brand (think Richard Branson and Virgin) or let the brand stand of its own accord (think Toyota). Just think about what best reflects your niche and overall business goals.

Brand Licenses

If you are teaching or practicing under a license agreement, I would absolutely advise promoting your own brand (yourself as an individual) at the same time, otherwise you are just working to promote someone else. If in the worst-case scenario that brand should crumble or change, you don't want to have your years of dedication and devotion wiped out with it. Think of it this way; if that brand was removed what would people see? Who is the you behind the brand? What do you specialize in? What would you like to be known for? Some licenses have great flexibility and others don't, so be really clear about whether you can be yourself and follow your unique path through it. If the brand you are licensed under allows you to deepen and broaden who you are, and what you are on this earth to do, then go for it. Understand that if you take on a license agreement there will be certain requirements you are expected to uphold for the integrity and clarity of the brand you are under. The beauty of working under someone else's brand is that the reputation they have already established in the marketplace helps to give your business a head start.

There is more on this in the licensing chapter. Balance yourself firmly between integrity with the brand you are licensed under, and your own unique flavour.

Brand and Intellectual Property

Intellectual property is a vast and varied subject and is discussed further in the IP chapter. Requirements differ in each country, so do your research on what is needed to protect your brand with trademarks and patents where necessary. Note that a trademark in one country does not cover other countries, so investigate global requirements too. I know this can go a little against the grain for spiritual folks to claim a name, and it may feel a little 'grasping' to you, but let me briefly explain why it's important. If someone else trademarks your business name after you've built your brand and business for years, they can actually stop you from using it. There is no need to become remotely litigious yourself if you have trademarks, but it will give you the security that your name is safe for you to use. Think of it like a business responsibility. In the same way you would insure your car against accidents, you can protect your business name with trademarks. If you are running a grassroots home-based business and your long-term goal is to improve the wellbeing in your local community, this may feel a little over the top for you. Trust your instincts and go with what feels right. It's totally up to you. If you want to go global I would say it's a no brainer.

Protecting your brand is just about keeping your reputation in your control as much as possible so some dodgy person doesn't come along and ruin the beautiful name you have created, or simply provide a less-than service that may be mistakenly attributed to you. You don't want someone who has purchased the trademark to stop you from using your business name, and benefit from all the goodwill you have created while you have to start again from scratch. It's been done many times before.

Another part of protecting your brand online is to be cohesive in your business name wherever possible across your website, social media and event urls, so you are easily recognizable. With names and customized urls fast disappearing on social media, I would get onto this sooner rather than later. You may not be able to get everything the same, but look for cohesion wherever you can from your url, to personalised domains, to your digital marketing/social media presence.

Brand Visuals

You should create a great visual identity for your brand too which is easily recognizable. Brand visuals consist of the colours, design, logo, name or symbol that stands out to your customers. Coca-Cola or Qantas or McDonald's are all prime examples. The visual identity of your brand should sit neatly in line with your brand personality. When I chose the Spirit in

Business logo I wanted to portray structure and flow, stability and creativity, colour and life, spirit and business. To me the wording is reliable, businesslike and dependable, whilst the flow of the graphic gives it life, creativity and a little magic. The stars symbolize inspiration, spirit and manifestation. The colour orange relates to wisdom and the turquoise to communicating from the heart. You can check it out here www.spiritinbiz.com.au .Your visual branding should be consistent through your logo, website, social media, business cards and other marketing. Try to find a symbol that is a little different rather than the lotus, a particular yoga pose, or ripples in a pond that a million other people have. The idea is to create something that is uniquely recognizable as you. Absolutely engage a professional to help you do this and be really clear on the feel you are after; take along examples of things you like. Words, a symbol or a combination is fine; just keep it clear and simple. Make sure your logo and brand visuals have the energy and feel of who you are.

Patience and Commitment

Building your brand takes time, but everything good does. Be patient. The fastest way to build a reputation is with clarity, consistency and integrity. You know your brand is getting somewhere when referrals start to come in. Your aim is to be the first person people think of when looking for a fabulous yoga teacher, naturopath, kinesiologist, skin balm, wellness centre or mindfulness facilitator. This has nothing to do with competition and everything to do with honouring yourself, your peers and your industry with the highest level work you can put out there. Le'ts all raise that bar. You need to behave as though you are the best in the world at what you do. And you are. You may not be the only healer in the world, but you are the best healer at what you do that no one else does, in your own unique inimitable way. So respect yourself, your clients and your spirit by owning it and sending it out there into the world to do a whole heap of good, because that's why you're here, isn't it?

The Wellness Brand

The evolution of the wellness brand is a very fascinating thing, especially for those of us who have been in the industry a long time. We used to be thought of as fringe dwellers – a bit out there and all about crystals, fairies, angels and rainbows (not that there's anything wrong with that). People had a tentative curiosity at best. Now we talk about yoga and mindfulness and eyes light up, people are fascinated, they have questions. They want to know if we can put together a program for their school or workplace. Due to some celebrity personalities, fabulous marketers, health trends and savvy industry leaders we are in the mainstream. Do you know there is now such a thing as wellness salami? Has it gone too far? In some ways yes, and of course their will be people behaving out of integrity in any profession, but in many ways the commercialisation of the wellness industry has done us huge favours. I for one celebrate it because I believe nothing happens by accident, and everything in the universe has been evolving as it should be. It has opened huge doors for us to step in and do the authentic work. We have a stage – and not just at the mind, body, spirit fairs any more. There are openings for us in schools, councils, the corporate arena and even in local government. Places where we can make huge changes.

So how do you build the brand for your business? You get out there; through marketing, advertising, social media, promotions, events, speaking, conferences, websites, blogs, webinars, interviews or e-courses. You choose a few punchy platforms that are the best for you and your brand and you go for it loud and proud, no holding back. How can you be sure your clients are aware of the benefits of your brand that add value to their lives? You tell people; over and over and over again. Let them hear you, let them see you and let them experience your work. Show them how you make a difference. Create a brand that engages the senses in a pleasurable way. Let people feel your devotion to what you represent. And when your tribe emerges from conscious contact with your brand, they should be glowing, delighted, uplifted, engaged and ready to tell people all about your amazing work.

Ask Yourself

What are the human qualities of your brand? Is it joyful, innovative, passionate or something else entirely?

What is your brand promise? What do you promise to deliver to your clients?

Are all the visuals and the experience of your business in line with your brand?

Is the language you use in line with your brand?

Are the prices you charge inline with your brand look and feel?

Is it time for a brand refresh?

How do you want to be seen?

Try This

Look at your brand from a detached perspective or ask a few friends or colleagues. What do they feel when they think of you or your brand?

Decide whether you are going to brand a business name, your name, or both.

Consider a trademark application if you intend to take your brand to a large platform.

Write five essential qualities any future partners must have for you to collaborate with them. We'll talk more about finding the right partners later.

Think of the impact you want your brand to have on the world. What changes do you want to make, what do you want to deliver that is utterly unique and inimitable? Create a desire statement and make it big and bold. What is your brand promise?

List as many ways as you can to ensure that your brand stays true.

Audience and Target Market

'Find your tribe. Love them hard.'
- Danielle La Porte

Those of you who know my work will know that I am often fond of saying it is more important to know your voice than to know your audience. If you look for an audience from the outside before you are sure of your core message or true purpose, you are going to end up all over the place, dragged around by the nose by trends and flashy ideas. That being said, once you are totally clear on who you are, what your purpose is and where you are going, from a deeply soul-centered perspective, you can target your message to those folks who really need you. When you are super clear on your message and your purpose, your audience becomes a no brainer. Remember always, always, always make your choices from the inside out (soulful, eternal and infinite), rather than from the outside in (egoic, limited and finite).

There is a huge push for the high-end market right now, but offering a lower cost option can be just as lucrative. I have a very successful client whose low-price e-course earns her triple what her high-priced option does. True, you will need more clients, but if your service offers great content at great value, the word is going to spread like wildfire, and you'll have a larger audience for your future work as well. Never base your work on a high-end market for the hell of it, or try to 'grab' an audience you think will be lucrative. Remember that if you are totally aligned with your soul work, abundance will follow, the energy will sustain itself and you will feel joy in the depths of your being. That being said, if your *purpose* calls you to work with a high-end market then absolutely go for it. We have to get rid of the idea that one market or group is any better or worse than another, especially in spiritual leadership;

it is purely about who you were *born* to lead.

I'm not a big fan of using a customer avatar model to speak to your audience. Although I did use it early on in my workshops, I found my clients getting all locked up over it. They were trying to create a fictitious character from the outside. They were getting frustrated and squirming and it was creating mental blocks on how to deliver their authentic work to those particular people. It was like trying to put a square peg in a round hole. So we turned the exercise on its head and started talking about who the best people were to support your soul purpose. We looked at qualities instead of demographics. Do you want just any woman aged thirty to sixty who is interested in yoga, buys organic food, loves nature and hangs out at markets on the weekend? What if she is stuck in her stuff or doesn't pay on time, or is disruptive in class or is always late? Can you call out to your tribe via their qualities instead? To people who are committed, reliable, fascinated, respectful, abundant, ready, willing and able to grow? How would a tribe like that make you feel? How would they energise you? Can you make your social media posts all about who you are to attract people authentically, instead of a prescribed array of things your avatar might like?

The more specific you are about your purpose, and the clearer you are on your niche, the more obvious it will become where you need to shine your light. Then you can head out to the obvious places your real tribe hangs out online and in the real world. Let's say you are a personal trainer who loves the physicality of the body, and your niche is training for endurance sports. Once you are super clear on who you are, you simply list as many places and ways as you can to tell people about that. You could join endurance groups on Facebook or create one of your own. Have a stall or warmup offering at endurance events. Collaborate with nutritionists for endurance athletes. Give a talk at your local gyms on personal milestones and endurance sports. Write a column for an endurance sports magazine. Train a high-profile figure or community character for an endurance event and get interest from a local paper. Create an endurance event to raise funds and awareness for a local charity close to your heart. Get involved with your local male or female sports club. Do something quirky by helping the local roller derby team to increase their endurance (good luck with that!). You could write blogs on the latest training breakthroughs. Create a LinkedIn profile for endurance sports and connect with triathletes, mountain bike racers, long-distance runners and so on. And so on and so on. Every time a new idea of where to share pops into your head, write it down. Be on the lookout for signs and synchronicity too. Do all the obvious stuff, and then bring your personality and step out the box with something unique.

So the rules are; get super clear on your soul work first, create some smashing programs, products or services, and then get super clear on who they will benefit. Then in every way you can possibly think of keep reaching out, engaging and informing your audience with love and devotion. Be open, but never, ever allow an outside influence to pull you away from your core work. Hold fast, be innovative and creative, and you will have a tribe that is faithful, engaged and growing in no time.

Ask Yourself

Are you confusing your niche (what you specialise in) with your target market (who you deliver it to)? What you do and why you do it always comes before who you will deliver it to.

Are you willing to get out in the real world and make as many connections there as you do online?

What kind of clients will best support you and your work? Don't think of it as begging or scrambling for clients. Stand tall and proud in who you are, see the value in your work and radiate that out into the world. Do you want people who are committed, spiritual, fun, passionate and great advocates? Do you want clients who pay on time, show up regularly and take responsibility for their spiritual growth? What kind of clients would make your life easier and support you supporting them? Think of your dream client rather than creating a customer avatar from the outside. That way you will attract your audience energetically too.

How would you treat these amazing beings who support your work?

Try This

Before you go hunting for your audience, get super clear on who you are first. Get coaching help on this if you need it.

Create some great material, products, services or programs first so you are really clear on your philosophy, the pillars of your business and what you have to offer before you send it out into the world.

List as many groups, businesses, publications, events, expos, fairs and people you can possibly think of that could help you get your message out there to your audience. This exposes you to a far greater audience reach. Be generous with your connections. Don't just think about what you will get; think about what you can contribute to others too.

It is often the case that in the rush to get new clients, you forget the old faithfuls, so how can you keep your current clients feeling valued, rewarded and engaged?

Get involved with as many high-profile events, people or venues as possible. Aim high, you may be surprised how easy it is to get your foot in the door. Apply to heaps of places. It's a numbers game, the more you apply for, the greater your chance of success.

Don't forget your energetic practices. You'll be amazed how many people this can draw in. Send people blessings as you email, pick up the phone or send applications.

Visualise yourself channelling light from the universe and radiating who you are in essence out into the world like a lighthouse. A constant stream of energy from an infinite source, pouring out with truth, integrity and wisdom is incredibly attractive. Doing this every day will create amazing shifts in your business.

You can't sustain your audience long term if you build it inauthentically or with tricks and manipulation. Always remember this not about grabbing any old people and pulling them in to get a buck. This is about radiating out who you are, getting out and communicating that physically, and visualising thousands of people moving into your audience freely, willingly and lovingly.

Business Model

'All existing business models are wrong, Find a new one.'
- Hugh MacLeod

Once upon a time business models were pretty straightforward. Now in the wonderful age of technology and creativity, the business models of old have undergone radical change and we are able to build business models in new and innovative ways. So what is a business model, and how can you create a business model that works for you? At a practical level your business model is the basic structure and function of your business that helps it to generate income, and make profits that sustain and grow the business over time. Make no mistake, part of building a successful spiritual business means treating money and business practices with integrity so you can continue to serve. Messy structures and lazy financials will sabotage getting your purpose out into the world. Once the nitty gritty is taken care of the main thing to remember is that you are unique, your soul is unique, your business is unique and your clients are unique. Therefore your business model should also provide a unique, strong, exciting, loving, enriching experience for you and your clients.

Once you have clarified your vision, you need to decide which business model will best suit your business in a way that is sustainable physically, mentally, emotionally, spiritually and financially. The key is to decide how you want to work, and create a sustainable business model around that. Bigger isn't always necessarily better. Remember to go with your heart, not your ego. If you do want to go big, you should do it the smart way rather than running yourself into the ground. That means lots of great infrastructure, controlled growth so you're on top of your systems, and yes, quite a bit more work than if you choose a smaller model. You may want to blend a couple of business models, or change your business model over time. For example while the kids are in primary school you may want to work from home building a client base in school hours, then when the kids are in high school you may want to open a wellbeing centre. The first business model may mean seeing clients from home 10am – 3pm Monday to Wednesday, leaving Thursday for admin tasks and Friday for your own time off. As a start-up, this model offers low overheads and greater profitability. Outgoing costs include massage and essential oils, towels, laundry, candles, relaxation music, insurance, associations, marketing, personal and business development. There may also be some additional start-up costs including a website, massage table, basic room decoration and of course training. This current business model allows you to work from home, be there for the kids, make a great profit, build reputation and still look after your own wellbeing, and have weekends free for friends and family.

In a few years' time when you open your wellbeing centre, your business model will change quite drastically. You will have higher overheads including rent, utilities, staff obligations such as wages and superannuation, equipment, insurance, fit out etc. You will still want to keep your old clients and will need to have a broader target market to pay for increased costs. The business model is a lot larger and will require stronger structure and systems so that bookings run smoothly, staff are trained, high standards are consistent and the financials are well managed so the business is still making a profit, and you retain your impeccable reputation. The cost of treatments will need to rise, and other programs and services must be put in place to ensure the business is profitable in the face of increased overheads. You can't just shift from one business model to the other overnight. So during your home business years you may be blogging, using social media and leading one wellbeing workshop per school term to engage, invite and entice future customers for your studio workshops and to build your reach and reputation. I thoroughly recommend anyone thinking of opening a yoga studio or healing centre to really look at the difference in these business models from a home practice to a larger retail outlet. Be sure you are aware of the increased money, time and energy you will need and ask yourself if you are prepared for all the hard work and energy needed. If the answer to that is yes, and if you have a carefully laid out plan for profitability, then go for it. But this is not something you do on a wing and a prayer, you need to honour the commitment and understand thoroughly what you're getting into.

So what sustainable business model best suits you and your passion? A lot of people would tell you to copy a successful model, but I would say think first of how you would love to work, and then create a model that supports that. Nothing too crazy or complicated, please. The larger your business model, the more important that you keep it clean and clear. A large business model has nothing to do with adding loads of services, and the most successful wellbeing practitioners, speakers and leaders today have one simple idea that they have taken to a large platform. The aim is to create a clear, reliable business structure that supports you and makes your life easier, not sends you around the bend. Always make it something you can live and thrive in. Want to work from home? How about using e-courses to get out there? Don't want the rent and utility costs associated with a retail space for your fitness wear? How about a pop-up shop followed by an online business? We are so lucky in this age of digital technology and social media that there are loads of delivery methods that grow day by day. So find what you really, really, really want to do and create a clear, clean, sustainable business model to take it out into the world.

Know that a small business model doesn't mean a small business spirit. You can do great things in a small and cohesive model delivered simply. Understand too that a big business model is going to require a lot more time, infrastructure and effort, so balance that choice with a long-term goal, patience and a strong wellbeing/lifestyle program for yourself, and know you need to start small to build big. It's not necessarily great to grow too big too fast, so exercise your management skills and put the brakes on when you need to so you are sure your systems can sustain your growth.

Ask Yourself

Do you want to go with a big, small or medium-sized model? Why?

How can you create a business model that supports you?

What does your current business model look like? Is it working for you? Does it reflect your unique signature and why?

Does your business model offer your clients unique ways of connecting with you, a clear vision and easy purchasing pathways? Will it add light to their lives and ease to yours?

Try This

A clear business model is essential for success, and if you want financial support from a bank or investors you'll need to show them why your business model is the one to back and how it will sustain itself long term.

You build a model for your business in the same way you would build a model aeroplane. By equipping it with the tools it needs in the right size, proportion and functional capacities that meet the needs of the vehicle to get it airborne.

Create a business model that balances both the structure you need and the unique personality or soul of your business.

Get super clear on what you need from your business model to support your work, and explore new technologies that might best help you get there.

Planning

'Opportunity is missed by most people because it is dressed in overalls and looks like work.'
- Thomas Edison

Planning is one of the most crucial aspects of your business. Without a plan you are floating aimlessly in a big wide ocean, hoping you'll land on a tropical island and not get lost at sea tangled in a bunch of seaweed. Unless that's the life you're after, in which case float away. I so often see wellbeing practitioners who have been slogging away for years with a great vision and a big beautiful heart, but no plan. Or an idea of what they want to achieve, but no step by step guide. I'm guessing you wouldn't get on a plane without a working navigation system. Nor would you look for job security at a company who said 'we don't really have a plan, we were just thinking about going with the flow.' You have a responsibility to your business, your clients and most of all yourself, to create a beautiful heart-centered plan. A plan that feeds and nourishes both you and the business; that helps you to express yourself, thrive and bring light to the world. So let's stop avoiding and get that big beautiful plan down on paper and firmly planted in the earth. Let's choose the right seeds for the right soil. Let's nourish it, water it, protect it from the elements and let it grow, grow, grow until it bears such beautiful fruit you can't help but burst with pride at what you have created. To get to that place you need to dig in and prepare the soil. The three most crucial elements in planning are; to get super clear about your purpose, to keep your plan aligned with your long-term vision, to break it down and to follow through.

Every year without fail in the late winter you should plan for the year ahead. Winter is a fantastic time for introspection and it means you will have sufficient lead-in time to start strong with your spring program. Unless you are working in the snow, spring and summer will always be your busiest months, so get ready to make hay big time. You can certainly market cleverly for winter clients as well, and I'm not suggesting you drop the ball here, but part of planning is about understanding the seasons of your business. Take your holidays, undertake further studies, rejig your website or tidy up loose ends in the quieter seasons and go ahead all guns blazing in the peak seasons.

I suggest you have a lifetime goal which is centered on your purpose in this lifetime. Then a ten-year goal with major milestones, five-year goal with more detail and a very detailed twelve-month plan on exactly what you want to achieve and how you will go about doing it. A detailed plan that you are committed to implementing is the only guarantee that your goals will be completed. The twelve-month plan is broken down into what you need to achieve by the end of the year and what you will do each month, week and day to ensure you get there. At the end of each week anything that isn't done goes onto the next, and at the end of each month you can evaluate how you are tracking with your tasks. If you are not keeping up something is wrong. Either you have too much on your agenda or you are avoiding doing the work, so check in and see what adjustments need to be made. A step by step plan, always keeping the end goal in mind, will stop you getting distracted. The last thing you want is to have a beautiful vision and wake up in ten years' time, exhausted by distractions and nowhere near what you wanted to achieve. If you do find yourself here, please don't give up. Take some time, meditate, be honest with yourself and throw absolutely everything you thought you wanted out of your basket metaphorically. Then get down to your true work. You'll find it's a lot less tiring to do your one true thing really well, than a load of small shiny projects that have no long-term vision. You'll have more energy than you've had in years.

Planning is the healthiest thing you can do for yourself and your business. A great plan can stop you moving into overwhelm in your business, or getting distracted by bits and bobs while meanwhile your opus magnum is gathering dust in a corner. A good plan should have great structure and purpose, with an element of fluidity and space; not so much space that you get distracted, and not so little space that you feel you can't breathe. Connect with your heart, follow your plan and your life will become your living, breathing purpose.

Ask Yourself

How can you create success markers in your plan for motivation and a sense of achievement?
How would it feel to have a plan that ensured your success?
Is there a balance of structure and space in your plan?
Is your plan full of heart, passion, authenticity and soul?
Can you lean back into your plan for support?
Are you super clear on your purpose?
Do you know exactly where you want to be in ten years' time?

Try This

Create a clear, bold statement on your life purpose and what you intend to achieve in your lifetime. When I say bold, I mean BOLD. Let go of the 'ifs and buts', and don't withdraw into your processing formula here (I think I'm holding back on declaring a goal because my babysitter dropped me on my head when I was three). I just want you to make one huge statement. Because there is no point in creating a timid statement and feeling more and more deflated as you work through your plan. It doesn't matter whether you are planning a grassroots business or a worldwide empire. A bold lifetime goal is still required. Now a bold statement on a grassroots wellbeing business may be 'I intend to revolutionise the level of health and wellbeing for men in my community' or 'I intend to empower single mothers in my region' and so on. In the goals section I talk more about being specific, or you can go to the purpose section if you need to as well, but for this principle let's just make it big and bold to start with. When you've written down your goal ask yourself, could I make this any bolder? Now remember that's not about adding lots of things, it's about one powerful intention born from your true purpose. How does it feel in your body? It should feel expansive, exciting and energising. And a little bit daring or naughty. Your vision has to be able to fly before we bring it down to earth, so let it lift, expand and breathe. Remember the seed holds the knowledge of the tree.

Where will you need to be in ten years' time to be closer to this vision? Think practical milestones and achievements. Where will you be working, who with, what associations will you be connected with, how many clients will you have, will you have a clinic or will you be travelling the world? The ten-year goal can be fairly broad based, and if you hit these milestones earlier, by the end of your five years for example, you can always expand your vision out to the highway again. It may actually be your goal in ten years to be closing down your practice and retiring, or working fewer days for better life/work balance or to travel more. There are no rules.

Now for the five-year plan to keep you heading towards your vision, you will need to write down what you intend to achieve by year five, and then break it into year by year steps. For example; what will you need to achieve by year four to be on track, what will you need to achieve by year three to support those goals, what will you need to achieve by year two to get there, and finally what will you need to achieve in the next twelve months to ensure your success? If you break things down, you'll realise you actually have heaps of time. Then you will focus on what you will need to do month by month from today to succeed. For instance if you want to have 500 people in your workshops within five years, you'll need 300 people in them within four years, and 200 people in them within three years, and 100 people within two years and 50 within the next year. So what you need to do now is make a plan for how you are going to get 50 people in your workshops within the next 12 months. You can do a similar breakdown with the number of consultations you want per week, the amount of people you want in your webinars, e-courses, and your mailing list, how much money you want to earn and so on.

So now you are really clear on your purpose, and you have a five-year plan of what you need to do to get there, the next step is to break it down into a plan for the next twelve months. In the same way you broke the five-year plan down into years, you're going to break the twelve-month plan down into quarters, and then months. Start at the end point, and ask yourself in order to achieve 'this' by the end of the year, what do I need to do each quarter, each month, each week and each day? Start with a big piece of paper and divide it into sections so you can see it all out in front of you. That way you will be able to see if you are a bit top heavy in one month and a bit light in another. Then when you are satisfied with what you have created, fill in your calendar.

Get your yearly wall planner out and the first thing you need to do is block out at least two weeks, preferably four, of non-negotiable holiday time for yourself. Choose a time that is low season for you so you won't be missing good business. Then decide which two days in a row you will have off each week. Then what hours you are going to work. Please *do not* put down a Saturday or after hours if you don't want to work then, it is a total illusion that you have to. Go with what supports you, your family and lifestyle. Now how many workshops or programs are you going to run this year? You may have just one major launch, with a huge amount of promotion leading up to it, or four per year. Remember for each event you need a certain amount of lead-in time to promote it. It is better to have fewer workshops with more people, than a lot of workshops with less. That way you spend less time and money on advertising, rent, preparation and travel. If you are on a speaking tour, be sure each town is far away enough from each other that you're not splitting the numbers. Always be thinking about working efficiently and you'll keep the energy clear and abundant. Be aware of the seasonal influences and opportunities and highlight the busiest times of the year for you so you can be sure you are stepping into that energy flow, not trailing after it. I have run several successful summer intensives, New Year programs, spring planning workshops and so on.

Once you have a clear vision of what you are going to do this year in front of you, you need to ask yourself what will I need to do this month to make that happen? What will I need to do this week and what will I need to do today? Write it down, do it, tick it off. Once you begin to fill in your calendar you'll see how important it is to keep your purpose really clear and avoid distractions. Rather than sitting down each day and doing what is in front of you, or letting fate decide, planning gives you the opportunity to take care of the nitty gritty while keeping you on track to fulfil a long-term vision you can be proud of.

Operations

'How we spend our days is of course how we spend our lives.'
- Annie Dillard

If planning forms your long-term, whole or broader vision, your daily operations are the one thing that determines whether you will see that vision through or not. So what do I mean when I talk about the operations of your business? Literally what you are doing every day to ensure your purpose is fulfilled. In short the day to day core activities that keep your business on the path to success. It is literally the hour to hour breakdown of how you will use your time. It is the most important influence on whether all your planning comes to fruition. It's how you organise your business from the roots up, and how you do that will drastically affect your productivity, your communications, how you are perceived, your visibility in the marketplace and your success. If your operations are all over the place, so are your results.

Now I am a creative spirit. A free spirit if you will. I don't like rigidity or confinement in any way, but I also know that too much freedom is like setting a garden hose on full and letting it fly. Not so much water on the garden, and an angry neighbour saturated over the fence. Without clear systems in place you can lose your best intentions, your focus, those tax forms and the list of hot contacts you've been meaning to call for months. It's sloppy. I don't want to be in a plane where the pilot's sloppy and I don't want my wellbeing in the hands of someone that's sloppy. I want to know if I recommend you, that you will give the same professional service to everyone; that you will be timely and responsive and in control. We have to let go of the idea that structure will smother us. It actually opens up the time and space for our soul work to be created, seen and heard.

You will usually only fall off your operational intentions because you are trying to get too much done. If you can't stick to your plan or timetable there's too much on there, so go back to the drawing board and prioritise. Keep a project book so you don't forget ideas for the future, and go there when there is a gap in your timetable, not before. Less done brilliantly is way more than a whole lot all over the shop. I have seen so many beautiful, creative, talented wellbeing practitioners who never get off the ground because they run from one thing to another. Or they avoid, or dawdle or refuse to set a timetable for their dreams. Their ego is pulling all the strings and that is one wild horse. They mistake a lack of discipline for freedom. They feel they will become trapped or twisted or conformed if they step into structure. And I get that – as a creative spirit I understand the fear, but I got over it and things opened up for me ever since. I am here to tell you that structure is going to shine a light on you and your beauty. It is here to promote your essence, not hide it. It is going to help you reach people you never dreamed of reaching. It is going to bring light, love, peace and healing to the outside world. The structure ensures you keep your integrity and vision. It ensures you say what you mean and do what you say. It keeps the road clear of stumbling blocks, has backup plans and systems to create more time for you to spend on your art. It teaches you to outsource to experts, so you have more free time for what you love. It is about spiritual maturity and whether you will fulfil the promise you made.

So get this really clear in your head; structure and systems won't trap you, or kill your art, your talent or your creative spirit. Structure will set you free. It is everything to the life blood of your business. It opens time and space not only for your business, but for holidays, to socialise, to meditate, to step back and see if what you're building is what you intended, and the opportunity to check on any gaps or glitches. Operations is about breaking your twelve-month plan down to a month by month plan, then down to a week by week plan, then down to a day by day, and dare I say hour by hour plan. The best thing about this is…you get a lunch break! The operational plan ensures you get everything done in a timely manner. Instead of avoiding the aspects of your business that overwhelm you, you open up time and space to better understand them. This gives you confidence moving forward. You set yourself up for success. You can timetable creativity, research or brainstorming sessions as well as marketing, writing programs and seeing clients. Your business model will give you a clear idea of what you need to set aside time for.

Operations will move you away from overwhelm and towards purpose. It will keep your body, mind and spirit in a state of relaxed alertness and efficient competency. An effective operations plan divides everything you need to do into bite-size pieces and measurable portions. It helps you prioritise, so what really needs doing gets done. It means you can balance working in your business with working on your business. It ensures you are seen as a professional, not some hippy out there practitioner who is unreliable and ungrounded. And yes, you can be deeply spiritual and deeply organised. There is nothing spiritual about flinging your energy all over the place. So respect your craft, yourself and your clients enough to operate from a vibrant, joyful, clean and clear space, and you'll find your work and your name becomes highly respected and your work expands to its rightful depths.

Ask Yourself

How structured is your week?

Do you have beautiful projects on the back burner because you haven't created space for their development?

How much energy is leaking from your business in the form of wasted time, distractions and dawdling?

Can you allocate more time to work on weak spots in your business?

What working habits can you engage to become more professional?

Try This

What are your values and commitments? Eg to respond to emails in a timely manner is a bit vague and depends on your definition, so I would say to respond to all email enquiries within 24 hours. That allows for times when I'm teaching workshops, and other than that I would respond immediately where possible.

What hours are you open? Think carefully about this because the pattern you set now may dig you a hole if it's not what you wanted. Start as you mean to go on. Don't make presumptions. As a massage therapist you don't have to be available in the evenings or Saturdays. No you don't. I know plenty of great massage therapists that work Monday to Friday 9-5 or even during school hours and are booked up weeks in advance. As a yoga teacher you don't have to work evenings if you don't want to, or daytime classes if that doesn't suit you. Want to work three longer days instead of five shorter days? Do it. Choose the times that support your lifestyle for the future and don't be swayed by opinion. If they want you, they will come. Over-availability can leave you exhausted and in a position of servitude. Clear boundaries will sustain you.

Create a weekly schedule. What days are you seeing clients or teaching classes? How much time do you need each week for your social media? Break down what you need to do each week and schedule it. Then sit and do only those tasks in those times.

Make use of the time in between clients or classes. You can get lots of nitty gritty stuff done in between awkward time slots like filling in your bookwork, responding to emails or sending out applications.

Create structural boundaries for areas where you might easily get distracted and lose time. For instance I only check my emails at 7am, 12pm and 4pm. I usually only go on Facebook once a day, to post and check out my news feed. Can you imagine how much time that alone frees up to do the work that matters?

Never forget what you do today, and every day thereafter is going to directly affect where your business is in the future.

Diversifying and Dilution

'If you don't stand for something, you'll fall for anything.'
- Malcolm X

The most successful practitioners around the world today have one thing in common; literally. They have one thing that they do incredibly well. They do not overcomplicate things by trying to be everything to everyone. They have an incredibly clear identity that they send out into the world. Marie Forleo has B-School, Liz Koch and her Psoas work, Wayne Dyer and his manifestation teachings, Doreen Virtue and her angel work, Eckhart Tolle and the Power of Now, Marianne Williamson and her teachings on a Course in Miracles, Mama Gena and her School of Womanly Arts and so on.

There is absolutely no confusion here, the message is clear; everyone knows who these leaders are and what they stand for. No one came to this earth with two purposes, and the more you try to do, the less successful you will be in fulfilling your true work. It may sound a little harsh, but by trying to be everything to everyone you are actually diluting who you are. Not only that but you are blocking abundance, deeper learning and an impeccable reputation as a specialist in your field. Can you imagine how the work of those successful leaders above would look if they branched out in many different areas? How it would affect the potency of their message and what a loss that would be to us? The same goes for you, because yes, you can have a voice every bit as powerful as the greatest leaders out there today. And your tribe needs to hear it, and they are waiting for your wisdom with bated breath.

You need to learn how to cut through illusion, and take comfort in the truth and courage of the soul, because the closer you to get to that one thing, the more the ego is going to start hopping from one foot to the other and producing 'evidence' that it can't work and why. I want you to stretch yourself, challenge yourself and be willing to be courageous; to leave everything but your one thing behind. Doesn't that idea sound pretty exciting? The capacity to diversify your services offers both the greatest opportunity and the greatest threat to your business. Diversify cleverly and discriminately *within* your core niche or purpose and you are on a winner. Diversify in a variety of practices with no clear intention, and you may find your business in a world of pain, with no clear identity and no clear market. Let's get one thing straight – you can't be everything to everyone. Your diversification should all sit neatly in your business model, each aspect feeding the other and reinforcing your niche. Remember we talked earlier about keeping your niche narrow and taking it *deep*.

I cannot stress enough how important it is to get really clear on your purpose before you start to diversify. With many people in recent years promoting diversification, folks have jumped on the bandwagon without thinking and totally diluted their message of who they are. Only ever diversify within your niche, not outside of it. And even then make sure it's valid and on point. Think about enriching and deepening what you have, rather than overloading your business with so much that people can't see the woods for the trees.

Staying with your niche makes you a master, rather than ever the apprentice chasing after the next new thing which will blow away faster than you can imagine. Take a deep breath; pause, wait, check in. Is what you're about to do coming from the deepest reaches of your soul, or is it just filler, or a reaction to the ego's fears? Let any diversification form the essence of what you are here for; let it shine from your bright heart so all the world may see who you truly are.

Ask Yourself

What scares you about just doing one thing?
    If you could do just one thing for the rest of your life what would that be?
    What would your one thing taste like, look like, feel like, sound like and smell like?

Who do you want to be known as, and what do you want to be known for?

Can you break away from industry lingo and prescribed language and find your unique voice?

How would it feel to step fully into your deepest work?

What do you tell yourself you will get if you diversify? Are they the reasons of the soul or the ego?

Are you diversifying powerfully and soulfully, or diluting your business and your brand?

A clear indication of whether you are diluting or diversifying is to ask yourself what motivated you to add another modem or branch to your practice? Was it through a pure love of learning, a deep inner calling or need to upskill and grow? Or was it as a reaction to what others were doing, what you thought might be popular or from a sensation of panic or fear? Be honest here.

Diversifying can have a very strong fear trigger around it, so ask first; am I doing this because I am responding to a fear about money or scarcity, or am I doing it because it comes from a soul calling? Is it an integrated part of my overall business vision, or am I diluting myself and my message and cheating my audience out of my deepest work?

Is there an end goal to your diversification? (To be everything to everyone is not a healthy goal.)

When do you tend to get distracted, and how can you stop yourself from heading off on another tangent? Become acutely aware of your triggers and resolve to sit with the discomfort rather than rush to act.

Try This

Write down your purpose, get as specific as you can, then list the products and services you could offer that are intrinsically tied to your purpose. Then how you could best deliver them, what the content would be, how long they would run for, how much time and money you would need for marketing each project and so on. When you get a realistic view of how much energy each project takes, you will be more likely to offer a few powerful options. Each product or service should keep purpose front and centre, make sense and feed into each other to create a strong brand.

Remember the call to your true work should always come from the soul. If in doubt sit, meditate and listen.

Write down all the modems you are currently trained in. Can you see a powerful thread or niche that ties all these together? Be specific, to say a love of wellness is not enough. What is it about all these modems that you love? What can it help you convey, what does it gift people?

Even if you are diversifying within your niche, you need to keep it clean and clear so your clients don't become overwhelmed. What dead wood can you chop from your business? Play around with this. Ask yourself what if I eliminated this and this? It may be practices or delivery methods (consults, classes, workshops or retreats). Can you see how making a few courageous changes could open up and clarify new options? Take your time with this and explore thoroughly. What do you need to exclude, and what do you need to add to offer a clearer vision of who you are?

What avenues are working best for you, and which are not? Make a list of which ones you wholly truly love and which are draining you. Rate each practice and each delivery model a 1 - 10, with 1 being not exciting at all to 10 being your most favourite thing of all. If the ones you love are not performing so well can you tweak them, or do you feel you haven't had enough time to nurture them due to other distractions?

If you're having trouble believing you can be successful with just one thing, write a list of your favourite leaders in the world today and ask yourself what they specialise in. You'll find that there is a specific thread that moves through their work. That is the thread of their soul.

If you think you need to diversify to succeed, try writing a list of the most successful wellbeing or spiritual leaders of our time who do a whole heap of different things. Mmm.....

Website

'Sometimes being seen is the same thing as being saved.'
- Mary Rakow

Gone are the days where a website could simply act as a brochure for you. Your website needs to be your number one employee, and you need to give that website a list of essential tasks it needs to do to fulfil its obligations to you and your business. It should be easy to navigate, express exactly who you are and what you do and have powerful integrations that seamlessly walk your clients through your sales process. They should be able to book into your events, make an appointment, buy a product, sign up for your e-course, join you on social media or subscribe to your newsletter effortlessly. So ask yourself what do you want your website to do for you? What essential products, programs or services does it need to promote? How can you keep it clean and clear from a branding perspective? How can you fill it with love, innovation and warmth? How can you stand out from the crowd and be easily found? Follow this essential checklist to make sure your website will take you to new heights.

A Clear Message

It should be totally clear in the first few seconds of landing on your webpage who you are, what you do and how you can help. Sell energy, an emotion, a vision, or an experience rather than just a list of services. Think about reinforcing your brand with clarity, love and conviction. Make sure the colour, style and feel are aligned with your brand image.

Design & Technology

Try to find a person or team who can cover both the design and technical aspects of your website. It should be easy to navigate for sales, whilst looking beautiful, spacious and clear at the same time. Too much clutter and your clients will switch off. Beautiful design without functionality is just a brochure, and your potential clients will be less likely to purchase if they have to jump through hoops to get there. Likewise if all the integrations are present and the technology is great, but the beauty and design doesn't grab the eye and engage the spirit, your website may feel soulless. Do your research, look at the folios of potential web designers and visit the websites to ensure they are functional and aesthetically pleasing. Never mimic another website, but you can certainly look at lots of sites to see what you like, what works and what doesn't, both from a technological and design perspective. See if you can find someone who gets you and remember to be as clear as possible with your brief. You will need to balance your personal vision, with taking advice from people who know what works and what doesn't. You will also have to be brave, and communicate well in the interim stages as your website is being formed. If something is not right speak up early!

Price

Get a clear quote on what your website is going to cost you, and be mindful that any major changes you make may incur further costs. Be really clear about your budget with your designer, ask when full or part payments are expected and ensure they know to advise you if a change you want is going to cost you. Then at least you can weigh up the pros and cons. Spend as much as you can afford to. Yes you can set up your own website in Wordpress, but get a professional to do it for you or you may be missing out on a load of business opportunities. There's no point having a website sitting there doing nothing. The more you pay the more your website will return to you. As in most things you get what you pay for.

Content

Keep your content original, relevant and fresh. It should be rich with keywords that attract your customers to your website without sounding like a shopping channel. Quality content always helps with your Google rankings, and it will keep your customers really clear on who you are and what you do. Don't overload keywords or you'll be penalised in your website ranking; good quality content always wins the day. If you are not a writer it may be a good idea to get someone else to help you with copy, but make sure they really know who you are, what you're all about and the feeling tone you want

Personality

Be yourself, inject a little fun, and let your personality come through. If you're quirky be that, if you're gentle be that or if you're wild be that. Authenticity is what engages people at the deepest level and will encourage them to linger longer to explore your offerings or feel brave enough to ask you questions and engage. Your customers want to buy from someone real, someone they feel they can connect with. The more they feel they know you, the more likely they will be to use your services.

Testimonials

Add some testimonials with photos. We'll talk more about social proof a little later, but there are some amazing statistics on how responsive people are to the experience of others. There's nothing like a testimonial to add recommendations for your services, and photos let customers connect to a real person and know you're not just making these up in the back room.

Website Templates

There are a wide variety of website templates to choose from today and each of them will have different capabilities, ownership rules and qualities. Some popular cheap and basic website builders won't let you transfer your website to different hosts, so make sure that is who you want to stick with long term before you begin. If you want to move it later you won't be able to. Also be aware of what integrations they are capable of working with. Integrations will become more and more important in the future. The most popular platform is Wordpress. Wordpress has a vested interest in insuring your website gets great search engine results, has a ready-made audience and it has a wide array of templates to choose from. You will have to be vigilant about your security though as it can be targeted by viruses (as can anything). Think about what your template does, not just what it looks like, and make it sure it is responsive or mobile friendly. Wordpress is clear and attractive to Google, and there are an incredible array of plug-ins you can add to make your website more effective (make sure you choose wordpress.org, not wordpress.com for your business for better plug-in options). You can get a tech person to switch you from one to the other if you have made this mistake and need to expand your website capabilities.

Newsletter Opt-ins on Every Page

An opt-in is an option for your clients to sign up for your newsletter. You should have this option on every page, as people don't have time to go hunting back through your website to find your signup button. You don't need to have a pop-up box if that's too full on for you, just an opt-in opportunity at the top and/or bottom of the page can suffice. Have a great lead attached to your opt in like; 'stay connected with our newsletter', 'want exciting tips and tools? Sign up now', 'want to be the first to hear about events?' and so on. It is also a great idea to offer a reward or thank you for signing up – sign up now for a free e-book, discount on our next workshop etc. Make it fresh, fun and exciting. There are lots of great email providers out there that can be linked into your website. More on that later.

Call to Action

Speaking of which…it is important to add a CTA or call to action for every blog you post on your website so you encourage clients to take action. I know it can sound a little cheesy if done badly, but if you do it with heart and good intentions people will respond. After all you want your clients to come, sign up, and join in, don't you? Leaving out a call to action is like saying, 'oh my God I just found the best wholefood cafe, it has such a great vibe and the most delicious salads, and they were so kind to my kids and they have some incredible events coming up you just have to go there. Ok bye.' Hang on a minute! Where are they? How do I get on the list for events? When are they open? Think of it more as an invitation…if you want them to come, have the courage to ask. You can ask clients to sign up to your newsletter, book in for an appointment, or join an event. Just choose a call to action that is appropriate and relevant to the blog article you have just posted. For instance if you are writing an article on aromatherapy you might add a call to action for your next aromatherapy workshop like 'want to learn more about aromatherapy techniques for self-nurture? Join our e-course today.' Simply add a link to the CTA so folks can easily follow through.

Have a Good CRM System

A CRM is a customer relationship management system. At its most basic this is simply about having good tech systems behind your website that help you interact easily with current customers and gather new ones. It takes the legwork out of things by integrating sales, marketing, sign-up data and responses. It makes things streamlined for you and your customers. Some systems are incredibly sophisticated (and slightly creepy) about the information they gather about your clients. Please balance any system with your ethics, some are very intrusive with tracking, just go with what feels right and works for you. You can get your tech person to integrate your newsletter provider, your appointment scheduler, a shopping cart, an e-course provider, or whatever you need into your website, and once they are in they work fine. Or you could choose a service that provides everything in one system. Please just go with what you can afford, and you can switch to more fancy systems over time. I sometimes have clients come to me who are paying $200 plus per month for a system they have no idea how to use and it's just burning a hole in their pocket and not creating any sales. On the other end of the scale you could get a newsletter service for free, a basic scheduler for $10 US a month, an event provider that either takes a percentage of sales or charges the clients a few extra dollars per purchase, and a shopping cart that does the same. I'm not saying always go with the cheaper option, you do get what you pay for, but if you are going to use a sophisticated system make sure you know what it does, and attend a seminar, webinar or training series to understand your choice better. Many of these are geared to the layman and have great instructional videos, so there's no need to feel overwhelmed.

Social Media Links

Choose the social media platforms where your audience hangs out, and that are easy for you to use. Add links to your website so your clients can like your pages and connect with you there, or you can also have a stream from your social media account embedded in your website. I would also add LinkedIn for a professional resource which adds credibility. Less is more, so choose what works for you. Three powerfully managed platforms is better than six you dabble in. It's also highly unlikely your clients will lead into each one from your website, but they may check in on a couple.

Regular Blogs

Regular blogs from your website will help your SEO (search engine optimisation) which is basically about how well you rank on an internet search. The more relevant, regular, fresh, new, original and exciting content you are putting out there, the better you'll rank. It also lets your clients know more about who you are. It showcases you as an expert in your field, and it is fun! Never before have we had the opportunities and platforms that we have today and I for one am very grateful. You can also link an rss feed from your e-mail provider to your blog, so that each blog post you make goes out to the people on your mailing list. The other alternative is to send a newsletter with part of your blog and an invitation to read more by clicking through to your website. The idea is to invite people to spend as much time on your website as possible, because that will help your SEO, so you want people to read your blog from your website rather than their inbox. The only danger here is they might not bother to click through so you'll need to make the lead-in and subject really exciting. It's a personal choice; you can experiment, look at your statistics and see what works for you. Check out the blogging section for more hints

Less Pages, More Clarity

It is better to keep the pages fewer and the message clearer. Remember the beauty of the blog and daily social media posts is that you can talk more about your expertise and who you are. Not every single thing you have ever done needs to become a page. In an increasingly busy world people want clear communication and choices. Take the work away from them as much as you can. Make it clean, clear and simple. Chop the dead wood from your business, get super clear on your brand, be brave and promote only that.

Make It Responsive

Having a responsive website is absolutely essential; being responsive means that your website will look great whether your clients are checking you out via iPad, iPhone or on a desktop. More and more people are using their mobile devices, and this will only increase in the future. Search engines will now punish sites that are not mobile responsive by pushing you down in their page rankings, and bringing others up. Most themes are now responsive, and if your website is not, get it fixed *today*.

It Needs to Make Sales

The primary role of your website should be to increase your exposure and make sales. It should be your number one employee. That means getting you more coaching clients, selling more products, filling up your training programs, selling more books and supporting whatever it is you do. You want your amazing work to get out there, right? What if you had a website that bought clients to you, and took away a whole load of that effort? How amazing would that be? Yes you still need to work your mojo, but you will have an incredible support system that is going to be gathering more clients and signing people up to your mailing list while you sleep. How cool is that!

Like all marketing, creating a great website is an art….and a learning curve. Get clear, get passionate, do your research and get a great website that supports and fulfils your calling.

Social Media and Content

*'May what I do flow from me like a river;
no forcing and no holding back.'*
- Rainer Maria Rilke

You are here to help people, to share your knowledge, to impart wisdom and to express yourself. Social media offers you a golden opportunity to fully express who you are, where you stand and what you are all about. We are so blessed to have social media to help us spread our craft. Gone are the days where we paid a fortune in fliers and print advertising. Social media opens up equal opportunity for everyone to get out there and be heard, and I for one think that's a beautiful thing. The most important role for your social media, apart from your soul expression, is to drive traffic to your website, promote your brand, build your email list and let people know about your products and services. Always remember your audience on the social media platforms you use is owned and managed by those platforms. They may feel like your clients or even be your clients, but all your interactions with them on social media, including how often and when you connect, is being controlled. Each of these social media platforms manage all connections between you and your followers, and can create or change rules about when and how those interactions occur whenever they want. And they will more and more as time goes on, and they try to monetise their services. A classic example is when Facebook started limiting who saw your posts. You may have had 400 followers but only a minute portion of them got to see your wisdom. This was done in order to encourage you to spend money boosting posts, and using Facebook advertising. It is absolutely essential now to make use of social media platforms to build your brand. It is a fantastic thing, but let's not be naïve about it. When you get your social media followers to join your mailing list, however, you can contact them anytime and let them know about your fabulous events, wisdom and services without any interference or someone stepping in the way.

By all means make new connections, showcase who you are, your fabulous events, products and services, and continue to engage and grow there, but never forget who controls that information. Keep building your email list and driving clients to your website and you'll be in a win-win situation. I would urge you to set up your social media platforms as soon as possible inline with your business name and personalise your url on each platform. You want everything streamlined as much as possible. You don't have to be an expert in social media before you start, just get in there, experiment and give it a good crack.

Content

What are you actually going to say? What will you talk about? Aren't we overloaded on inspirational quotes? Aren't there enough wellbeing practitioners spruiking out there? Haven't people heard enough? Obviously not, because they keep logging on and liking and following us. People are still searching for something, and it's your job to find out what that is for your clients, and how you can help.

Have you ever had the experience where you learn something a few times, but then a particular person comes along and says something to you in a particular way, and it just clicks? Or that you knew something but needed a reminder. Or you were waiting for an answer and exactly the right words, video, motivation or inspiration fell onto your screen at the right time. Or there was something there so great and so spot-on you wanted to share with all your friends? Well you are the messenger that your clients are looking for; the one with just the right experience, just the right knowledge, just the right manner, just the right voice at just the right time. Not only that but when you are clear about exactly who you are and what you have to say, a little window opens up. People start to tune in because, well, blow me down if that isn't exactly what they needed help with. And you start to shine a little brighter, and more people take notice. Pretty soon you're a lighthouse.

To get there I want you to go back over your heartland/niche chapter from earlier; your unique message. Be really clear about it. Make sure this is your true message, not something you've concocted because you think it will sell, or be successful, or be popular. Double check, triple check; how does it feel in your body, in your mind and in your spirit? It should make you fell energised, inspired, light, and free (a little afraid is okay too because you're going to be putting it all out there). If you feel really uncomfortable, constricted or unsure go back to the exercises again. There's no point building a reputation on one thing, when you really want to do another. I see this all too often and it really wastes a lot of time, money and effort, so be clear or get some help to be clear from me or someone else. Don't ever let anyone tell you this is what's trending in wellness; this is what's hot, this is the way of the future, this is the modem to teach or practice. You can explore trends in your delivery method (e-courses, videos etc) but not with who you are. The *truth* is the hottest thing out there and that's eternal, not just seasonal. Always, always, always go with what you love and who you are in essence.

Your goal is to broadcast exactly who you are, and what you are willing to devote your life to. Everything stripped back, open hearted, wholly present. To be truly successful in mind, body and spirit this is what it takes; the whole truth and nothing but the truth. Something you're willing to stand for. Every single thing that radiates out from your being will contain the essence of who you are. And that is going to heal you, your clients, and the world, so it's totally worth it. This will take time. Don't give up at the first hurdle if you're not getting the responses you wanted. Make sure its exciting and inspirational, experiment with different content, play around, check in. Your niche is going to bring you bliss, and of course there will be challenges, but there will absolutely definitely be challenges on any other path. Don't imagine if you stay away from your true message that you will avoid criticism or heartache in your life. In my experience with clients avoiding your deepest calling brings nothing but a sense of loss, pain or regret. So if you are to be criticised anyway, let it be for something worthwhile, something sacred and something worth fighting for.

Before we go into deciding what themes or content to use in social media to connect with your clients, I want to bring in a note of caution here. I have often seen practitioners deciding who they would like their clients to be before fully immersing themselves in who they are. It's a bit like choosing the coolest kids in school and then realising you have nothing to talk about, or being involved with situations that leave you empty and cold. Who you are, and what your niche is, are the single most important factors in determining who your authentic audience is. If you don't know who you are, you sure as hell won't ever know who they are. Any old person won't do. You need to find the people you are here on this planet to help and get to it. Stepping fully into that will drive your success and give you great personal satisfaction in the heart and soul. So…

Who Are You?

Who are you?
　What are you here to share or teach?
　Why do you want to do it?
　What are you passionate about?
　What experience do you have?
　What training do you have?
　What do you have life skills in?
　What do you teach?
　What are your best qualities?
　What are you intuitively gifted in?
　What fascinates you?
　What would you like to specialise in?
　What are you here to share?
　How can your positive stories influence others?
　Where has your life led you?
　What are your five best talents?
　How did your journey bring you to this?
　What do you know for sure?

What services do you provide?
Where is your heart leading you?
What positive stories can you share?
What is it above all else that you want to say?
What would you hate to leave this planet without saying, being or doing?
What were the three hardest lessons of your life and how did you move past them?
What are the best tools you have for dealing with difficulties?
If you saw someone alone, afraid or lost what are the three things you would tell them to get them back on their feet again and why? (No platitudes here like everything will be alright, your real deep down truth please)

Connecting With Your Clients

Once and only once you are super clear on who you are, start to join the dots on who you might help. Ironically (or should I say beautifully) your journey will often directly relate to theirs. If this is the case when you think about how you can help, also think about what would have helped you back in the day. If you want to build a rapport with your audience you will need to be consistent and cohesive. You will need to speak directly to their heart from yours. So ask yourself a few simple questions – then answer them;

What do they need help with?
What worries them?
What do they want to know?
What are their doubts and fears?
What do they wish they could overcome?
What would change their life?
What would make everything easier?
What would help them breakthrough?
What do they need encouragement with?
What tools could support them?
What experts could advise them?

What could you say that would set their mind at ease?
What experience do you have that you could talk about?
What wisdom could you impart?
How can you increase their faith, courage or confidence in themselves?
What books would help them?
What diet, exercise or philosophy might help?
What skills do you have that speak directly to their needs?
What services can you offer them?
How can you be generous with them?
Where do they sabotage themselves?
What are their hobbies and interests?
How old are they?
Where do they go online and in real life?
What is important to them?
Do they know you are an expert in this field and are here to help?

I want you to really take your time on this (no, not a couple of years). Set aside a couple of days, create a sacred space, make a cup of tea, light some candles, meditate, and consult your spirit. Create a really strong clear vision of how you can be of service. Feel it, explore it, and test it by tuning into your mind, your intuition and your body. This is not something you can just pull out of a hat. If you are still totally stuck after giving it an honest go, head to your nearest kinesiologist to shift any blocks. At the end of the day you have to feel any fear and do it anyway. 'Even though I'm scared I am committed to working with my passion.' Pulling back is getting old, so just get to it! So how do you take your niche and create good content around it? Take your message, mind map it (check out the Mind Map chapter) and brainstorm ideas from there. Let's look at an example. Jenny is a massage therapist. She is well qualified and could work with anyone, but she is really all about connecting women 30-55 with their sensuality. It's her passion, so how can she get that out there on social media? Jenny can use her own material, products and services, or share others' to explore a million different aspects of women's sensuality, with the intention to inspire, ignite, inform, heal, transcend, explore, create, discover and engage. By sticking with her niche Jenny begins to achieve a great reputation as an authority in women's sensuality over time to grow herself, her business, her client base and her passion. Let's brainstorm some topics and ways she could achieve this – a mind map is a great option or you could just list some ideas. I totally recommend having a file for ideas on an app like Evernote. You can add ideas straight to your mobile when inspiration comes when you're out and about. Open your Evernote account from your iPad or laptop, when you get home and its all there in one place. Of course if you are more artistic and hands on you could have a special book with quotes, ideas, pictures and so on and return there to add ideas or for inspiration. Please don't do what I did and end up with about twenty notebooks because you'll forget what is in each and never end up using the information. *One* notebook or one app for inspiration is ample. Or just use the notes section on your phone. So back to some ideas for Jenny and how she might use her social media posts to strengthen her brand and live her purpose on social media:

Sensuality for Women Topics
TED talks on female sensuality
Beautiful photos of the female form
Inspirational quotes & messages on being in your own skin
The road from motherhood to sensuality
How our perception of sensuality changes as we age
Benefits of massage for sensuality
History of the art of massage and sensuality
Massage during pregnancy, menstruation, menopause or change
Massage as healing touch
Sharing other sensual arts & events like Tigress yoga, Tantra studies, belly dancing
Videos of sensual dance
Art exhibitions on the female form and how ideas have changed culturally and historically
Small e-book on sensuality

PDF top tips to reconnect to your senses
Aromatherapy for sensuality
Blogs on sensuality
E-courses on sensuality
Workshops on sensuality
Events and retreats focussing on body reconnection
How massage reconnects us to our sensuality
Self-massage tips to reconnect to our body
Why she's passionate about it
What services she offers
Articles she's written on the subject
Photos of her at events and workshops
Ten top reasons to connect to your sensuality
Seven tips to love your body
Conferences for wisdom on women and sensuality
Book recommendations
Her personal journey, stories, experience with sensuality and so on....

You'll see I have just generalised on the topic of sensuality and massage, but Jenny would take each subject and break this down ever further into subjects that are meaningful to her. And then break those down again and again. Remember how we talked about making your niche narrow and taking it *deep*? This is just how you do that. Deep doesn't mean complicated by the way. And this is how we can have many experts on sensuality and each person is still unique due to their specialised field, personality, identity, experience, brand, passion, delivery and services. The closer you stay to your own heart, your own truth, the more successful you will be. The trick is to gather, gather, gather everything about the topic you love, and be sure to write a lot of your own stuff from the heart. Write down as many points about your niche as you can and then expand on them, and then expand on them. Once you start setting your creative juices flowing in a subject that you love, you are going to start getting ideas left, right and centre. What you focus on grows.

Because Jenny's niche is sensuality, her language and tone should match.

Pictures should be warm and inviting, language should be soothing. When Jenny is advertising her massage treatments she may use text like; when is the last time you had a beautiful, nourishing treat, slip back into your own skin, dive deep, feel the bliss, nourish your soul, the room's warm, the music's soft, are you ready to take the journey back to your self, and so on. If Jenny's message is clear across all social media platforms, pretty soon when you think of her you feel warm and nurtured. If she writes general stuff, it's like oh, she just does massage, and we all know there are a thousand different massage therapists out there, right?

Out in the real world Jenny goes on retreats, to expos, fairs, wellness events and talks to people about sensuality for women. She goes to tigress yoga classes, red tent events, seven sisters festivals and anywhere else where her peeps and potential customers hang out. This is her tribe, this is where she can have fascinating conversations, meet new contacts, friends and YES do a little business. Raising her profile and having the chance to chat to people personally means she is someone people go to, because they trust her, they have got to know her. Jenny stands in who she is. She's not all about the sell, sell, sell. Everything about her says this is her passion and people trust her enough to happily pay for her expertise.

There is a lot written about using platforms where your audience hangs out, but I would also say use only those platforms that are aligned with your brand and easy to use, because if it's too laborious or it doesn't feel right to you, you won't be consistent there. Personally I find Pinterest laborious. I do have an account there but rarely use it. I know that a lot of my client base hang out there, but they are also on Instagram and Facebook which are easier for me to use. Maybe at a later date I will get into it, but right now I am happy to let it go. Better to have less that you are using well, than too many platforms that overwhelm you. Remember you don't need to be dictated to, always choose with your intuition. You need to control your social media presence, rather than letting it control you.

Platforms; What to Post and Where

As well as going with what platform works for you, there is no point spending hours creating your pinterest boards if your clients are all on Instagram, or offering inspirational gems on Twitter that would be better received on Facebook. So how do you find out where your clients are hanging out? You can check out the stats on each social media platform to see which sex and age groups are using which platforms, talk to people in your area about what they are succeeding with, look at the websites of clients and industry experts to see what social media they are using, check out people who are successful in your chosen field and see where they are getting most engagement, see how many people are using each platform and so on. The absolute best thing you can do though is to really, really know your clients and that will teach you where they hang out.

I can't stress enough that you need to do your own research here and stay on top of industry changes by attending social media events, researching platforms, experimenting and following instructions to get the most out of each platform you sign up to. There are constant tweaks and new tools on each platform, so stay on it. The Spirit in Business conferences offer deep soul work and the latest social media breakthroughs to get your work thriving out there from an authentic space. All of the social media platforms have great information on how to get started and make the most out of their services, because your success is their success.

So What Kind of Stuff Could You Post Across Your Chosen Social Media Platforms?

TED talks
Beautiful photos
Inspirational quotes & messages
Statistics, studies, amazing facts
FAQ from your students and answers from you
Benefits, tips, tools and tricks from your kit bag
A challenge or exercise for your clients to try

Problem solving – nominate an issue and how to solve it
Try this – wellness practice, home spa products, healthy meal
Cutting edge information
Industry research
Videos – your own, YouTube, TED, Vimeo
Live Feed broadcasts and Q and A sessions
Wellness expos, markets, events, conferences
Slide shows
Free events, resources or information
Networking opportunities
Invitation to share your stuff with someone who needs help
Publications
Recommended books
Podcasts – audios from Soundcloud, iTunes etc.
E-books; yours or others
PDF info sheets
Downloads
Blogs – yours primarily and others where appropriate
E-courses
Product - benefits and features, new releases, new ranges and launches
Services you provide – benefits and features, new programs, special offers, packages and exciting news
Your workshops, courses, retreats and events
Your stories, personal journey, experience (they don't have to be sad stories to inspire)
Competitions
Laughs, play, fun, surprises and light stuff
Faith, confidence, inspiration
Surveys and results
Interview an industry expert or share a talk they have given
Top 10 industry leaders, spa destinations, wellness tips, exercises
Success stories from your products/services
Compare and contrast – eg different yoga styles, menopause approaches,

osteopathy & chiropractors, different dance styles, healthy diets and so on
Why – you're passionate about what you do
What – products, services you offer
Who – don't be afraid to say who you love working with
Celebrate other practitioners authentically
Be visionary - make a prediction on where you see your wellness practice going
Be innovative – be the first at introducing a new way of doing things
Write a review
Write a blog on a conference you recently attended & what you learned
A call to action
Articles you've written
Sneak peeks on coming events, books, services, products
How to avoid – injuries, stress or anxiety
Photos of events and workshops
Ten top reasons for this, seven steps for that, six reasons why you must do this, eight essential tips, five things to avoid when.
Book recommendations
Wellness sheets or demos - meditation practices, yoga poses, massage techniques, home spa treatments
How to series related to your craft on blog, video, PDF or e-book
Products – candles, yoga mats, inspirational posters, dancewear
Newsletters
All about your modem and why you love it
Behind the scenes, a day in the life of your work, setting up for an event, pics at the airport, gift bags, you at work, your workshop manual, the venue, talks, relaxing afterwards, taking people on the journey with you
Anything that inspires and connects with your audience

Whoa! Feeling like it's all too much? Don't worry you don't have to do all these things. Not at all. The trick is to use the social media platforms and the materials that work for you. If you love to write then the blog, info sheets and stories you share are going to be great for you. If you love to take photos then Instagram, Pinterest and Facebook will inspire you. Just grab a pencil and circle what appeals to you. Or take one or two things at a time and explore it over a week and see if it works for you. You do want to mix things up a bit though so there is variety there. At the end of the day, it's all about the quality of your information and the connection and engagement with your audience, so keep it real. Keep sharing from the heart and soul. Make sure it's all relevant to your niche and speaks to your audience. Keep an eye on the engagement on your page and notice what seems to excite people, and what they are not engaging with. For example I notice my followers are used to hearing my voice, so when I share from others I rarely get much interaction. I still share from practitioners I wish to support, and information I feel is important, but not too often. Experiment, test waters, readjust, keep going and you'll find a pattern that really works for you and your audience.

Most importantly, really engage with your audience – if they comment, then reply, affirm, engage, and get to know them. Every one of your online clients is a real flesh and blood person with hopes, dreams, a family, work, problems, tragedies and triumphs. Let them know their input is valued and always be generous in what you share. Make it easy on yourself and create files with links to interesting articles, create a playlist on your YouTube channel for inspiring talks, videos or music, list the people you find inspiring and like to follow, the best Instagram, Facebook and Pinterest accounts you can share from, keep writing articles or subjects of interest for later blogs/posts etc. That way you have a load of go-to information you can draw on, or you can store these on social media manager platforms.

Scheduling Posts

You can schedule posts for up to six months ahead on Facebook and use social media management platforms like Hootsuite, Buffer, and SproutSocial that allow you to schedule and plan across several social media platforms. For some people this makes everything so much easier, for others it's all a little overwhelming. Check it out, but I would suggest getting a thorough understanding of each social media platform you use before launching into social media management. Your first priority will still be to get proficient in what to post where, because in the same way you would slightly change your tone for different audiences you speak to, you will also need to change the language slightly for each platform rather than send out a blanket post everywhere. For instance the Twitter audience has a different personality from a Facebook audience, and a different amount of characters you can use for each post, so I would introduce my book launch differently in each place. Social media management tools give you the option of doing this, but you will be paying a monthly fee, so explore a little and then decide whether it's worth it for you or you can just do it yourself. I guess the best benefit is if you go away and want to keep your social media active in your absence. After a particularly bad holiday where I just couldn't switch off, I made a conscious choice to totally abandon all my social media for two weeks so I could recharge properly. Remember above all else you should be teaching sovereignty in your clients and students, so if they can't do without you for a week something is wrong. Leave a lovely automated response from your email saying when you'll be back with a link directing them to your website, blog, e-courses, books, and so on while you're away.

Integrating Platforms

Be sure to integrate all your business social media platforms with one another. A quick Google search or YouTube Video will show you how. For instance because my Facebook and Twitter accounts are integrated with my Instagram account, I can instantly share my Instagram post with Facebook and Twitter. Do be aware though that Facebook will always deliver a video to more of your followers if you post it direct to Facebook or via live feed, rather than through Vimeo or YouTube, because they want you and your audience to be spending more time there than on other platforms. Because Facebook owns Instagram sharing from there isn't usually a problem.

Understand Your Clients' Behaviour and Lifestyle

Again it comes down to knowing your audience. If your clients are corporate their behaviour online will be different to stay at home mums. Think about your client, their behaviour and when they get their downtime to check in on social media or search for inspiration or solutions to their problems. For instance many of my clients are avid meditators that rise early and teach early classes. At nine am they may be in transit, setting up the classroom and getting into a centred space, so they are not likely to be online then. So I usually post on Facebook at 6.30 am. If your clients are full-time workers they will likely check into Facebook at lunchtime, maybe tweet on their commute in the morning or night and check out LinkedIn after hours. You can check in with statistics to keep on top of any trends.

Your Intention

What is your intention? What do you want to use social media for? How big a business do you want to build (check Your Business Model)? If you feel you just want to go with the flow and let your posts come out organically, there is absolutely nothing wrong with that. It doesn't mean you can't still be successful, but know that your voice may end up like a needle in a haystack. If that's okay with you then that is totally cool. If you want to really get out there you'll need to do the hard yards initially to get clear on your brand, but you will get into a flow where it all becomes fun, creative and expressive, it may just take a while. Be patient and remember many larger places have a full-time person looking after this, so do your best, you're going great guns.

Calender Plan

Look out for coming events and special dates that are relevant to your niche and put them in your calendar. For example if you teach dance and your niche is in mental health, look out for International Dance Day, International Wellness Day, RUOkay day, National Mental Health Week and so on. If you grow organic produce you may put in Earth Hour, Sustainable Living Expos, and National Nutrition Week. It's great to include niche-specific events wherever possible, but you could also add events that run parallel to your industry. I know a lot of my wellbeing clients are passionate about nature so I would certainly include Earth Hour in my calendar. For many practitioners like spas, retreats and massage therapists Mother's Day would be a huge opportunity to engage, promote and sell their products and services. And to showcase your personality you could add a few quirky events just for fun, especially for weekend posts, but don't go overboard on these and make sure they are aligned with your values. You are only limited to your imagination here, so get creative. If it's sustainable living week you can post about events, articles on sustainability, TED talks on the future of sustainability, organic recipes, solar power, blog tips for living more sustainably, showcase pictures from your organic farm and so on. A calendar plan means you can look ahead for inspiration, save articles for future promotion and keep your message interesting and varied.

Must Do's for Social Media

Set the tone. What is the tone of your content? Is it interesting, helpful, professional, conversational, funny, informative, or quirky to keep readers engaged? Make sure the voice you use is yours and not just a vibe you like, or your followers will pick up on it. Make sure your social media content is in line with your product, is appropriate and enhances your reputation. For example Virgin and Richard Branson have a reputation of being quirky. At the luggage carousel with a few impatient travellers, I was waiting for the luggage to appear when a lone apple made an entrance. The laughter that ensued eased the tension and we all had a little chuckle. But even though I love a great laugh, as a nervous flier I don't want any tricks being played on me up in the middle of a flight, no thank you. If I was following Richard Branson and it was all about tricks, I would change carriers, but his reputation is balanced by professionalism so it works for me. Make sure your content adds value to your clients' lives. They don't want to be seen as a commodity, they want to be helped. Be prepared to share your information and knowledge freely, build rapport, trust, reputation and goodwill, and you will find you'll be the first one to come to mind when they need to buy a product or service, or make a recommendation.

Analyse What's Going On

Being able to analyse the results of your social media is priceless. It shows you what works for you, and what you're wasting your time on or need to tweak. If you don't look, you won't know. If you are not getting much response from your Facebook posts go into your insights and see what's happening. Are you being authentic? What posts do people respond well to? List as many reasons as you can why you think they worked. Then check the posts that didn't and ask the same question. Remember to see it as guidance from spirit as well. Are you avoiding speaking your truth by sharing too much from others or speaking in diatribe? Is your content true, but your voice too harsh or negative? Is it wishy washy? Connect to your heart, meditate and see if you can pick up on what's wrong. Then test your theory. If you know for sure you are speaking your truth just keep going, expand, enlighten, encourage, be patient and you will be heard

Make Content Consistent and Cohesive.

Think about your soul purpose, your brand and what message you are trying to get out there. What you post, who you follow, what you share, the platforms you use and the media you use should all reflect on you and your business personality. Use a theme each day of the week in the same way Facebook groups often do to help you focus your intentions.

Choose Your Platform

Decide what platforms you want to use and how much time you are prepared to devote to it. Choosing a few selective platforms and delivering powerfully is better than dabbling inconsistently in every one. Be honest with yourself. How often do you think you can post? What platforms best suit you and your business? What scares you about social media? Do an upfront evaluation and decide whether you are experiencing technophobia which can be overcome, or you have totally overloaded yourself. Take one platform at a time and spend a month studying it. Google the latest breakthroughs, look at in-house guidance videos and help sections.

Know Your Tribe

Post the right content at the right time to the right people. Know your audience; what they are interested in, what they need help with, who they are, what they love. Know what they love to see or read, what gets the biggest reaction and shares. Know where they hang out online and on what times and days.

Ask

Ask for recommendations; this is something I really struggled with in the beginning. Ask for people to share your posts, write a review or recommend you in a good, strong, clear, sunny, 'no strings attached' voice. And don't take it personally if they don't. Many people will share automatically, but please go ahead, be brave and ask. Reviews and recommendations help give potential customers a better idea of who you are, and let you know what they loved most about you. With plenty of good reviews, if you do get a bad one, it won't make a huge dent in your star rating.

Use Positive Tools and Language

You are here to inspire, inform, educate, entice, lift hearts, minds and souls. Give it your best shot. Get your best stuff out there. You are tapped into an infinite well of knowledge from the universe and it will never, ever run dry. Don't hold back on your best stuff, get it out there. That's the stuff others will share and that's what you will be known for. Your inspiration will never run out, the deeper you go, the more you stretch yourself, the more the floodgates to greater inspiration will follow.

Stay Up to Date

Attend digital marketing events and social media workshops continually. This is a fast-moving industry and you want to be all over new tips, tools and apps that make your life easier and engage your clients. There are many free or very cheap options available to help small business run by local government and plenty of successful marketing firms whose newsletters or blogs you can subscribe to. If you find this world a little overwhelming, the more things you attend, the more the penny will start to drop. Trust me.

Research

Remember when sharing research matters. Always check that the person you are sharing from has a good reputation and is aligned with your values. The last thing you want to do is share from someone who has great marketing tips but is racist, sexist, and homophobic. Consider sharing from someone less well known. If we are all sharing from Richard Branson, Oprah Winfrey, Dr Libby and Deepak Chopra, then our material starts to look the same. Think about local people you admire who work hard to help others and open generosity channels to support them. You may well find it is reciprocated and your clients start to know you as someone who uncovers unknown gems.

Balance the Shares

Share a little; use your own stuff a lot. Absolutely share wisdom from others, just not so much that you lose your own voice or identity. If you continue to share other peoples' words, material and wisdom don't be surprised if your clients switch to them. You don't have to be a writer to say what you think, love or feel. It may feel awkward at first but with practice you'll find a flow that's true to you. I find a lot of my clients sharing wisdom from other people, and then asking for money for their own workshops. Remember if you want people to spend money with you, they need to know who you are.

Be Creative

Be spontaneous too. If all this sounds a bit prescribed, it's fine to break out of your social media schedule as long as you keep it in line with who you are. The plan is for you to express yourself freely in all your glory, but you need a plan for that otherwise all that creative energy will just fly all over the shop, never truly connecting. Each post, link or inspirational quote should come from the essence of who you are. What if all this social media stuff was just play and all you had to do was reveal yourself truly, madly and deeply? Be unique, be exciting, be engaging, find out what matters to your peeps and make it your mission to solve their problems and make their life more joyous and wonderful.

Things to Avoid in Social Media:

Reputation Damage

Remember your reputation is on show 24/7, so photos of you drinking with a wild party background, or lying around in a bikini are not going to get you that industry speaking gig. You don't need to be perfect in private, but you do need to be aware of your professional reputation. Think of the person you most respect in wellbeing and ask yourself if they would do it.

Processing Online

There's such a thing as too much information. When I worked in retail, my area manager used to visit the store and tell all the customers about her recent hysterectomy whilst I cringed behind the counter. By all means share the wisdom you have learned at a higher level *after* all your processing around it is done, but only if it benefits others. As a professional it is essential that you keep working on your stuff privately with a professional natural therapist of your choice. Not everything needs to be shared. It won't build confidence with your clients if you keep posting about your weaknesses. It can come off a little victim oriented. If the emphasis is on how you're going through this or that, they'll start to think if you can't sort your own stuff out, how you are going to help them? And I don't know about you, but I'm a bit over sad stories.

Don't Dictate or Patronise

No one wants to be told what they're doing wrong, missing or behind on, so never post a problem without a solution attached. Presume that your audience are beautiful, capable, intelligent and vibrant souls at heart. They just need a little help, as we all do. See yourself as someone with wisdom to share, rather than a dictator with rules to dispense or a disapproving eye. Make spreading light, confidence and joy your priority.

Stay Conflict Free

Avoid passive aggressive comments or masked insinuations – I hate these in real life and they are just as bad online. It's cheap, tacky and immature. If you have any issues, call that person directly, send them a private message or ignore it. Never, ever vent your battles online or in public. I have received a surprising amount of newsletters from successful leaders, venting about problems or justifying their position in conflicts. I don't want to know. Even if you have been wronged, keep the collateral damage, negative energy and further gossip contained, by keeping it to yourself. A mature spiritual leader should deal with conflict directly and confidentially.

Don't Brag Too Much.

I'm all for a good boast about your achievements; photos from speaking gigs, upcoming events, retreats and classes will let people know all the great stuff you're achieving. But just a constant list of what you've done; 'this year I've doubled the size of my income and doubled the size of my business' tells people nothing about who you are, what you do and what you care about. Reach out your hand to pull someone else up onto the dance floor, share what has helped you from the heart and reveal doorways to help others. This will win you much more love in the long run. Always leave others feeling good, rather than less than. I'm not talking about shrinking yourself, but saying to others if I can do it, of course you can too.

Don't Beg for Compliments

Stay away from remarks that make your clients feel they have to pump you up. Remember you are there to emotionally support your audience, not the other way around. It's okay to be vulnerable every now and again and ask for support, but retain your mastery at all times and see another practitioner in private if you need help.

Watch Your Ethics

You want to be proud of what you put out there; today, tomorrow and in the future. If there's one thing I can't stand its psychological manipulation. By all means blow your own trumpet, get people excited about who you are and what you do, offer them incentives to buy, but always, always, always keep it honest. Let them know about the absolutely beautiful gem you have to offer and what it's all about in a thousand different ways. Tell them the features and benefits, celebrate it, showcase it, live it, love it, breathe it. But don't ever make anyone feel 'less than' if they don't sign up for it, manipulate their weaknesses or stir up their fears to make them buy it. This is all about ego, it is preying on people's mental, emotional and spiritual vulnerabilities and that's about as far away from the sacred as you can get. That's not spirit in business, that's ego in business, and it always ends in tears. As a wellness practitioner you are in a powerful position where you often have insight into the weak spots of those before you, and to manipulate this is absolutely not acceptable in any way. Stand in your integrity and you will always do well. You have to have faith and believe they will come. And when they do they will be honest, faithful, true, fantastic advocates and most importantly there of their own joyous free will. Do you honestly want people to come to you because you made them scared not to, or because they are celebrating you and following their own unique, independent spirit? At the end of the day you need to rest your head on the pillow and be proud of who you are becoming.

Be Careful Who You Like and Follow

You don't need to like or follow everyone who asks you to, or everyone you know. If clients notice you're following or liking brands that are out of alignment with them or what you're presenting yourself as, you may find they disengage swiftly. I have left a couple of coaching groups that were very mentally manipulative because that is not who I am, nor do I want to be aligned with them by association. There are some amazing soulful coaching groups out there, and it is all about being aligned with the energy of integrity, professionalism and love for me.

Don't Take It Personally

As in life, don't take any of it personally. Do the best you can and if people don't like you, so be it. That could be for a thousand different reasons and most of them are none of your business. Check to see what you are putting out there is what you intended and if you're sure you're on track, carry on. If you are being authentic, ethical and dedicated in your work you will succeed. Better to have a solid tribe who listen and will stay with you for the long haul, than thousands of people who never check in or purchase.

Don't Copy

Never copy, imitate or mimic another person. It is totally understandable that there is an overlap in information out there, but what you definitely don't want to do is copy or mimic someone else. Dig deep to find your unique voice and your soul purpose and stay true to delivering your message from deep within the soul.

Try This

Pretend you are writing a book. Write down all the subjects you would talk about to cover your niche, leave no stone unturned. These are your chapters. Then for each chapter have smaller sections or subdivisions that explain the subjects further. If you create twenty 'chapters' and just four subdivisions per chapter, and each week you focus on a different subsection you have enough information for over a year!

Write a list of local practitioners that you admire and would like to share from. Save links to articles, You Tube videos, TED talks etc that you would love to use to magnify your message and support them.

Download a free calendar template of your choice, then Google some events or weeks that might relate to your niche. Then check out your local council or government calendar of events and see what's coming up locally, nationally or internationally. And pop them in your calendar or phone with an alert of what is coming up. I actually like to put these on a good old-fashioned wall calendar, so I can flip through and see what's coming up.

Schedule time for your social media in your diary; choose a day, afternoon, or hour every day that you will work on your social media presence. Think about how much time you realistically need. For instance you may start with allocating one or two full days a week if you need to do some intensive research, and once you are feeling more confident just an hour a day may suffice. If it's driving you crazy short bursts may be best. Don't bully yourself into it or have outrageous expectations, just take things one step at a time and you will become proficient.

Social Proof

'A tribe is a group of people connected to one another, connected to a leader, and connected to an idea. For millions of years, human beings have been part of one tribe or another. A group needs only two things to be a tribe: a shared interest and a way to communicate.'
- Seth Godin

Humans are pretty tribal folks. We take the recommendations of others, particularly those we know and trust, seriously. I can tell you all about how fantastic my programs are, but of course I would say that. You want proof from an outsider, someone who has nothing to gain from endorsing me, except your best interests. Studies show recommendations influence actions more than any other technique, and that includes price point and discounts. If you say 'join three thousand other passionate women in our exclusive leadership training' it will have more influence than saying 'save $100 on our exclusive leadership training course'. Because we are tribal, we want to be included. If lots of people are working with you and recommending you, this has a watershed affect on your numbers and sales figures. So always, always, always ask clients to write a review for you and endorse your services.

If you are worried someone will write a bad review one day that is all the more reason to get the numbers on the board now. One bad review against hundreds of good reviews doesn't affect your ratings much, but if you have one bad review and haven't been asking the folks who love you to contribute, its going to stand out like a sore thumb. Clients are not silly, they know there are some people out there who just love to complain and be negative. If my hubby and I are reading through travel ratings we take bad reviews with a grain of salt, and usually end up saying things like my God how fussy is that couple, or they have no idea of that culture and so on. We look for reviews from people who sound like us.

High-quality photos alongside testimonials increase the sense of trust in potential clients; so photos with website, product, service and event testimonials are an absolute must. That way they know you're not just sitting in a back room with your computer thinking of the best things you can say about yourself. Reviews or endorsements on social media carry great weight too because your clients can follow those profiles and see who is recommending you. We are always more likely to go with the opinions of people who we consider to be just like us.

Storytelling via case studies also helps as it enables us to put ourselves in someone else's shoes. If we as buyers can connect with a story we are more likely to respond, especially if the problem mirrors our own and we want to get to the solution or happy ending.

If you can get endorsements from leaders or influencers in your industry, then so much the better as people start to link your reputation with theirs. For example Marie Forleo has endorsements from Richard Branson and Oprah – how's that for powerful recommendations? A little note of caution here to never recommend or endorse someone yourself unless you have worked with them, or experienced their products or services personally, because if they turn out to be kooky or totally opposite to your philosophy you don't want that trail leading back to you. But where you love someone, please go ahead and endorse them with all guns blazing.

Getting folks to share your content means you will get a further reach, more engagement and a wider audience. Most importantly your insights can help more people to heal. Sharing is also evidence of your expertise and respect in the industry. That's why it's really important to always make your content authentic, powerful and full of great tips that folks just can't wait to share.

Ask Yourself

Can you feel the fear and ask for endorsements anyway? Most people are happy to help.

How can you create a vibrant tribe around your business?
How often do you ask for reviews or testimonials?
What industry leaders could you ask to endorse you?
What groups could you connect with to help build your reach?
What platforms are best at building your social proof?

Try This

Ask clients to endorse you after a talk, consultation, retreat, or workshop. I usually say to clients if you have really enjoyed this talk, found our session helpful, or learned something from the retreat, I'd love for you to jump onto our Facebook page and write a review. It's great to send a follow-up email with the link to do this soon after your talk or retreat or they may forget. The easier you can make it for people in a hurried world the more likely they'll step in to respond. Do it as soon after the connection as possible while clients are still on a high.

At the bottom of a newsletter or blog, add a call to action. 'If you know someone who; needs to hear this…loves meditation…is looking for a holiday…please go ahead and share it with your circles.' Asking people to share your posts, blog or newsletter increases your audience, social reach and proof that your wisdom works.

Ask clients who have made great breakthroughs if they could write a short story about their journey, what advice they would give to others entering the program, what their problem was or what they were worried about when they started and what your product or service did to solve it and lead them to a successful outcome.

On LinkedIn list your skills and ask your connections to endorse you for them. Ask clients and especially industry influencers to write recommendations for you.

Newsletters and Email Marketing

*'Sometimes reaching out and taking someone's hand
is the beginning of a journey.'*
- Vera Nazarian

Whilst the social media and digital marketing platforms available to us today are fantastic tools, you need to remember that these platforms are constantly making changes about who sees your content and when. The most important thing you can do on social media is to drive clients to your website and get people to sign up to your newsletter. Your newsletter list is the only guarantee you can speak to your audience directly without outside interference. You may think people are sick of getting emails but that's not the truth. People are sick of getting emails that they didn't sign up for, that are uninspiring, irrelevant or too sales focused. If you have something funky, inspiring, fun, short and jam packed with info and value, people will be queuing up to get on your list. People like to be in the know, they like to be valued and cherished. They want to know the best tips, the latest developments and feel connected to something special. They want to be treated like a person, not a sales opportunity. They want to be a part of something. You need to make your list feel special, to show respect and attention. You can give your tribe your best work by sharing from your heart, really knowing who they are, what their worries are, and doing everything you can to help. Above all, meet them at a personal level and connect authentically.

First up you need to choose an email marketing service that works for you. There are a lot of options so do your research. I recommend starting with someone like mailchimp, which offers a free service until you get to a certain amount of subscribers. There is no point paying for something you don't need to when you're just starting out. Bear in mind that costs will increase the more people you have on your list, so you may want to reassess your provider once your numbers start increasing. There are fantastic videos and training supplied by most newsletter providers, so take your time to really understand what you can achieve with a great newsletter. The design elements may seem complicated at first but you will soon get the swing of things. You could even get a designer to set a template up for you, and then all you have to do is insert new information each month into the template. Some services are more responsive or intuitive than others, but most of them will allow you to send out automated thanks for signing up, links to a free gift and so on. It makes everything so much easier.

Once you have opened your account you will want to integrate it with other marketing opportunities, so that every time your audience engages with you they can join your list. On a digital level you can integrate it with your event booking service, e-courses or webinars. You can gather subscribers through offering competitions, free tools, resources or e-books. On your Facebook page you can integrate a newsletter signup button in your tabs. Have an opt-in (the opportunity to sign up to your mailing list) on every page in your website, and a link to signup at the bottom of every blog. In real life have a sign up opportunity at every talk, fair, market, meetup, conference or expo you attend. Conference venues now offer easy digital signup options and you can add QR codes to your print marketing material so clients can just scan to opt in on their phones. You can also ask your clients to share your newsletters with others by including social share buttons on your blogs and emails. At the end of the day the quality of your content is what is going to build and sustain your list and if you are offering real solutions, there is absolutely no reason why your clients wouldn't want to share. Never *ever* contemplate buying a list; you need to do the hard yards yourself to be sure you are connected with the right people and not spamming strangers.

It is only natural to have a few people unsubscribe from your list, so don't panic, but that makes it all the more important to keep your list growing strong so the drop offs are only a small portion of your audience. Segmenting your list can also help you target events and news to particular clients or areas, and the more relevant it is to them specifically, the less likely they will drop off. If you are having a lot of folks unsubscribe you may want to take a look at the content and ask yourself if it is too salesy, or if there is enough valuable content there. There are plenty of measuring tools available, so be sure to check your stats on how many people are opening, following links, purchasing and sharing your newsletters. Newsletter titles can also vastly impact whether your clients open emails or not. The idea is to have a bit of fun; make it quirky, problem solving or something that invokes curiosity. There are plenty of ways of doing this without invoking fear so play around.

Are you sending your emails out so frequently they annoy customers, or not frequently enough so they forget who you are? Frequency is a very particular thing to your unique business. Ask yourself how many emails you would like to receive from a particular service in a month. I would recommend between one a fortnight and one a month. You could create an rss feed from your blog to your email list too, so that every time you post a blog it automatically goes out to your list. Then you can balance the two so that something goes out every fortnight. Once you choose your frequency the key is consistency; it is better to send something every month, than send something once a week then nothing for two months. Just do your best. Sometimes if you have a huge project on it can be difficult to keep up and this where a bit of batching at the beginning of the year helps, so you can just insert a juicy newsletter when you are short on time. Apps like mailchimp snap are really handy too if you just want to throw out a quick howdy, or news from a talk or wellness conference you are at. It literally just takes a few minutes of your time, and in many ways a less polished version of your official newsletter can create a deeper sense of connection, and the feeling your audience is travelling with you.

When it comes to your content think more loving, less selling. If your customers feel like you're only in it for the bucks, they'll withdraw. Quality, originality and value of content is the key to building a list that people love, plus it gives you a vibe of generosity and abundance. Talk to your clients as if they are your friends and they will reciprocate. Keep yourself distant and clinical and they will withdraw. Connect from the heart and soul and they will engage with you at that level. Don't be shy to let people know what you stand for. What do you believe, what are you dedicated to, what do you wish for, and what can you envisage? Share your stories of triumph, success, wellness and courage. Your stories should naturally tie in with your brand and who you are. A good rule of thumb is to dedicate one third of the space to a personal greeting, one third tips and tools, and one third a product or service you have to offer.

Don't forget a call to action for every newsletter you send. It's totally okay to ask someone to book into your workshop, come to your class or let them know about your amazing new massage service. Otherwise you are just giving everything out and asking for nothing back, and that's not good energetically for you or your clients. You don't need to sound like a shopping channel, but you do need to encourage people to try your amazing products and services. You can add a link to your website or programs available so they can read further. Don't list every single thing you do in one email. Choose something particular to feature each time, and try to tie it into an event coming up, or products and services you offer. Include your logo, keep the format aligned with your brand look and feel, and include pictures that offer a sense of who you are.

So the key to a great email list is to make authentic connections, sustain quality, commit to growth, offer great value, innovation and information. The graphics and language should reflect your brand and what you're all about. It doesn't have to be perfect to start, just do your best, be warm and generous, and watch yourself evolve over time. Ensure you are inviting people to connect at every opportunity and across all platforms, and pretty soon you'll find you have a unique engaged tribe who are just thrilled to hear your news.

Ask Yourself

How does your newsletter directly reflect who you are in essence?

Do you need to practice a call to action to get folks signed up for your newsletter? Try something warm, inviting and uniquely you.

When was the last time you checked your newsletter statistics?

How frequently are you sending out your newsletter and is it a consistent, high quality in line with your brand?

What percentage of your newsletter is sales, and what percentage is content?

How much effort are you putting into growing your mailing list?

Try This

Do your research to find the best email provider for you. Set aside some time to look through templates and portfolios on each option. Look through their training videos, what they offer and decide which one seems most user friendly and compatible for you, your business and your clients. Watch a few YouTube videos on how to put your newsletter together. Sometimes regular folk may explain it a little better.

Decide how regularly you intend to send out your newsletter and ask yourself if this is doable time wise for you, right for your clients and in line with your particular business.

Do some research on all the ways you can build your list; there are some dodgy and cheesy ways, so please just follow those options that feel good to you. The more practiced you get the easier it will become, but remember your list is one of the most vital steps to building a successful business so it needs to be done. This requires action on your behalf; you can't just sit back and expect the list to grow automatically, you need to ask people to sign up.

Create a plan for your newsletters for the next 12 months that is in line with your business and marketing plan. Seamlessly blend upcoming events, products or services with valuable information for your clients.

Practice making up quirky, inviting titles. Really have fun with this and think about what you could say to engage curiosity. Unfinished sentences work well to invite and entice. Follow up with a few dots and folks can't help but click through.

Check that your email service is integrated with your Facebook page, event ticket provider, e-course provider and so on.

Have links to your social media platforms so people can connect, and share your news on their own platforms, with friends and so on.

Write a list of twenty ways you could build your email list and start moving through them methodically today.

Ask people to sign up, and by all means offer a special reward or treat in return for their commitment like a pdf of tips, a discount on products or services, an instructional video and so on.

Try to keep fear out of your newsletter titles. Inspiration and curiosity works just as well statistically, and I know you don't want to spark fear in your clients' systems just to get them to read your stuff, right?

Blogging or Vlogging

'The currency of blogging is authenticity and trust.'
- Jason Calacanis

Blogs are very much about showcasing your expertise in your field. It is an opportunity for potential clients to connect with your vibe, your level of knowledge and your tone before they commit to working with you. It is also an important way for current clients to stay in touch and engaged. The term blog comes from web log, and vlog refers to a video log. It is at its simplest a daily, weekly or monthly entry by you to offer wisdom, tips, tools, assimilate a journey, or to impart information. Many people do write blogs about personal journeys from platforms where it literally becomes a diary, but for these purposes we will focus on a business blog. It is great to connect with your audience at a personal level, but please be mindful that what you write will never go away, so if you are sharing something deeply personal give it a day or two, meditate on it, check in with the body and if it all feels good, go for your life. That may sound a little over the top but I recently had a client who shared something very personal and the next year felt like she had betrayed herself deeply. You can be warm, open and personal without selling your soul.

If you don't like writing you could use video instead where you just get to chat away. Given the prevalence of video, new video apps and the favour it is shown in social media now, it is definitely worth a try even if you identify more as a writer. Video tends to personalise the experience for your clients and seeing you in the flesh with your voice, mannerisms and tone can give them the feeling of knowing you better, which helps build trust and connection. Put together the most professional video you can in this moment.

If you need to Blu-Tack your iPhone to a shelf and film yourself, so be it. If you can afford to hire a professional, go for your life. You could even check out the local film schools and colleges and see if a student wants to film you as part of their portfolio. As you become more financially successful you can polish things up a bit. If you can only afford a few professional videos I would focus on using them for any courses, blogs or YouTube videos or social media. Then you can post additional, more amateur day to day stuff on social media platforms. In a world of polish, people actually respond really well to unpolished video on Facebook and Instagram, but if you paid for an expensive course and there were blurred or dodgy videos as content you probably wouldn't be too impressed.

Time is money when hiring a professional videographer, so aim to batch a whole heap of work in one day. This is where being crystal clear on your brand and plan for the year comes in. Don't hold anything back; give them your best stuff now, because by next year I guarantee you will have a whole heap of new, juicy material. Have a time sheet; be organised, clear and ready to go. Remember to write scripts and memorise points for your vlogs so you can come across as informative and professional, rather than just waffling. Warm, personal, generous and succinct will work wonders. People are watching for help, information and solutions so keep it on subject. Practice on your phone in the days before to see how you come across. You'll be amazed what weird things you do with your face and voice. Of course you want to come across as naturally as possible, but a few small tweaks can make the world of difference to your presentation. When you talk to the camera, try to imagine a person at the other end to give it a feeling of connection and authenticity. You could imagine you are talking to a particular client you love who is struggling with the issue you are discussing. Preparation is the key; the more clear you are on your content the more confident, relaxed and warm you will come across.

Whether you are vlogging or blogging, try not to cater to everyone, but to use your authentic voice to talk about the stuff you are deeply passionate and knowledgeable about. Keep it on niche and on brand. The trick is to produce original, practical and exciting content that will rank well in search engines.

If you are just replicating other articles, that doesn't go down very well with Google, and the tools around this are getting more sophisticated all the time. Take care not to load it with keywords to the detriment of the content or you will be penalised here as well.

I think that's a great thing because we should be pushing boundaries, encouraging innovation and deep thinking across all industries rather than just regurgitating the same old stuff. Post your blog across all your social media platforms, and see if you can guest blog for other sites or associations as well. It is totally fine to ask people to share your blog too, so don't be shy. After all something you have written may offer the perfect solution for your clients, friends or colleagues. Break up the subject matter with photos or heading titles so the reader stays engaged.

So what is the difference between a blog and a newsletter? Your blog sits in your website and should share knowledge, how-to guides, opinion, professional guidance, case studies, industry breakthroughs, new techniques or experiences. Blogs are a great opportunity to increase your website traffic and SEO optimisation as well as build your brand and expertise. The blog is more the professional voice, whilst the newsletter is the more personal one, with special offers and treats to reward the clients who committed to sign up to your list. You can also set up a rss feed from your blog to your newsletter list as we discussed in the newsletter section.

You should have a lot of 'evergreen content' on your blog, which means it stays relevant longer as opposed to a coming event on a particular date, which may be better for the newsletter. Consistency is really crucial for success, and studies show that a blog once a month will rank better than a blog that posts sporadically every couple of days then nothing for four months. Think about what is realistic given your lifestyle and time on hand. You may have years of information swimming inside your head, but having the time to curate it and turn it into an engaging article is another matter altogether. Think about your clients too. I'm sure they would prefer amazing, practical, quality information less often, rather than be bombarded with filler all the time. Speaking for myself, I usually like to receive a blog or newsletter once a fortnight or once a month. If it more than that I will most likely unsubscribe. It is also about not giving away *too* much stuff for free. There is a lot to be said for generosity of information, but if your clients get the impression that you are available on tap for free, there is no need for them to purchase your services. It is vital you impress upon your clients that the best stuff and deepest learning occurs in consultations, classes, workshops and retreats and the blog is just a taster of amazing things to come.

Blog titles should contain a catchy lead-in, relevant information for your audience and great keywords. For instance if you are a meditation teacher who specialises in stress relief for parents, you may want to call your blog 'Ten Reasons Not to Murder Your Children at Exam Time', but let's face it, you don't want to pop up in a keyword search for murder! So perhaps you might try 'How to Keep Your Teens Calm at Exam Time', 'Seven Essential Tools for Talking to Your Teens', and so on. When you are writing a title think about what words your clients might be using in a search; teenager exam stress, anxiety in teens, talking to teens and so on. When you know the problems you can supply the solutions. It is essential that you stay on topic and have great engaging content so that your clients read through. Never misrepresent your article through your title. If people find you through a search, then follow the link to your website but click straight off your page, Google assumes that your information is not of a high quality and this will penalise your rankings on SEO.

Tags should focus on specific topics at hand that are relevant to your business and the article. Categories are the wider titles, and the tags form the index. If you are a massage therapist writing an article on aromatherapy your category may be massage styles, whilst your tags might be aromatherapy, massage therapy, relaxation, massage techniques and so on. Photos too should be given an alt text; a simple description so Google can locate them. Be sure to use original images too, or pay for and acknowledge the artist.

Each blog should include a call to action at the end with a direct link readers can click on to follow through. You could ask them to sign up to your newsletter, join your workshop, or enrol in your webinar. The call to action should be relevant to the article and take them somewhere for a deeper learning experience. For instance if you article is on 'Ten Reasons You Need a Coach Today' then your call to action should be an invitation to your talk on coaching, your coaching book or a link to the life coaching appointment scheduler within your website.

The jury is out on how long a blog should be. Some say to hold your readers' interest it should be less than 600 words, which makes it easy to digest, assimilate and share. However longer posts will rank better on Google as it is seen as holding more quality content, keywords and time spent on your website, which is all good for SEO. Longer posts may also help you establish your reputation with in-depth information. At the end of the day it is up to you. You could try a longer post every three months on an in-depth topic and check the difference in your stats to make a decision. Always remember to analyse results and be responsive to what you see.

Your blog is an amazing way to showcase who you are and what you do. The more authenticity, quality information and warmth you can inject into your blog the better. Always come from the heart with the intention of making a difference. The primary reason should always be to help, serve, showcase your knowledge and solve problems for your audience. You are blessed to have the opportunity and the platforms to be seen and heard in this modern world, so make the most of it. It will be far from perfect when you begin, so just give it a crack. Understand your writing and vlogging will get better and better over time, so just make a start. As well as serving your audience it is an amazing opportunity to become clearer and clearer about who you really are.

Ask Yourself

What is it I really, really, really want to say?

What do my clients seem to need the most help with and how can I answer their questions simply and clearly?

What practical tools can I offer that will work for them at home?

What tasters for up and coming programs can I entice them with?

How can I be innovative and creative about the information I share?

What is the best stuff I have ever written and why?

Could I write a guest blog for a wellness partner to help increase my audience?

Try This

Decide how often you will post your blog. Be realistic and remember consistency is the key. Err on the side of caution and aim for once a month, then if you find that is a breeze, try for once a fortnight for a few months and if that is a walk in the park you might want to go for once a week. Or not, remember this is your lifestyle too, and if a blog once a fortnight means you can spend more time with your kids or caring for yourself, choose that. Stick to the time frame that works for you. You could try writing a couple of articles to completion including pictures, tags and categories and seeing how long it takes you on average to give you a realistic idea of how much time you would need to set aside every week, fortnight or month to follow through. Find your rhythm and stick to it.

Batching your blogs (writing a few at a time or even a years' worth) is a great idea. Although it may seem a little contrived, it is actually a great way of keeping your information aligned with your niche or core purpose. Each subject tends to roll and deepen into the other. Remember you can always slide an extra one in, or change the line-up order, or edit it if you feel there is an article you want to write. If you are writing once a month you could even write twelve articles at the beginning of the year. Just be careful with your settings on your blog and rss feed or it may shoot them all out at once! It is best to save them as drafts or on your computer to prevent any mistakes.

To write a blog plan for a year simply list twelve subjects about which you care deeply, are relevant and tied intrinsically to your brand. What are the major foundations of your work right now? If you were blogging on counselling you might focus on twelve essential principles about counselling, or run a series about a different counselling technique and its merits and benefits. Remember the idea is to sell yourself, so don't go raving about a service you don't provide. Focus on educating your clients about what you do and what you know.

Take some time to take great photos relevant to your core subjects in your blog plan; that way you will have a library of images on hand to choose from. If you don't have a load of good-quality photos or find this too time consuming, you can break up your blog with subject headings instead. The times you really need photos are more for instructional blogs like how to, step by steps or examples.

Don't forget to add a relevant call to action at the end of every blog.

Make a list of all the things you can help people with. What do you know? What is your expertise? What do you love? How can you help? What are your favourite topics?

Batch Your Work

'No business can succeed in any great degree without being properly organised.'
- James Cash Penney

In the brave new world of digital marketing, social media, blogs, video, articles and so on, your time has never been more in demand. There is a lot expected of you, and the same amount of time in which to do it, as well as get on with your actual work. You need to find systems for working *on* your business so you still have time to work *in* your business. Batching your work is a great way of doing just that. Now it may seem a little disingenuous to do your work in blocks, but actually it will really help you to stay firmly aligned with your purpose and core message, it will give your audience a sense of cohesion, and of each subject deepening and expanding in succession. Then when you're busy you can rest assured your information is still going out as intended; on time and on point.

What to Batch

You can batch your Facebook posts, your Instagram photos, your newsletters, your blogs, and your videos. Really whatever platforms you use, you can batch information for them. If you are using video consider the subjects you wish to talk about, write basic script outlines for them, and have a few different outfits on hand that you can change into for each video. You can get a professional videographer lined up for the day, and each topic should be intrinsically tied to your niche and follow a line of deepening wisdom.

Pair Up with a Friend

Get together with a fellow practitioner and help each other build up content. For instance yoga teachers may have multiple snaps taken of yoga poses in various surrounds, massage therapists may have action massage shots taken in their studio, and they may both take lots of photos of nature for inspiration quotes. With a plethora of relevant photos to choose from on your phone, you will never be short of material. Take shots of anything that catches your eye, and have fun with it. You can always delete the dross later. These can be stored on your mobile for later use. You can use Facebook's inbuilt scheduler, or for Instagram, apps like Latergram, Hootsuite or Schedugram can be used.

Copy

For written content (copy) for video or blogs, go back to your core message and brainstorm important themes and aligned topics. Think of the most important things you wish to say to your audience, pick a catchy title and a basic framework that you can expand on. Most blogs will allow you to schedule your releases, otherwise store them on your laptop with an alarm in your phone to post them once a month, week or fortnight.

YouTube

Create a YouTube channel and a playlist of videos relevant to your passion and purpose; from inspirational TED talks, to how-to videos, to inspiration music. Anything that resonates with your work, then you can schedule them into your digital marketing. Store them under different playlists or titles and remember to keep subjects on brand and on niche.

You will always have plenty of room to pop up current events, coming talks, courses, advertising, photos or inspiration in the moment, but having a load of prepared content on hand will make your life so much easier and your content so much more relevant. It creates a platform and structure you can lean up against and trust when your schedule is busy. You will need to put aside time to batch your work, but in the long run, you'll save heaps of time, anxiety, repetition and trouble trying to come up with ideas in the moment. Most important of all, everything you post will be totally tied into your soul purpose and your brand. Winter, or your slow season, days or times in between classes or appointments is a great time to batch your work.

Networking

'The currency of real networking is not greed but generosity.'
- Keith Ferrazzi

I used to think networking was, well…a bit of a wank to be honest. A bunch of shiny, successful business people puffed up like peacocks, walking around a room congratulating themselves on their success. Maybe it used to be like this, maybe there are still some of these groups around, or maybe I just totally made that up in my mind. So what is networking and how can it help support you, and grow your business? Now I'm not talking the hard sell marketing groups here. I'm talking soulful, heart-centered and authentic groups – both online and off. People who really want to see you succeed, just because, well why not? I think we're all over the groups that just sell, sell, sell, and if you look at them there's not much engagement there. In a world that's already hectic, people don't respond to bombardment.

Networking to me is all about authentic engagement. At live events your ability to listen will do far more for your reputation than your ability to sell yourself. The capacity to listen to others, ask questions, show an interest and engage will be well remembered. Then when people are referring to you after an event, or see you online, they'll be more likely to engage or recommend you. The most important factor people consider before booking into your courses is who you are and what you're all about. This trumps straight-up selling every time. I encourage you to get out wherever possible so people can see you in the flesh. Even if you are online quite a bit, if potential clients see you out at a networking event, talk, expo, market or business workshop, it gives them a personal experience and will encourage them to become a client. With such wonderful wellness offerings around these days, it's hard for clients to choose where to go. Once they get a feel for who you really are in person, they are much more likely to buy. On the business to business end, look for groups that have marketing and business tips, interactive events, networking nights and a philosophy that is aligned with your own.

Networking is also about making authentic connections with people in your social or professional circles to offer mutual support. If you can't help someone with a particular issue, recommend another person who may be able to step in, and keep that circle widening so you foster inclusion. If you practice making good connections, and offer your own advice when others need a hand with something, you'll feel less shy to ask for assistance when you need it. The truth is people love to help, feel like their advice is valued, and offer direction. It's a beautiful thing. Ask for advice on a Facebook page and the interaction is almost immediate. In its essence networking is all about making connections and building relationships that will enable you to thrive, and to help others to do the same; authentically, generously and professionally. Who knows, some of these people may just wind up as some of your best customers or greatest friends.

Ask Yourself

When was the last time you went to a networking event?

What local groups could you connect with?

What events, expos, conferences or gatherings could help you gather more connections?

What parallel industries could you become better acquainted with to help you extend your reach?

How can you build your confidence with networking?

What online groups could you become more connected with?

What networking groups are not working for you and is it time to extend your circles?

Try This

Remember to listen rather than just self-promote

Speak *to* others, don't speak *at* them.

Keep your tone authentic, but warm and soft. People back away from loud pronouncements, they move towards a gentle invitation.

Offer generosity. Ask yourself is there some way I can help this person, a connection I can offer them, without going over the top or needing to rescue them.

Bring your business cards and promotional material – there is often a table set up specifically for this purpose, and be sure to gather others' material too.

Have cards easily accessible for people you feel a connection with – struggling to wrestle one free from a tight spot in your wallet while balancing your handbag and champagne looks a little awkward.

Practice your 'elevator pitch' aloud alone or with friends before you get there. You should have a one liner that explains what you do, and then you can talk further if people ask questions.

Invoke curiosity; let people know a quirky project you're working on or what interests you. Surprise them with something left of field.

Know when it's time to move on, a graceful exit is a godsend sometimes. Learn to extract yourself from conversations going nowhere, the awkward pause or an hour of free wellbeing advice from someone who will probably never become a client. At a networking event it's totally okay to say 'oh well I better go and mingle, meet a few more people, I'll catch up with you later.'

Don't shut yourself in a corner or with a friend because you're feeling shy. Be brave, most people are really friendly, and those who aren't you can quickly move on from.

Have a sense of humour. People love a laugh and a sense of lightness. Be okay with laughing at yourself too if you get home and think 'why did I bring up nude yoga with that accountant?'

Practice makes human. Be yourself – this gets easier over time.

It's important to network with groups that are in line with your target market, colleagues and industry leaders, but remember to keep your feet on the ground and head out to a local networking event full of tradies, retailers and bank folks sometimes. You never know who you might meet and it can get you out of wellbeing land for a night. A shake-up is always a good thing.

Look people in the eye. Is there anything worse than someone looking past you at other people while you're in a conversation?

Set your intentions before you leave home. Make them achievable so you don't feel like you're under pressure, and be flexible so if you wind up in a fantastic conversation with a valuable contact stay there.

Put the mobile phone away.

And most importantly don't get stuck in to the alcohol (especially you wellbeing one pot screamers where two glasses of champagne can often look like you've had five).

You could network at conferences, expos, small business events, meetup, social nights, industry events, workshops, training, markets, demos or talks.

Create your own events to support, fundraise or connect with your demographic.

List as many relevant groups as possible that you could network with online; like LinkedIn groups, Facebook groups and so on. See how these feel to you over time and expand your interaction in groups that feel great to you and cut back on those where you don't feel connected.

Getting an Unknown Out There

*'Everyone has been made for some particular work,
and the desire for that work has been put in every heart.'*
- Rumi

So you've found a modem you're totally passionate about. The trouble is no one seems to have heard of it before. So how do you get a new or unknown wellbeing art out into the world? You start by telling them all about it. Write a short powerful blurb on what your service is all about. Brainstorm lots of different explanations until you land on one which encompasses the heart of what you do, will be comprehendible to novices, and has a professional ring to it. Practice verbalising that too, so that when people make enquires you have a clear statement you can give them. Then if they ask you for more you can expand. Keep your verbal or written language clear and simple. If you launch into a complicated or 'out there' conversation many people will zone out. I consider myself a very spiritual person, but if a practitioner is explaining something in a really ungrounded manner, I'm not interested. Even the most spiritual work must be grounded enough to be able to articulate clearly to potential clients.

Who your target market is will radically alter the language you use even around the same modem. If you are promoting dance to a gym group you will focus on language around cardio, tone, strength, flexibility and fitness. If you are promoting it to a life coaching group you would use language around inner power, strength, courage and freedom. If you are promoting it to teens you might focus on body image, self-confidence or self-esteem. The important thing is to blend who you are with the art. People don't buy a thing – they buy the person, the energy or the passion behind it. If you keep your descriptions general, potential clients will have trouble connecting. What do you love about what you do? What blessing has it bought to you? How can it offer the same thing to your students? Get that really clear in your head, and then create offerings that are in line with that.

Network and make contacts by getting out there and talking to as many people as you can about your service, both online and in person. That means other wellbeing practitioners, local business groups, friends, families and contacts. Hold information nights, market stalls and attend expos where you can discuss your craft, give people brochures, put them on your mailing list, let them try a treatment and answer any questions they may have.

Create some great video footage. Video is a huge growth market and a fantastic way for people to connect to you, see what you do, understand the benefits and features, and be drawn to your service. You're not just telling them – they can see it for themselves. And they can get a feel for who you are. Videos that use testimonials from clients make a really powerful statement and give validation to your own promises.

You need to be persistent. Decide whether you're in it for the short haul or the long haul. You will need to keep sending your message out there on a thousand different days in a thousand different ways, whilst keeping it 'tight' with your niche. Look for publicity wherever you can. Write magazine articles, blogs, contact local radio and media outlets, and have a social media strategy that reinforces your passion. Keep at it. When you feel your confidence waning, ask for help and advice, take a break and look at business courses that can show you new ways of doing things that may not have occurred to you.

Be creative. Think of any way you can create an interest story around your service. Collaborate with other wellbeing practitioners on retreats or workshops where you might pick up more customers and raise your profile. Have an article in the local paper offering a discount. Give current clients a special discount pass for a friend. Run a competition to win a treatment or class and build your mailing list. Offer case studies explaining ways you can make a difference and *why* you do what you do. Don't just sell, sell, sell, you need to give, give, and give. Be patient, dedicated and follow through on your marketing plan every single day. Cultivate warm-heartedness, integrity, generosity and passion around what you do and your success will come.

Ask Yourself

What are you prepared to do to get your work out there?

If you really think it can change lives, why wouldn't you follow through?

Where can you go, what can you do and what can you say to get your heart work out there?

What can you do to ensure people have a real experience of what you are offering?

Try This

Use language people can relate to and avoid over-complications when you're explaining it. They are not studying it; they just need to know how it will make them feel.

Try preaching to the choir by introducing your practice to open-minded folks at wellbeing centres, MBS expos or spiritual festivals.

Take heart. Remember when kinesiology was totally new and everyone was like 'what *is* that?' Then it took off like a rocket and is one of the most popular healing methods available.

Leverage the fact that your modem is new and exciting by using enticing language like 'the latest breakthrough in deep relaxation' or 'the new body, mind, spirit explosion'. People love to be in the know about breakthroughs early on and will be thrilled to tell their friends. Sometimes it is easier to launch a new product, than to enter a flooded market of yoga teachers. Everything has its drawbacks, the question is how much do you love it, and how hard are you prepared to work to get it out there?

Finding Work

*'Small disciplines repeated with consistency every day
lead to great achievements gained slowly over time.'*
- John C. Maxwell

There will come a time when people will seek you out for your knowledge and expertise, but initially you will need to create the work yourself. That's what running your own business is all about. So sure, you can look out for advertisements for practitioners wanted in yoga forums, wellbeing colleges, online employment services, word of mouth and so on, but you also need to actively create the work yourself. So first get clarity on your niche, purpose, target market and message, and then actively seek out work in those areas that are aligned with who you are. For instance if you want to work in schools, you'll need to contact all the schools in your area. If you want to work in the corporate field, you'll need to contact HR, the social club, or any contacts you may have already working in those companies. If you want to work in resorts, you will need to email all the resorts in the area you like. The trick is to keep sending out as many applications as you can and someone has to say yes eventually. It's a numbers game. If you pin all your hopes on one place, it can be devastating if the answer is no, and its easy to fall into the mind and defeatism, but the more applications you send out, the better your chances and the less sensitive you'll be about any rejections. Even if you don't get your dream position immediately, the jobs you get along the way will help build your resume, body of experience and hone your skills.

It may seem scary, but look at it this way; the people you are writing to are waiting for you. In fact they are desperate for you to get in touch. Imagine you are a really busy teacher who has been asked to put together a wellness programs for the teachers and students in your school. Where would you start when it's not your area of expertise? How do you know who to choose or if they are going to be good or not? And then lo and behold an email arrives outlining your passion, your expertise, your program proposal, testimonials and you have just taken a huge weight off this woman's mind. Imagine you run the social club at a large corporation and you have been asked to put a mindfulness program together for staff; where would you go, who should you choose, what should you look for? And again lo and behold an email arrives offering a comprehensive professional program and you can just message your boss that the problem is solved. And he/she is going to be so impressed at the efficiency of this staff member. You may think these people are being inundated with requests, but chances are they are not. You'd be surprised how few people do the legwork.

Even if you set up your own studio, you can't expect people to just rock up and stay there, you'll have to work at it. You'll need to create relationships with local community, business groups, schools, mums and so on to keep them coming in the door. Your programs need to be unique, professional, creative, and innovative. There should be absolutely no fear about other yoga studios, gyms or natural therapy centres opening up around the corner if you have established yourself as a leader in the field. In this new creative age you can't just put on a variety of classes and leave it at that. You need to run innovative programs, workshops, classes, and consultations to be seen as the authority in your field.

I know it can become a bit overwhelming, but if you love what you do, get on the front foot and make this exciting instead of on the back foot and making it hard. It's just a mental shift you have to make to thrive. And if this is really what your life's calling is, why wouldn't you? No one is asking you to do anything unaligned with your ethics. This is the universe saying to you if you want it, you need to step up and say it. If you want to fulfil your purpose, the time for hiding or holding back is over. Remember too what this is all about; being in service to others. The more people you can reach, the more people you can help. It is negligent to do any less. Get out there and take it to the edge. Get a stall at the local market where you can chat to people, do a demo at a wellbeing expo, reach out to show your tribe who you are and where they can find you. You have to see this engagement as an ongoing part of your business. Keep building.

You need to decide if this is your career for a lifetime, a calling or it's just something you want to dabble in. If you worked for someone else, you would be expected to turn up at work during certain hours and move through a list of pressing tasks. When you work for yourself it is no different. You wouldn't just wander off for hours at a time and leave your work undone, or start roaming the office looking at what other people were working on; you'd do your job. You need to fulfil the obligations to yourself, your purpose and the universe by going about your business with the same dedication, efficiency and professionalism as you would if you worked for anyone else at the very least. So let's get to it.

Ask Yourself

Could you be doing more to find work, or are you just expecting work to find you?

What people, groups or companies could you contact?

How many networking events have you attended?

What conferences or talks have you attended?

How many expos, festivals, or markets have you had a stall at this year?

What folks are aligned with your niche, and how could you create greater contacts there?

Try This

Get really clear on your niche, choose who you want to deliver it to, and align yourself with partners who can help.

Send out the message of who you are and what you do with consistency, clarity and courage every day on social media to build your brand.

Don't forget sometimes doing things the old-fashioned way like introducing yourself at places you would like to work, and taking fliers and business cards to cafes, can get results too.

Keep sending out emails to potential clients.

Get out to expos, festivals, fairs and markets and do a demo, have a stall, give a talk or all of the above.

Join LinkedIn group networks, post articles and invite connections in your niche area.

Network, network, network – authentically.

Look out for jobs online via industry websites, colleges, relevant groups, and employment sites.

Keep the faith and keep going. Ask the universe for signs on where you should go and who you should contact. Ask for synchronicities and meditate daily for guidance.

Write down as many partners as you can to align yourself with. For instance is there a natural therapy centre or community centre near you with a good mailing list where you can run a talk, class, course or workshop?

Get out and meet a few people. If I appear at expos, people will often say – oh I've seen you on social media – and yet they may never have liked or commented on my posts. The key here is that you complete the circle by meeting people in real life, and that's the tipping point that makes them book for an appointment or a workshop.

Write down as many places as you can that you would like to approach with wellness programs, classes, talks and so on. Email them and follow up with a phone call. Keep emails simple. People don't have time to read a whole load of waffle. Choose your own words, but make it honest and succinct. You can attach a CV or a link to your LinkedIn page, but please make sure they are up to date, powerful and relevant. The key rules are to make it relevant to your niche and target market. For instance if your target market is schools and your niche is mindfulness, take the time to read about each school's key values by making a visit to their website. Personalise the email by using the school's name and philosophy (you can cut and paste the rest, but be careful and reread it before you send it – the last thing you want is to send the wrong school name or values out there). Send out a load of applications, rather than pinning your hopes on one place. Think about the time you are sending it out as schools will probably be too busy first thing Monday morning and tired Friday afternoon, so maybe try for a Tuesday morning. Follow up with a phone call within the week. If you're nervous about this, trust me it gets easier. Feel the fear and do it anyway, because it's time.

Use the same process for corporate, councils, aged care or whatever area you want to move into. Keep the language specific to the industry, emphasising relevant benefits. If you don't have extensive experience emphasise your passion and your qualifications instead. Remember two short paragraphs with two sentences each should be ample as a teaser. Short, sweet and powerful. Add a link to your website and your phone number.

If you are having trouble finding work in the beginning you could offer a free demonstration or do some volunteer work for a while to build your experience, gather testimonials, take some photos for your website and get some references. Voluntary positions can often become permanent jobs too.

Business Coaching

'In the end, it is important to remember that we cannot become what we need to be by remaining what we are.'
- Max De Pree

There is only one thing worse than not having a coach for your business, and that's having two coaches. If you are with a coach who is working for you, stick with them. Don't go chopping and changing or you may have to face the fact you're self-sabotaging. Likewise if you are not happy with the coach you're with or you're not getting results *after* following through, then by all means change them. If you are looking for a new coach, ring around, talk to coaches, ask what their philosophy is, don't just choose based on price. Make a decision and stick to it. When I was starting my business there was no such thing as a business coach, and certainly not for the wellbeing industry. Mentors were more concerned about our spiritual and personal development than how to take our soul work out into the world, and rightly so. We are so blessed today to have a wonderful array of coaches, so you are bound to find one that is perfect for you. I would also like to add how important it is to have a healer, kinesiologist, yoga teacher or spiritual mentor as well so you are looking after your own self-care and spiritual development too. If you can get a business coach who has a strong understanding of soul work, so much the better.

I know a lot of wellbeing practitioners resist the idea of a coach because they think they'll save money by doing it all themselves, but I can't tell you how often I have seen practitioners flounder around in circles for years, because they have no clear marketing or business plan, or they don't follow through. A coach means that you get to work with someone who knows your business as well as you do; who will encourage, support and push you to grow beyond your own limited view of what you are capable of, and help you map out a clear and direct path to success. It makes you accountable. How often you attend will depend on the cycle your business is in and how fast you want to grow it. To me the ideal is every six-eight weeks, leaving you enough time to complete tasks in between each session. Or you may want to launch your business with a bang and start intensively, and then drop back to a check-in every eight weeks, or so. You should be responsive to the needs of your business, so if you are going through a time of change or expansion, crank those sessions back up. If you are following through you will be making more money than before so this will offset the price of your coaching, and of course it's a tax deductable expense.

Remember your business coach can only work for you if you work for them. Always ask yourself what you will get back on your investment instead of thinking about what you can and can't afford. At Spirit in Business we pride ourselves on affordable coaching options. Don't make a poverty consciousness your excuse. Trust me it will save you a fortune in time, stress and money if you just invest a little in your future. As the saying goes, a year from now, you will wish you had started today.

What to Look for in a Coach

Confidentiality

Someone who has built a successful career in health, wellbeing & spiritual leadership

Someone who has experience in the health and wellbeing industry

Someone who can take into account the heart and soul of you and your business

Someone who understands purpose and calling

Someone with ethics and integrity

Someone with smarts and intuition

Someone experienced in business and marketing

Someone who makes sure you're clear before you start moving. There's nothing worse than being five years down a path you don't want to be on. Tell your coach you want to be crystal clear on direction before moving forward.

Someone who can open professional doors for you and help you with industry contacts

Your Responsibilities

Be coachable; don't resist, make excuses, self-sabotage or hold back.

Get out of your sad stories and your fears; the healing is in the doing.

Follow through, follow through, follow through and follow through. Honour yourself, your spirit and your money enough to make use of the wisdom at your fingertips and work your little butt off!

Be honest. Let your coach know if you haven't followed through and why not.

You need to take full responsibility for your business. If you are unsure about something question your coach, if something doesn't feel right ask them about other options.

You don't abdicate your responsibility when you get a coach, you actually increase it, but this time there is a clear structure, plan and road to success.

Keep going. One session, no matter how amazing your coach is, just isn't enough. Rome wasn't built in an hour. Although you may feel clear after one session and think you can take it from there, the truth is you have barely begun.

Flicking your coach a quick email to clarify any questions you have is better than sitting on your hands doing nothing. So if you're unclear about the goals set in your last session just ask.

Cultivate a relationship of mutual respect.

Let your coach know if they are going too fast, too slow, or doing an amazing job.

Never be afraid to go back. If you haven't been to your coach for a while and you're embarrassed that you haven't followed through, swallow your pride and make a phone call. Make an appointment and start again.

Speaking

'Life is short. There is no time to leave important words unsaid.'
- Paulo Coelho

First let me say that you don't have to be a speaker if that's not who you are. There are plenty of other ways to get your message across to people. I'm all for challenging yourself, but by the same token, you don't have to spend time, energy and money perfecting an art you have no interest in pursuing. Maybe you're better at writing or communicating via images, podcasts or video, and there's absolutely nothing wrong with that. I do encourage even introverts to be able to communicate clearly and effectively who they are and what they do at networking events and so on, but speaking on a stage is a whole different matter. If you have a calling to get out there, speak your truth, and deliver your message to the world, let's look at where, how and when you might do that.

First of all as always get really, really clear on your message and your niche first. The point is to impart amazing information and inspiration to your audience, to boost your following, social media engagement and clients. There is no point talking about mindfulness if that is not your core work, otherwise when people get on your website and see it is all about massage, you'll lose them. So keep it specific. This is about becoming *known* for something. Break down your niche into a few relevant options. Then decide who you can deliver it to, where you may be able to do that and find some industry partners to help you on your way. It is good to have a few talk options available, whilst keeping the central message clear. Keep your audience in mind; if you're speaking on mindfulness in a corporate arena, on a retreat, at a school or a festival, you would tweak the language slightly for each audience and venue. If you are trying to get a speaking gig at a particular event, take a good look at their website and social media and pitch it towards their values (as long as they are aligned with yours).

Make sure you're delivering to the right audience. There's no point delivering your core message to the wrong audience. If you want to target mums in their 20s – 40s, then you can ask to speak at school events, women's gyms and kinder groups in the community to build your risk muscles. For larger stages you may apply to speak at expos and festivals. If in doubt about what groups or events to target, ask yourself is this the audience I want to work with in ten years' time? Look for affiliates or people who may want to collaborate with you. Get a really clear feel for who they are, and whether they are aligned with you and your philosophy. The last thing you want to do is be associated with people who have a fundamental difference in ethics. Don't presume just because you're all in wellness industry that you will believe in the same philosophy and methods.

Always ensure your information is accurate, fun, engaging, informative, stimulating or breathtaking. You should intend to wow people. Watch some really great TED talks and ask yourself what did you love about the best speakers and what did you dislike about the worst? I have seen many celebrities speak and each time I ask myself, if you took away their celebrity status, would the information they gave be valuable and life changing for me? It's usually a fifty-fifty split. To me the most interesting speakers are the researchers, people who have lived an interesting life, lateral thinkers, people talking about the brain, behaviour, spiritual leadership, social or humanitarian issues. I'm also a fan of anything a bit kooky.

Types of Speakers

Although some of these speaking roles overlap, here is a basic breakdown;

A keynote speaker is usually the highlight of any conference or event. Although these days it tends to be more of an equal playing field or collaboration, one might say that the keynote speaker is the major drawcard, and the other speakers are supporting acts. It is still a fantastic opportunity to be given a role as a supporting speaker though, as the keynote speaker may have bought the crowds, but if you deliver a resounding speech you will be well remembered.

An inspirational speaker is someone who tells their own personal story of triumph against the odds, their personal road to success or encourages you on what is possible through human nature, determination and hard work.

A motivational speaker is usually one whose job is to stir action or change in their audience. You may motivate people by telling stories of your success, talking about why folks are resistant to change, what happens in life when we don't change and how to overcome blocks to success.

Essential Tips for Preparation

For every talk I give I first take into account how long the talk is and what key points I want to get across. Then I write five subcategories below each point. I then memorise these key points over and over again until I can recite them back in my mind, and out loud. No matter how many times you have given a speech, don't presume you have it down pat, always give it the time and respect your audience deserves, and never ever try to wing it without prep time. No matter how good you think you sound, you can always do better with solid prep. If this sounds too rigid, remember structure allows for flow. That way you can go with inspirations that come to you throughout the talk, and always find your way back to your core points. Ask yourself what you want your audience to know for sure by the end of your talk.

Nerves will always be there, but the more prepared you are the better things are bound to go.

Take a few moments before you leave for the event to meditate, calm and centre yourself.

Don't leave this centring time until you get to the venue, because chances are the co-ordinator will want to talk to you, or guests will arrive early and you won't get the chance.

Leave plenty of time to get to the venue because running late will just kill your calm and muddle your mind. Sit outside in nature and have a cup of herbal tea while you wait.

Take a bit of rescue remedy, some calming essential oils, or a grounding crystal to support you. Ask spirit to talk through you to ensure you are touching hearts at the deepest level. If you get caught up in nerves just remind yourself that you are here for a reason; to inspire, educate and motivate people to a deeper, richer, more peaceful life, and that is what is important here.

If you go totally blank, don't panic (don't worry it's unlikely to happen). Don't let everyone in on the secret, just tell the audience you are all going to take a moment to centre or try a breathing technique or meditation. Close your eyes along with the audience, guide them through some breathwork, and then take a few moments of silence together. Allow your mind to empty and wait for illumination, then bring the audience back into awareness of the room. They'll never know the difference and will appreciate the sense of rest and calm. And you'll be ready to go. Remember this is why preparation and memorising your talk is key. If it is planted in the subconscious mind, it is much easier to find.

If you feel you didn't do as well as you could have, keep it to yourself and discuss it with a trusted colleague later. It is not up to the audience to stroke your ego or reassure you after your talk. Keep it professional; try to make up for any shortcoming by engaging with the audience after and giving short, concise, relevant advice to improve your standing.

Keep everything relevant and succinct. Don't go off on crazy tangents or be sidetracked by yourself or your audience.

Keep your introduction and conclusion short and sweet. Introduce yourself, what you're going to talk about and when questions will be. Then follow with the body of your speech, and conclude with thanks, what you offer and how they can get in touch. Don't overdo the sales pitch, if your content is really good, they'll be clamouring to work with you. Usually one call to action, one offer and your contact details is enough. Your host should also have a blurb about you and a link to your webpage and social media that their audience can use to get in touch.

If you are giving a TED talk, no self-promotion at all is allowed and you will need to memorise your speech, so be sure to read the speaker expectations and obligations for any event you attend and abide by rules if you want to be asked back.

Make sure you have plenty of relevant marketing material on hand where appropriate, like your business cards with your website and social media links, a banner, books, coming events and products. If you are talking about nutrition, don't have a massage flier out, you should have a coming nutrition workshop or consultation flier. Once again keep everything aligned, streamlined and relevant. If you have a table it shouldn't look like an op shop or be littered with all kinds of fliers. Keep it simple, clean, clear, and professional.

If you are a guest speaker and your host has created an event page via social media, try to engage with attendees before the event to make contact with your audience.

You may be asked, or choose, to speak for free or for a nominal amount when you are starting out, so make the most of any marketing opportunities to help your business and reputation.

Decide if you'll allow questions in the middle or just at the end of your talk and let attendees know before you begin. If you allow questions partway, just let your audience know that if you start to get sidetracked or short on time you'll continue with the talk and allow for further questions at the end. I recently attended a talk on video production, and was increasingly frustrated by the amount of irrelevant or incredibly specialised questions all the way through the talk. It was running 45 minutes over time and the speaker still hadn't got through the presentation material. Several guests including myself started leaving. I definitely wouldn't book him for video work, because I thought if he's being paid by the hour he could easily get distracted and run up the bill. Which may or may not be true, but the moral is first impressions count. You need to be in control of the audience interaction. My personal preference in a talk is to leave all questions to the end, because what is most important is that you impart all your information in a timely manner. Leave plenty of time for Q & A at the end so that you can offer real examples and problem solving options for people that are relevant to them. Then invite guests whose questions were not answered to email you or talk to you afterwards.

Practice your talk by speaking out loud to yourself by memory at least ten times before the event, more if you're nervous. Saying it out loud is totally different to saying it in your head, and you'll iron out any linguistic stumbles and get to hear how it sounds, which can be quite different to how it reads. It will also make an incredible difference to your timing. You can certainly record yourself too and listen back to the feeling tone you are sending out with your words.

Let the organiser have a blurb for your talk that is just as exciting and engaging as the talk itself. Create a dynamic bio that you can tweak slightly for different audiences or occasions.

Make sure you talk to people before and after the event by introducing yourself and showing an interest. If you feel talking before an event will throw your prep time or calm time, some time after will suffice.

Keep your voice relevant to your audience. You will need to tweak your language (not your innate message) so it is appropriate to your audience. In some places you can get away with the f-word, in other places it will be frowned upon. Your language with teens will be different to your language with older adults, and kids will need a lot more variety.

Keep the material relevant to the industry.

Use variety. There is nothing worse than hearing the same story over and over. I love comedian Anh Do and he has such a powerful refugee story to tell, but after I've heard it ten times it loses its power. Every interview and standup act involves the rotating of the same stories. I just keep waiting for the next episode. Your work should deepen and expand over time.

If you don't feel connected to the subject, do yourself and someone else a favour and pass it on. Let the organiser know that this is not your subject but you are an expert in such and such if they would prefer a talk on that now or in the future. If you take on a subject you're not familiar with and people ask some tough questions at the end, well…you won't be hired again.

Speaking is a fantastic opportunity to let people know who you are, what you are all about, and how you can help them. Start small and build, or if you're given a great big speaking opportunity, accept it and work your butt off to get it right for the night.

Slow down. Don't race through the information, sit back in it. Let it vibrate out of your being. Embody it. It's fine to have a little pause every now and again. A moment in time makes the audience lean forward.

You will probably always look back on speeches and say to yourself I forgot this, or I should have said that, but trust me when I say you'll get better and better with time and experience. The audience wants you to succeed.

Always remember the golden rule; preparation, preparation, preparation.

Hiring a Speaker

If you are hiring a speaker ask for references from previous speaking gigs and their general experience in the industry.

Check feedback from previous talks by checking out their website, social media or asking for testimonials.

If you are hiring a speaker make it very clear to them that although they may sell themselves in the last 2-5 minutes of their speech, this is primarily an opportunity for them to engage and inform the audience. Be crystal clear about what is and isn't appropriate selling.

Be very clear around the boundaries. What they are being paid (or not), what time you expect them to arrive, whether their talk will be taped or not, how long they are expected to engage with the audience after the speech and what are absolute deal breakers for you.

Clear expectations are a recipe for success for everyone involved.

Writing and Publishing

"The art of writing is the art of discovering what you believe."
- Gustave Flaubert

I absolutely love writing, and feel it always has and always will be, an incredible way to inspire and empower others. Words have power. Writing is an amazing way to get your work out to a wider audience, be recognised as an expert in your field, and build your brand. The trick is to always, always, always write from your heart and tell people who you really truly are, what you believe in, and how you can help. This is what creates connections and openings that speak to the heart and soul of whoever you are here to serve, and at the end of the day that is what it is all about. Words that are filled with truth, love and wisdom change lives for the better, and you can be a part of that with a little time and effort.

Whether you are writing a blog, a feature article, copy for your website or a book; don't borrow words, ideas or subjects from others. Write from deep within the heart and soul on subjects that you feel passionate about and who you are and you can't go wrong. Don't search for topics from the outside that you think may be popular; tune in and connect with the message you are here to offer with words that will move and inspire others. For larger pieces or blogs, break your topic down into subjects or subheadings that are relevant, digestible and cohesive. Mind mapping is a great way to brainstorm ideas and create a plan to ensure your message is heard. Rest assured that as you start to write you will become more inspired along the way, and the content will begin to generate itself. Don't hold back, but give your audience the best information you have right now, and you'll release a beautiful flow of wisdom that just keeps coming. Ask yourself what the intention of your writing is.

What do you want to achieve with your message? Who do you want to reach, who do you want to serve?

Think about the format, the platform and the feeling you want to impart, when deciding on the voice or tone for the article. Should your voice be professional, knowledgeable and informative, or relaxing, deepening and softening? Try to think of the material and embodying your soul's voice rather than stressing about what your audience might think, or how it will be received. I would go so far as to say that trying to write for an audience can lock you up. If you know exactly who you are and what you are here to do, you'll know exactly what to say. Give yourself permission and let it go. Always speak with your genuine voice and your tribe will hear you.

When I wrote my first book *The Art of Joy* I felt I had so much knowledge that could help people, and I needed to get it out there before I burst at the seams. It was a very cathartic experience and I felt a deep sense of achievement and relief when it was done. I would have hated to keep that wisdom to myself or go to the grave without sharing everything I knew. In fact what we know is not our information at all, it comes from the pool of all wisdom, so holding it back really isn't an option, we are simply caretakers of universal wisdom and our responsibility is to get that wisdom out to as many people as possible. My knowledge comes from deep within my soul, and so does yours. I remember going to see Deepak Chopra and a man in the audience asked him if there was anything he didn't know, to which he honestly replied no. When you are tapped into infinite life force energy and wisdom, all knowledge flows to you. This is nothing to do with ego or thinking you 'know it all' in the human realm. I felt the same way with my book. I was aligned with an incredible flow of energy and wisdom and to put a stopper in that would be unfair for others, and actually unhealthy for me. It was the book I wished I had when I was younger. So I listed every single subject I could think of and wrote what I knew about that, and some questions and actions to help people move through it. Along the way more subjects came up and I added them to my list, took each subject at a time and wrote until I was done.

The tone is incredibly important when you are writing. When I had finished *The Art of Joy* and was going back through to edit it, I was shocked to find quite a harsh voice running through parts where my ego had snuck in. I wanted this book to be full of love, support and encouragement, so I had to go back through and soften the edges with more spirit. There are certainly strong and challenging parts there, but the overall feel is one of connection, truth and love.

I believe your writing voice should be a combination of your human experience and your spirit. Let it flow and edit only at the end of each blog, article, chapter or book. Feeling like the writing police are hovering above you with a red pen will do nothing for creativity or truth, so give yourself absolute permission to express yourself to the full edges of your being and curate it later. Writer's block is usually caused by internal criticism, disconnection with your message, or fear of being heard. It is never because you have nothing of value to say. Be daring, open up and let it flow; nobody is going to see it until you send it out into the world, so write freely and wholly. Be careful not to edit out those beautiful morsels that will touch another's soul and create shifts for them. Sometimes the scariest things to write are the most powerful. If you are hiring an editor be very clear about what you do and don't want edited. It's not all about punctuation and grammar. Get them to do a section first to see if they are aligned with the message you are trying to convey. Most editors now use programs where you can actually see what they are editing out as they go so you can keep abreast of changes.

There are so many options for self-publishing a book these days that you don't have to endure the heartbreak of sending your precious words off to publishers and endure the rejections as they come back one by one in manila envelopes. By all means go ahead and try submitting your manuscript to publishers that specialise in your genre as well, but rest assured there are other options if that doesn't work out. Create a list of publishers that specialise in self-help books by searching online or simply looking inside the cover of your favourite books from popular authors. Check out the website and be sure to follow submission guidelines for your best chance for success. Many publishing houses like Louise Hay will only accept manuscripts through an agent, so you will need to decide if you want to go down that road too. Know that an agent will get a cut of any deal, but it could certainly be worth the effort if they broker you a great deal.

If you are successful in getting a publishing offer be sure to read and understand all the fine print about the rights on your book once you sign. Even if you have a publisher, don't expect to sit back and put your feet up. You will still be expected to get out there and promote your book, give talks and generate your own publicity as well. You will also be paid less per book than what you will earn if you self-publish, but a publisher has a further reach, so you'll need to weigh that up against how many you can sell and promote yourself. Also bookstores are more likely to order your book through established publishers, but you can counter this with some good book distribution partners.

I don't want to turn you away from publishing traditionally, but understand it is no longer the Holy Grail it once was. Advancements in technology have opened up a whole new world of self-publishing options and opportunities for you, so be sure to explore them thoroughly. You can self-publish through a group that handles it for you but be very aware that many self-publishing packages will keep the rights to your book, and charge you through the nose for the pleasure. A popular alternative is to handle the self publishing yourself through avenues like CreateSpace, Amazon and Kindle. Although it may seem daunting to connect the dots yourself, with a little time, effort, research, and help, you can get your own book out there on Amazon. You will need an editor and/or proofreader, someone to format your book into both the print and e-book versions, and an eye-catching cover. You can then load it up via CreateSpace and Kindle and sell it on Amazon, online and order some yourself to sell at classes, talks and workshops.

If you decide to self-publish make sure all your legalities and copyrights are in place and *please* get a decent cover. Pay a graphic designer to upload a design if the options offered are dreamy, misty seventies lookalikes or cheesy photos of you with sledgehammer fonts. The cover should be a representative of you and your material in essence; magnetic and beautiful to the reader. Go to some bookshops and see what covers stand out to you and why. Then feel into your work, and use your intuition to choose the colours, design and energy you wish to impart. The best option of course is to raise your profile so much that people are falling over themselves to buy your book, whether you publish traditionally or self-publish. To me the best way to do this is a combination of social media, website, PR and getting out there to expos, fairs and markets.

Tell people who you are with your words. That is what they really want to know. Leave behind any old fears on spelling, grammar, being seen, heard and understood. Truth and integrity is valued above all else in my experience. People don't want or need perfection, they need to connect, and your words may be just the thing that breaks the ice on living their most beautiful life ever.

Ask Yourself

If writing is your thing, what are you waiting for?

What platforms and mediums could you use for your wisdom to be read and heard?

What partnerships with other brands could help you get your voice out there more often?

What is the one thing you don't want to leave this planet without telling people?

Can you overcome judgement about your writing by remembering there are people out there who need your words, perfect or not?

Try This

Read over your website copy, the description of your products and services, your bio, your LinkedIn and social media profiles and ask yourself if it is a true and accurate representation of who you are in essence and what you do today? If not go ahead and make some updates.

If you are not much of a writer, there are some areas in your business where you will find it necessary to hone your writing skills or hire a professional copywriter to do it for you; such as the copy you use on your website, social media and promoting your products and services. If you do get someone else to write for you, make sure you don't abdicate responsibility. You will need to be absolutely confident that the copy is an accurate reflection of who you are and what you stand for. Copywriters are used to doing several drafts, so speak up if it doesn't feel or sound right to you. It's actually a great exercise on articulating who you really are.

List all the print and digital media avenues where you could publish relevant articles or stories. Make sure your values and audiences are aligned.

Get really clear about the subjects that inspire you, writing is as much about self-discovery as anything else. Every time you think of something else jot a quick note in your phone or on paper. Open the flow.

Create a blog plan (see the blog section) that is all about delivering your most important message with the most loving, inspiring, empowering voice you can.

Try writing up a few courses, workshops or e-courses that include wisdom, exercises and activities to help your clients grow.

If you are planning on writing a book, be sure to have a great outline and plan before you begin, then allow inspiration to flesh out the bones. Balance structure with organic growth.

Enrol in a writers' group or course if you feel you want inspiration, motivation or to improve your skill set.

Create a writing schedule. Put aside the time to write; at the end of the day it's about sitting down and doing the work.

Check out Sarah Barbour from Aeroplane Media. She has some amazing tips, warnings and information on writing, editing and self-publishing.

Consultations

'Did I offer peace today? Did I bring a smile to someone's face? Did I say words of healing? I must trust that the little bit of love that I sow now will bear many fruits.'
- Henri Nouwen

Consultations, especially those of the healing kind, should be ripe with ritual. They should have a beginning, a middle and an end, and be timed to perfection. Going over the allotted time drains energy from both the practitioner and the recipient. Keeping right timing ensures the depth and breadth of the treatment is perfect for that point in time, and don't forget your client will continue to process over the coming days, weeks or even months, so you certainly don't want to overload them. You will need to create a space that feels safe, warm and professional. Be conscious of your clients' comfort and ask them if they are warm enough, like the music and if the lighting is okay. If you are massaging ask them if the pressure is okay during the session just once or twice, as often people will be shy to ask you to back off or dig in. If your client is feeling a little cold or being agitated by the music they won't be able to let go and reap the full benefit of the session which will reflect on you, so make their comfort paramount in your mind.

If you are conducting a healing or massage session, for goodness' sake be quiet. Don't engage in conversation other than what is necessary, and try to leave any insights for the end of the session. Coax your clients into a state of deep relaxation by getting them to focus on their breath and let go on every exhale. Let them know it is like going into a lovely meditation that provides deep rest for their body, mind and soul. The right music should help here. By keeping silent you allow your client and yourself to go deeper. This means a much more intuitive, powerful session. You will be guided through the session in new ways and pick up more insights for their benefit. Leave the guidance until the end or you will bring them back into the mind by sharing during the session. Write a quick note if you think you will forget anything, but usually messages from spirit are short and poignant, rather than a dialogue. Leave enough time at the end of the session to discuss any insights and for your client to slowly come back into their body fully. Guide them out as you would from a meditation; asking them to slowly wiggle their hands and toes, allow their breath to lengthen, and have a nice stretch. Then ask them to sit on the edge of the treatment table when they are ready before standing up. Ensure they are fully grounded before they leave your treatment room; the last thing you want is them spaced out in another realm when they jump in their car.

Of course leave the room for privacy if your client is not clothed and follow all necessary draping procedures throughout the session. No matter how at peace you are with nudity, presume your client is not and offer them all the benefits of privacy. Whether from being raised conservative, experiencing negative body image or from a traumatic experience, for some even getting down to their knickers can be terrifying. If you are working from home, please ensure your partner or family is not heard to be moving around in the next room closing and opening doors, or this can make clients feel unsafe.

Listen to what is said and left unsaid during all consultation sessions. Rather than try to show off your prowess, listen for what it is your client needs. It may be less than what you want for them. It is one of the toughest lessons not to want too much for your clients, and I have struggled with this myself, but people learn at their own pace, and remember just because you have incredible insight and a broad vision, it doesn't mean they can see all that you can for them right now. Perhaps if they could they would run for the hills. People need to integrate and assimilate at their own pace, otherwise their system can get overloaded and you can do more harm than good, so check that ego and help them with what they need right now. If you like you can put it out there to work with clients who are more advanced, but know they come with their own resistances as well. It's your job to act as a conduit for spirit and practice your craft to the highest level possible, not to take control the results. The rest is up to them and spirit.

Creating a different ritual or spa menu is all about creativity and authenticity. Gone are the days where you have to keep it the same old, same old or use conservative language. Many of the top spas in the world are now using indigenous treatments, smoking ceremonies, drumming, native sea scrubs, crystal and energetic healing techniques. The language is peppered with soul, spirit, dreaming, quests and calling. In fact those who are keeping to conservative lines are being left behind in a quest for the deeper experience. From a broader spiritual view, I believe this is a call from the human spirit for something deeper, more spiritual and profound. It is a yearning to get back to the healing arms of mother earth. It is a cry to connect.

What are the most amazing rituals you can put together to create space for your clients to connect to their soul? Not just something that looks or sounds good, but something that will transport your clients to a place of deep peace, love and connection with who they are in essence? What herbs, what lotions, what oils, what sequence and what ritual will do it and why? Feel it in your heart and soul. Ask spirit for guidance. Think of each session as a sacred meeting of souls and elevate your results to a whole new level. Can you imagine the referrals that will pour in from this kind of session? You can certainly do this in a more subtle way in coaching appointments too. What oils can you burn to support your clients' opening? How will the session be run from a heart and soul level? What can you do that is unique, different and wholly engaging? How can you make huge shifts in your work and your clients' results by going deeper?

Whatever one-on-one work you do, ensure you are fully present, clear and engaged. Take care of your own wellbeing. Be sure to clear the space for yourself and the next client because as you know a lot of stuff can be shed, and you don't want that old energy hanging around. Take adequate breaks and get some fresh air and good food into you. Some plants, a salt lamp, natural light, smudge stick, space clearing spritzer and fresh air can go a long way to keeping the space clear. There are many other practices you can use in the grounding, clearing and protection section too. If you are a new practitioner, just start with a couple of clients a day and build up whilst you learn to handle the energy.

Get yourself a great appointment scheduler integrated into your website, Facebook page and phone apps. Investigate some schedulers specifically designed for wellbeing practitioners like Acuity (my favourite), Timely or Mind Body Online. Many services offer a free trial so you can see if it works for you first. You can choose from different levels of service that offer different inclusions for different price points. That way the service grows with your business. They should offer appointment scheduling, gift certificates, various payment methods, be responsive to you and clients, and easy to use. It is also good to look for a system that allows classes and events too, so if you are running a workshop or teach classes as well, you can have it all there on one system. This will help organise your calendar, availability and cut way back on cancellations.

A consultation is a sacred space. It is a meeting of souls where amazing things can be achieved. Keep a high level of integrity, be innovative, creative and warm without surrogating for your client and you'll have an amazing reputation that follows you through the years.

Ask Yourself

Does your consultation have a beginning, middle and an end?

What is unique about your treatment menu? How is your essence communicated there?

How can you bring more magic and soul to your sessions so the results are transformative?

When was the last time you freshened up your consultations?

Are you able to do your highest work and then detach yourself from results?

How can you integrate your education and your unique soul path to create something fresh, new and inspirational?

How present is your spirit in your work?

Can you let your clients shift and grow at their own pace?

Try This

Create an etiquette document so clients know what is expected; switching off their mobile, cancellation or appointment change policies, what payment types you offer and so on. The clearer you are, the less surprises and the more you can just focus on the work at hand. You can set these guidelines up on your scheduler, website and on any brochures.

Let clients know what to expect before, during and after the treatment.

Let clients know what is needed on their behalf after the session to continue their self-care; to rest, drink more water or complete a set task.

Create a new spa ritual menu that is both innovative and soul quenching. Start with three new treatments that address a particular need. Remember the golden rule to always keep it in line with your soul work, brand or essence. What are you here to do and how can you translate that into a ritual with a beginning, middle and an end?

Balance a beautiful creative ritual with a sense of process. Keeping it simple and profound is better than turning it into some mad sideshow! You might want to practice on a few friends and get some feedback before you launch it.

Check out the professional conduct and ethics section in this book and ask yourself honestly if you need to tidy up some corners of your practice. This is as much about supporting you as your clients.

Find an appointment scheduler that works for you. See what resonates, is affordable and easy to use.

Consider offering a reward for regular clients. For instance make your coaching packages cheaper than an individual session. Or offer massage clients a free session, extra thirty-minute facial or skincare pack if they pre-purchase multiple treatments. Or put a time-specific offer out there like a reward when they have had five massages within six months and so on.

Explore options for coaching consultations via Skype or other technology. You may be surprised by the level of connection you can get, and it allows your wisdom to be available globally to those who need you.

Classes

So I said to the gym instructor: 'Can you teach me to do the splits?'
He said: 'How flexible are you?' I said: 'I can't make Tuesdays.'
- Tim Vine

So you teach a weekly class like Yoga, Pilates, Tai Chi, Qi Gong, Nia, Dance, Meditation, Spiritual Development or something equally as exciting, and you want to build numbers. You need to let people know all about you and your classes. In order to come to your classes, your potential clients need to get to know, like and trust you. They need to see you out and about talking about your stuff and giving demos online and in the real world. So depending on what you're teaching, here are just a few ways to get out to a wider audience, build your tribe and keep them.

Commitment

The best possible advice I can give you is to book people in for the term and not offer a casual rate. What!!? I have never offered casual rates for any of my regular classes and I'll tell you why. Casual means exactly that; float in, float out, no commitment. You don't know who's going to turn up, how much you're going to earn, or who's going to walk in the door. If you went for a job interview and asked how much you would be paid, and your employer said 'oh I don't know, just whatever we feel like week by week', I'm sure that would make you feel a little uneasy. There's nothing worse as a dedicated teacher, than sitting in a space waiting for people to arrive and feeling your heart sink as two people walk in the door. In effect you are teaching for free, or in the worst case scenario even paying money to teach. As the saying goes you teach people how to treat you. When you ask clients to pay up front for the term, you create a far deeper energy and experience for your class. Students grow both individually and together. You can deepen the content in each subsequent class so it becomes a personal development *experience* or a course. You build community; people talk, invite friends, bond, and are more likely to continue together. They see results in their lives.

If your clients have paid the money for the term, they will come to class. They will rearrange their schedule, decline invitations and temptations to skip class, and come on cold and rainy days. And if they don't, you have still been paid for your time and effort. By asking clients to commit to their personal development and self-care you are offering them a sacred opportunity. It may sound counterintuitive, but offering too much to the consumer, without rules or boundaries, is actually the fastest way to ruin your business. If services are too available, and they can go to class anywhere, anytime there is no incentive. How many times have you closed a class and then had people say 'oh I was going to try that one day'. If you take a stand and value your time, energy and effort, you radiate a certain quality that lets people know that what you offer is precious, and if they want to come they have to commit.

You have to be courageous and hold strong on this because every man, woman and dog is going to test you on your boundaries. Your clients will come up with a hundred permutations and combinations of why they can't book for the term and they need to be the exception and pay casually. The answer is no. Have a line ready. You can say to your students 'I put a lot of time, energy and commitment into my classes, and I expect commitment in return'. Or 'the experience builds week to week, and if you don't book for the term, you'll miss the full experience or the opportunity to advance.' Get people excited and intrigued about what you're going to do. Will you miss out on people who want to pay casual rates? A few, but I can tell you for sure after eighteen years of teaching to date, that there are a very small number of people who really have to go casual, for most it's a lack of commitment.

There are millions of casual classes around if that's what folks want. You should never try to cater to everyone; you should do what feeds the authenticity of your practice and respects your wellbeing too. Imagine the gift you are giving your students by asking them to commit. Like a new mum who desperately needs to get out of the house; offer her casual and she will only make it when her hubby gets back from work on time, but ask her to book for the term and she may call in mum to babysit every week so she can get there. Which option would make the biggest difference to her life? Sell it on the bonuses too. If you run several classes a week you can offer students to make up any missed classes by attending extras within the term if they are away on holidays. Make the price attractive so that booking for the term is a reward, and remember this is not a ten-class pass that they can stretch out over the next three years; it is a ten-week course *within* the ten-week term. This may not always be appropriate if you run a yoga studio, but still seriously think about integrating it at some level. Can you be competitive with other gyms by offering a membership style business model, or can you offer a significantly better price for buying in bulk? I would still strongly urge that you make any ten or twenty class passes to be used within ten or twenty weeks because otherwise it's the same as a casual rate, but cheaper. Value yourself, your time and your work.

Community

Community builds commitment, connection, joy and authenticity around your classes. If you build community your students bond with one another, share the journey and are more likely to continue term to term. Try having a celebration at the end of each term, or encourage your students to have a cuppa after class, have a Christmas lunch, set up a Facebook group where they can connect, have a special night a few times a year where you offer a deeper practice so people from all classes can get together and meet. Go on a relevant excursion together; for instance if you teach dance, you may all go to a dance performance at the local arts centre. Offer free talks or wellness workshops that are on brand. Brainstorm as many ways as possible you can foster connections within your tribe and they'll form an incredible net under your business and recruit others as well. Everyone wants to feel they are a part of something.

Print Media

Pitch an article to your local paper; in some cases you may need to pay for an advertisement, but often you can get the paper to do a local interest story. Try to tie it in with current affairs in your community; if you work with seniors you might tie it into seniors' week, or international yoga day for yoga teachers and so on. Pitch it as an exciting and engaging story. If you just come across as wanting to sell yourself they will probably switch off, but if you can make it relevant, personal and of interest to the local community they will be excited and happy to help. A fascinating personal story will also engage your audience. Tell them how you overcame stress and anxiety with meditation, and are now a qualified meditation teacher determined to help others do the same.

Make the most of your exposure if you get published by offering something at the end whether it is an upcoming workshop, talk or new class. You could offer a free class before the new term begins so people can come and try your class. This always gets great numbers, and even though some people are just there for the freebie, it creates great local buzz, word of mouth, and can be an amazing opportunity to gather photos, reviews and testimonials. Just offer the freebie once or twice a year until your numbers build. This is especially valuable if your class or practice is new or unknown.

You could also try applying to write a regular wellbeing column for your local paper or wellbeing magazine. This helps build your reputation as an expert in the field and you can usually include a little blurb with your bio and website. Some media may pay you for a regular column, or you may get a free advertisement in lieu of payment.

Getting Out There

Network to your target market; if your target market is mums, see if you can connect with the school committee and offer a free class at their next social night or fundraiser. Go to local small business nights, join a meetup club and talk to people about what you do. Do a demo at the local market, wellbeing fair or community event. It's a numbers game, so the more people you can get out to the better. Wherever there is a gathering of people that fit your audience, you should be there. You don't do this once, or once a year, or wait until someone asks you; you do it over and over and over again. You reach out at any opportunity to let people know who you are, what you're passionate about and how you can help. I often hear practitioners say they went to business nights but it didn't work, then they reveal actually they only went once. It doesn't work like that. It just takes one week to make an amazing connection, and it's really vital to be generous at these things too, and think about what you have to give, rather than what you can get, because there's nothing worse than being sold to when the person speaking doesn't give a toss about who you are. Read the networking section for more ideas.

Expos are a great way of getting out there as well. Your clients can come and meet you and have a chat before they commit to your class. If you can book a spot to talk about your passion, take a movement demo or give clients a little taster of what you do, they are more likely to sign up. You should offer an incentive to join on the day and get folks on your mailing list too.

Check out the social media chapter for great suggestions on how your clients can get to know you, the modem you practice and how it is just right for them. Don't forget to do a few things the old-fashioned way too and get some fliers or postcards out to cafes, health food stores, wellness centres, shop windows and so on. It is estimated that people need to see you at least seven times before they buy from you and if those seven times come from different avenues, it becomes even more powerful. Hence the marketing mix. So let's say they see you on social media, see your business card in a local café, see your flier at the health food store, they hear someone talk about you, see you give a local talk, have your newsletter forwarded by a friend, meet you at a small business night and then see you at an expo. By the time they see you at the expo, the client has begun to know, like and trust you and is far more likely to give your class a go.

Job Opportunities

Local community centres can be a great resource for starting new classes as they often have a large established mailing list that can expand your reach in the community. They may pay you a tutor's fee and advertise your class for you, or you could hire a space from them in which case they may advertise you in their program, or for a nominal fee you can pay to be put in. If you want to offer a free class before term begins, community centres are often happy to help you promote that.

Approach small businesses, corporate companies, councils and schools and see if they want a regular class for their staff. Businesses can either pay you a set tutor's fee, or their employees can pay you. I would charge more for corporate than small business if the employee is paying, and more for private than public schools, taking their resources into account. You could also try working at local gyms, retreats or five-star resorts, but make sure you are getting a reasonable fee for your service, and you are keeping it in line with your niche and target market. There is no sense applying to companies if wellness in schools is your thing.

Create great partnerships with local businesses. See if you can work from an established natural therapy centre, have a wellbeing night with the local health food store, become a guest presenter at a wellness retreat or gym, or put together a wellbeing day with fellow practitioners.

Discounts and Rewards

I would far rather offer people a reward than a discount. A reward is something people earn for great loyalty to you and your brand. For instance if they book in for the term they might get 10% off your workshops, retreats or products. If they buy a coaching package they are rewarded with a cheaper price. If they pay upfront for a year of yoga, they may get access to a video series of the classes and so on. Strange as it may seem people want to make an effort for a reward, and will be more likely to tell their friends proudly that they get their reward because they've done this. There is a bit of a push on the flash sale at the moment, but know that if you offer your treatment for half price, you might get a bit of quick cash in the door now, but it's going to be an uphill battle to get people to pay full price again. They'll either wait to see when your next sale is, or look around for someone else offering a flash sale too. If you offer discounts for their own sake, it slices a little energetic value off what you do. Rewards mean a lot, create great word of mouth and make your clients feel recognised and valued. Most importantly they celebrate your clients' self-esteem, pride and commitment to their own growth and self-care.

Have a Target

You should have a target for the number of people you want in your class and focus all your energy and effort towards achieving that target. Once your targets have been achieved, celebrate and set a new target. Don't just wait to see what happens, or how many people come, *intend* to reach the number you set. Intentions work best with a combination of visualisation and action. Each week check in on how many clients you have in your classes and how many more you need to reach your target in each class. Don't get stressed or disappointed by numbers; instead create some excitement about moving towards your target or asking yourself what else you could do to get there. This will also let you know which classes need a bit more of a push. Don't just average the numbers out, be really clear about how many you want in each class, set your mind and your spirit to having them, and build from there.

More in Less Time

It is far better to have four classes with twenty people in each, than to have ten classes with eight people in each, especially when you are hiring a venue. Four full classes means less rental costs, less advertising, less overheads, less time away from home, and less prep time. Of course you can put on a lot of classes and hope to fill them over time, but that's a big drain on your business financially and timewise in the meanwhile. Better to fill a few classes to the brim, and then explore expansion from there. If you have a studio where you are already paying rent, you might as well make use of your money by pivoting classes at popular times, but don't go overboard. Consider using spare time to invite consulting practitioners, or aligned teachers to share something different, contribute to your rent and broaden your audience.

Overavailability means your services may be undervalued. By having full classes with people on a waiting list, it creates the impression that your classes are valuable and popular. Don't play that game of trying to block all time spaces so that someone new can't come to the area and create a business. If someone new comes and people want to try it they'll do that anyway, so just work within your integrity and you will be fine. Consider moving to a larger venue rather than putting on new classes when your numbers build.

Build a List

Keep in touch, deepen your relationship and offer your clients a wealth of information via your mailing list. Social media interaction can be very enticing, but remember that your mailing list is the only direct way you have of contacting all your clients. At any and all opportunities you should be getting people on your list. Make it a priority. We are so lucky to have great newsletter services now that mean you can be super creative or make it simple as pie. You can include video demos of particular techniques, student testimonials, special offers, coming classes and news. Be inventive. Why not include a video of a particular pose, sequence or technique you are working on in class this term, explaining the deeper benefits of a practice. Above all else be sure you are offering your clients great information, not just selling to them. Think of it like a conversation with friends. Fill it with great content, genuine connection and rewards to enrich your clients' experience.

Concentrated Areas

Depending on your business model I would recommend concentrating your work in one particular area to help build your brand and reputation. If you are community driven choose to run your classes in one suburb or town, or depending on the population, or three to four surrounding suburbs at the most. If you are corporate wellness driven, choose to build your reputation by focussing on the corporate area. If you are passionate about wellness classes in schools focus your attention there and so on. This is how you create word of mouth and a great reputation in concentrated areas and this will be vital to your success.

Professionalism

Handle everything about your classes professionally. Hire the best venue space you can afford, make it beautiful, warm, welcoming and energetically clear. Make sure you are set up at the venue, and sitting in a centered space well before any students arrive. Have receipts ready, change on hand and take the money in your hands thanking everyone personally. Try to remember your clients' names and introduce them to others. Keep your timing tight, don't run over time, and try not get caught up talking to people for hours after class finishes. Have a very clear direction for the class, including a beginning, middle and end. Prepare fastidiously, and then you can flow within the boundaries where appropriate. Offer fantastic customer service without bending over backwards. Respond to phone calls or queries as soon as possible, and please dear God if you have one of those 'convert your message to a text' voicemails get rid of it yesterday. Your clients may be feeling excited, shy, nervous or inquisitive when they call you to ask about your classes, they want to have a real voice at the end of the phone and to be able to leave a message that will be heard and understood.

Online Classes

We are so lucky to live in this incredible age of new technology. Personally I prefer to teach in person and really feel the energy in the room, but I have a lot of clients interstate and overseas who love to get into my online courses. Although travelling, talking and running seminars will always be my favourite part of my business model, I must confess I have loved connecting with people from all over the world in the online space. For those of you who are hesitant, but think it could fit, I really urge you to give it a go; you'll be amazed with how the quality of your work shines through. In fact it forces you to create something really schmick and cohesive. If you teach a class like yoga, Pilates, tai chi or other movement practices, before you create a DVD, look at live streaming and other tech options for delivering an online option. You can certainly monetise this if you're clever. If this isn't your thing and you prefer to teach in the flesh, you could still set up a course that complements your classes in real life.

Perhaps you could run a pranayama series for your yoga students or a gut health course for your cooking class or a lead-in course for your retreat. There are lots of complex course delivery systems, and lots of super easy ones too. You can have your techy guru integrate it into your website. You can offer video, audio and written downloads or all three so your clients can learn in the way that best suits them. The great thing about running online courses is that once it's up and running, people can access it any time day or night as the lessons are automatically downloaded to their inbox. So while you are sleeping, clients can be enrolling in your courses. It also cuts way down on your overheads, and many courses will just take a small amount from each enrolment, rather than charge you a monthly fee. Try Course Craft for a simple introduction or Google the top ten online course providers, read the reviews, and see which service seems like the best match for you. Play around. Most providers understand that a lot of people accessing their services may be a little technophobic, so the instructions or videos on how it all works are incredibly comprehensive. You can also just use the same content, framework and downloads for your online meditation class that you offer for those you conduct in person, hence no extra work and your brand is reinforced. These courses don't just sell themselves as soon as they are up there though, so get a good marketing plan in place for success.

You could even offer a free mini e-course for a reward or to let people know a little more about what you do. Even though it's free, make sure it has value because it needs to be a reflection of any paid courses you may run in the future. If you have a paid course listed alongside the free one, it gives clients the opportunity to get to know your style before they invest in your more expensive offering. If you link enrolments to your mailing list it's a great way of getting new clients on your list too. There will be a huge growth in live stream classes in the future too, so take a good look at this technology where students pay a fee for a subscription that they can watch at home, on holidays or at work.

Pricing

Basically it is up to you what you charge; don't be persuaded by the 'market value' or just plucking a figure out of the air. Sit, meditate and really think about what *feels* right to you. Check out the pricing, costing and value section to examine all possibilities. If you do feel you can't possibly just offer a term rate, please just offer a casual rate and a term rate; two options, that's it. The only exception to this is if you have a studio, but then be *very* discriminatory, and don't go overboard with your options. It will make a mess of your books, your marketing and confuse your clients. Too many options don't solve problems, they turn people away.

Ask Yourself

If I am disappointed with class numbers, is there more I could I be doing more to get my classes out there?

Could I consider offering class term rates without a casual option to build commitment and community?

Is all my advertising across all media cohesive and easily recognisable?

Who could I partner with to help create a mutually beneficial relationship?

How is your social media interaction on your page, in local groups and in building your message and your brand?

Are you confident with what you charge, and can you tell clients in a clear, strong, loving voice? (It's kind of funny recording yourself practicing this. Listen to your voice and energy and practice, practice, practice!)

Am I letting people know who I really am?

How can you create an abundant mindset?

Even if you feel a little technophobic are you willing to at least look at the online class option?

Try This

Write a list of how you could build community around your classes in as many ways as possible so that your students can get to know each other and you.

Look back on your journey and think about all the reasons you got into this field in the first place. Was it from personal experience or watching someone else struggle? There's no need to sell your soul or come across as a victim, but sharing your story is inspirational to others. Let local media know about your story to help you gather your tribe.

List all the papers, magazines and radio stations you could tell your story to.

List all the wellbeing fairs, expos, markets, and community events you could attend this year to get out there. You should be out there at least once a month.

Choose which area you will focus your efforts on whether it is geographical or niche based.

Depending on your business model, write a list of all community centres, schools and corporate businesses you could approach to hold your classes. Please note choose one (or another specialty area), not all three.

Write a list of possible rewards you could offer your students for their loyalty. Not too little, not too much, but always from the heart.

How many people would you like to have in each class? Make it feel achievable and realistic. Once you hit that target you can always raise it, but setting huge numbers when you're struggling could sabotage you before you begin.

Make it your priority to build your mailing list, asking people to sign up at every opportunity.

Do an inventory of your professionalism and attitude. Is there anywhere you could improve? How is your punctuality, customer service and class content?

If you are creating fliers, try to buy in bulk and rather than print dates and times, leave a blank place for stickers so you can print any details there, rather than throw out fliers if times or venues change.

Keep your branding, logo and style consistent across all advertising and marketing mediums so people can easily get to know you and recognise you.

Workshops

'I've learned that people will forget what you said, people will forget what you did, but people will never forget how you made them feel.'
- Maya Angelou

Workshops are an amazing way of giving your clients a deeper experience of who you are, and some incredible practical tools that could change their lives. If you are running classes I would thoroughly recommend running at least four workshops a year. This gives you the opportunity to get to know your clients better and vice versa. It also gives them the opportunity to bond more deeply and be vulnerable with each other. Wherever people create community through authentic communication, mutual respect and trust, they will stay because that's where they feel safe, seen and heard. Keep developing your programs into a rich experience for people to learn and grow and they'll stick with you through thick and thin.

Although retreats are a wonderful way of taking your clients' experience further, don't be surprised by what you can achieve in a workshop format. In terms of your own health and wellbeing, workshops will take much less time, money and energy than a retreat. There are fewer overheads, and you won't have to be 'on' for twenty-four hours a day to deal with any problems that might arise. With the right content, environment and intentions, a one-day workshop can feel like a weekend away. You could also run a two-day workshop where people are responsible for their own accommodation throughout the course.

The most important thing to remember when creating a workshop series is to keep it in line with your niche, brand and purpose. I would thoroughly recommend having a plan for your four workshops at the beginning of the year. That way there will be a natural progression and you won't head off on a tangent. You can promote it as a series and encourage people to follow through to deepen their experience. You may decide that your clients can do each workshop individually, but let them know they will get the most benefit by doing all four. Or perhaps you will promote the series as a level one to four and they must attend each workshop in succession. You can always offer an online version in case they can't make one of the scheduled dates.

You could run workshops more frequently, but it is much better practice to have twenty people in four workshops, than eight people in ten workshops. You'll have less prep time, fewer overheads, less overlapping promotions, less marketing costs, less planning and more time for your life. There is nothing wrong with a little space between workshops to let people process, and build momentum for the next event. If you have really blown people away, don't be shy to get them to sign up for the next workshop while they are still glowing from the last one. If you have a wellness studio where you are already paying rent and overheads, and have a lot of traffic coming through the door, you could run workshops more frequently. Having a specialised workshop once a month, or every two months, could be a great way to get clients connected and feature different practitioners. Just be sure to measure your results and adjust accordingly. Always try to get larger numbers in your workshops. When you have bigger numbers your clients create an energy of their own that promotes independence, whereas with smaller numbers they will tend to latch on to you a little more for their answers.

Each workshop should tie strongly into your business and marketing plan by feeding into other services and products in your business. For instance people from your classes can come to your workshops and vice versa. Books, wellness products and coming events can be promoted at your workshops. You can offer a door prize of a free term of yoga for workshop participants. And so on. This is where your niche is really important. There is no point selling products and services that are totally irrelevant to your niche. Each aspect of your business should reinforce your message, and take your clients into a richer experience of your unique wisdom and specialty. This is how you build your reputation and become *known* for something.

Break each workshop down by the hour. This may sound a little anal, but it is as much to create space as to fill it. I mean literally what is happening from nine to ten, ten till eleven, eleven to twelve and so on. How long will you have for lunch and tea breaks? When you break it all down you will realise it is better to focus on key points thoroughly than to offer a load of material your clients have little time or space to feel and integrate. There will need to be time for sharing with the group and questions too. I know you want to give them value for money, but value doesn't lie in a whole heap of information. It lies in how they feel afterwards. Usually from one full day each person will get one key breakthrough or takeaway, and chances are it will not be something you expected or intended. You don't need to focus on outcome, just keep deepening into the truth and integrity in your work, and your clients will grow and heal in the way their soul needs to in that moment. And that is a beautiful thing.

Don't hold back on your best stuff. Pretend like each workshop is going to be your last ever opportunity to teach. Leave nothing behind. Use your deepest information every time. I can guarantee you another spring of knowledge will open up and pour forth. You will never run out of material. Make it new and innovative and breathtaking. Don't even *think* about modelling it on someone else's workshop or work. It must come from deep within your heart and soul; a combination of your training, your experience, your history, your unique voice and your soul calling. That is powerful stuff.

Ask Yourself

Are your workshops a living breathing experience of your soul purpose?

Are your workshops exciting, innovative and creative?

Are they filled with practical information that works?

Do they fill the senses with delight? How do they feel, taste, smell, look and sound? A beautiful sensory experience will stay with your clients for a long time.

Try This

Write down the most important message, skill or gift you want to deliver to the world. For instance it may be to help women get in touch with their personal power, it may be to deliver wellness programs to teachers, or equine assisted therapy for teens. Then break that intention into the four most valuable experiences you could ever provide. Trust me next year there will be four more, so don't hold back.

Know that people will feel a little nervous at the beginning of any workshop so be sure to set them at ease, introduce them to other participants and give them something to occupy themselves until the workshop commences, such as helping themselves to a cuppa or looking at the oracle cards or books you have set out.

Add an element of ritual to your workshop. Rituals are a powerful way of helping your clients step over a new threshold. They will help facilitate your work and assist attendees in stepping into a whole new level of being. Rituals can be sweet and tender or wild and powerful, so choose according to your workshop energy and focus.

Give your clients a little unexpected treat at the end, whether it is a goody bag, a follow-up email with a free meditation podcast, PDF or video series. Or even just tell them one by one what you have seen in them that is beautiful this day. This will probably touch them more than anything.

Make energetic boundaries really clear before the day too by setting intentions, and you can do this in a way that is warm and welcoming like; 'Hey everyone, I'm really looking forward to our beautiful workshop on Saturday. To create the warmest and most welcoming environment possible we will gather in an attitude of mutual respect, honour, integrity and kindness.'

Let clients know punctuality is essential for the smooth running of the day, and to allow plenty of time to get to the venue. Ask that they be sure to arrive fifteen minutes before the workshop to offer respect to themselves, the teacher and fellow classmates.

Send out a Google map link to the venue, a parking map and let your participants know what to bring. Let them know if they need to bring a plate to share, if you are providing food, or they need money for lunch. Do they need to bring a mat, cushion or blanket? Ensure their comfort and wellbeing has been top of your mind. You may get a few people with back problems or mobility issues so be sure to provide appropriate seating. Not everyone can sit in the lotus position or even on the floor for hours. The clearer you are with your instructions, the more at ease they will feel about the day.

This is an oldie but a goody; get attendees to write a letter of inspiration to themselves which you can later post out to them. As you know the best of intentions set in a sacred space can soon be forgotten in a busy world, so ask participants to write a letter from this powerful space to remind them of who they are and what they are capable of. Get them to seal the envelopes and address them to themselves. Keep them in a safe place for four weeks and then post the letters out. You will usually get an email from a few attendees saying 'oh my goodness this was just what I needed to hear that day', or 'what a timely reminder' and so on.

Never forget a good workshop can change lives. Never be afraid to try something unique or innovative even if it breaks the popular line. Teach what is impeccably true for you. Make sure you are centered and clear before the day begins, listen carefully, heighten your intuitive responses and follow guidance from spirit throughout the day.

Running Retreats

'In order to understand the world one has to turn away from it on occasion.'
- Albert Camus

The first retreat I ever ran was a comedy of errors. My participants had a great time, but little did they know I was a nervous wreck, fending off one disaster after another. From
being told there would be a town meeting in our space on the first night, to arriving to a huge mess I had to scramble to clean up, to scooping up cockroaches, to having to get someone in to repair the hot water service (it was the dead of winter), to dealing with two aggressive attendees and more! I left the weekend trembling, swearing never again. Thank God for the teacher trainees who were with me, and raced into action alongside me. Although I did go on to run plenty more retreats, I took my lessons seriously and made big changes. And here's the thing; your retreat has to support your central nervous system as well. It has to bring you joy, allow you to be totally present, relaxed and alert. So here are just a few things that I hope will help you and your beautiful attendees.

Make sure you visit the venue before running your retreat there. Even if you have been there in the past, make a visit if at all possible in the weeks leading up to your retreat. This will give you a realistic experience of the service, cleanliness, feel, light, facilities and location in the moment. Ask the centre or venue to give you an assurance on cleanliness and readiness for your arrival. Be sure to arrive early yourself to make sure everything is up to standard. Understand that if you pick a cheaper venue you can't expect the best of everything, so know that lowering your prices may mean lowering your standards, and you'll need to think seriously about that. Think of it in terms of your tribe. If they are earthy folks they may not mind bunks or camping, but if you run a schmick, modern studio with a middle-high income clientele, they will probably be horrified. Be really clear with participants on what to expect from the accommodation. If it is back to basics shared bunk room, they need to know. If it is a five-star experience, then they will understand why it is priced as such. Be very specific about whether the room has an ensuite, it's single or shared accommodation, bunks or queen beds, or bedding is needed. Also list any special features such as whether it has a balcony, kitchenette and so on. An informed choice keeps everyone happy.

Play to your strengths and your brand. If you're all about women's leadership, don't run a retreat on getting fit. This may sound like a no brainer, but you'd be surprised how many teachers go off brand with this. Sometimes practitioners spend all year saying I'm all about this, then offer a generic retreat and wonder why they are not getting the numbers. Clients expect you to deliver a deeper experience of what you do day to day on a retreat, not something left of field. Think of what extra juicy, new experiences you can add, while keeping it utterly aligned with your brand.

Take your participants *deep* whilst at the same time keeping it simple. Don't underestimate what people are capable of taking in. It's easy to run a retreat that has meditation, yoga, nutrition talks, tai chi and massage. The trouble is everyone is doing that. So think about what you really want to offer people. Find a powerful intention and build your retreat around that. Choose wellbeing practices that support that intention instead of just throwing them in willy nilly. It's not enough anymore to say relax, soothe, get into your body, mind and spirit. What is really on the menu? How will they feel when they leave? Why are you running this? Do you want them just to be relaxed for a few days when they get home, or do you want to *change their life*? Preparation, forethought and follow through are vital. This isn't something you just throw together to make some money.

Leave plenty of room for participants to do their own work, connect with others, assimilate the information and make their own discoveries. Encouraging them to share what their illuminations are throughout the retreat will ensure they are taking ownership over the experience. The last thing you want to do is send them home in overwhelm to process there. You don't need to heal them; you need to give them time to heal themselves in a safe environment.

Please dear God, don't make it full of hard-core physical activity and no time to rest. Even if your niche is fitness and weight loss, participants need time to rest, recover, and look at the psychological aspects of why they are here. Otherwise they will simply go back to everything else they were doing before. You need to create a full picture. So often I see people arrive at a five-star retreat with the intention of a healthy experience. Their adrenals are exhausted because they often work in a high-level, high-pressure job. They need an understanding of where they are at, how to make lasting lifestyle changes and choices, why they are running themselves into the ground and so on. What they get is a few lectures on healthy food, mad physical workouts, chase one activity after the other, go home just as exhausted, and start all over again. So where is the insight, the learning, the growth and the change? Are we in service just to make money or are we really invested in making lasting change in peoples' lives?

Be creative and innovative. Make your own mark. In what is thankfully a more creative world, you can really generate something special and different. Just like the fashion industry has before it, the wellness industry now runs on trends. Don't less this be a distraction to your work. Hold fast to your unique blend. We have just come out of a trend on hot, Ashtanga and very physical yoga and are now switching to Yin Yoga and LSD (long, slow, deep yoga). Hold on long enough and something new will be trending. You can't rebrand every time there's a new trend because it will decimate your identity; keep to who you are and believe in that for longevity.

Give clear directions. There's nothing more likely to result in a tired, frazzled attendee than to give really unclear directions to the venue, or hold the retreat at a venue where you have to drive through boggy marshes to get there. If you are running a high-level retreat you should certainly have clients picked up from airports, so they don't need to worry at all. Other than that offer a printable map, Google map link and have your phone ready in case anyone is lost on the way. If you are running overseas retreats be clear about how they get from the airport to the hotel and how much they should expect to pay if you're not collecting them. Let people know about travel insurance, inoculations (their choice), weather and visas. Ensure you have a working visa that allows you to teach in that country and that your professional indemnity insurance covers you there. The last thing you want to do is be turned back at the airport whilst your attendees are arriving. Some insurance companies will cover you overseas but most won't for the United Sates and Canada, so extra insurance will probably be needed. Do your homework.

Don't forget your customer service. You should meet and greet each of your guests and welcome them warmly. A lovely flower or gift is a nice touch. Show them to their accommodation yourself preferably, or have someone else do it. It can be a very vulnerable experience arriving for a retreat or training, so you need to offer a warm welcome to set a lasting impression. Arriving feeling a little scared and awkward with no one in sight, or no idea where to go, can leave participants feeling a little vulnerable. The personal touch makes for a great first impression. Ensure that your customer care extends beyond the retreat to a thank you letter when they get home, and perhaps even a free bonus meditation or PDF with tips and tools to keep going on their journey.

Create strong boundaries. Be very clear about the boundaries, expectations and etiquette of the retreat from the first advertising, through the sales process, to when you open the retreat at the official welcome. Things such as; everyone is to be treated with respect, to not take anything personally, to own your own stuff that comes up, to be an active participant in your own healing and so on. That way if a situation does arise, it's a lot easier to deal with by referring back to the boundaries that were clearly laid out.

Perhaps most important of all is to have crystal clear intentions for your retreat. Get super clear on the energy you want to bring into the retreat; from the venue, to the experience for participants and yourself, to the outcomes. For instance; I want this retreat to be in a beautiful, modern, clean venue in natural surrounds, with views of the sea. I want to feel relaxed, confident, professional, at ease, joyful and well organised. I invite participants who are positive, light, self-aware, respectful, open, loving, capable of taking responsibility for their own growth, fun and playful. I would go so far as to see a kinesiologist to set yourself up for success and remove any blocks towards getting the numbers or experience you want.

In case of emergency details are essential. In the unlikely event of an emergency you will need first-aid basics, emergency details, medical details and contacts to follow through calmly and professionally if anything goes wrong. Emphasize to attendees that they must have their own travel and medical insurance for the retreat.

Be clear on content and who the retreat is and isn't suitable for. Sometimes in the desire to fill your retreat and make it a success, you may not be picky or clear enough about who you want there. Trust me this can actually help fill your retreat, and with all the right people. For example; this retreat is for women wanting to learn and grow, to take a deep journey into themselves, to explore the soulful life and what that means. This is not for you if you prefer a fitness experience or are uncomfortable with introspection. Whatever you do or don't do, be honest about it. That way you'll gather a tribe who are incredibly connected and on the same page to create even greater shifts for the group.

Be really clear about your refund policy for the retreat. Will they get a full or partial refund if they cancel, or will there be no refund at all? Are there time factors involved such as a cancellation three months before will give you a 50% refund, two months before will give you 25% refund and a month before will give you no refund? Always state specific dates like by November 30th. Add a statement saying the refund policy is strictly abided by, and follow through, or you may find you get a reputation of bending rules, which is a delight for the non-committers. Can they pass their ticket on to someone else or not? Can they have a credit for another retreat or not? The refund policy should be clearly stated on all marketing, the purchase page in bold or red, and in follow-up correspondence. If there is no refund available (check your legalities here) it's a good idea to say please choose carefully as no refunds, transfers or changes are available. You will also need a policy in place in case the retreat is cancelled, which should include a full refund to all participants.

Let clients know what they are expected to bring on the retreat. Remember the more informed they are, the more relaxed they will feel leading up to the retreat. Let them know what they need to bring, and what you will supply. Do they need a pen and paper, loose comfy clothes, a jacket, a water bottle, bedding, torch, sunscreen or sunhat, runners, walking boot or anything else? It's essential to also take note of dietary requirements, allergies, medications and food intolerances.

Integrations these days make for a seamless sales process, but don't forget to get in touch with your participants and give them the human touch by saying 'hey everyone, I'm so excited you are booked in to the retreat...' and maybe give them a teaser of what's to come. This confirms the purchase (let's them know they have made the right choice) and gets them excited, which also encourages them to tell their friends.

Is it your deep burning passion to give people a retreat experience, are you after a holiday yourself (ha, ha, ha, ha, ha, ha, ha)? Running retreats is a lot of work. There is a huge amount of prep and research, marketing, organising, planning and logistics. Slapping together a poor retreat could actually damage your brand. You need to be committed to offering a memorable experience for all the right reasons. If you are running a retreat at a hired venue, you will need to be available on site for participants throughout the retreat. This doesn't mean you can't have a break, of course you can, but should an emergency arise you need to be on the premises. You will also need to take into consideration if you are in a bushfire, flood or natural disaster area. What! There's no need to catastrophise, I'm an optimist, but when you take on care of a group of people, you need to take that very seriously. Running a retreat at an established retreat venue gives you backup, should anything go wrong if you're more comfortable with that.

Find out from the retreat hire venue what your financial obligations are and don't put down a deposit unless you are sure you can get the numbers. You may need to put down a deposit of $1,000 or more depending on the venue, so ask yourself if that's money you are prepared to lose.

If you are thinking of running a retreat with someone else take into account first that you are on the same page with the retreat intention, philosophy and that you work well together. The cost will need to cover both of you for travel, accommodation and teaching time. You will need to split the profits so you will need to increase the prices. You may be able to strike a deal with another practitioner by offering them the weekend free if they teach a class while they are there, although I am always in favour of paying your teachers fairly for their expertise.

Take the seasons and environment into account. If you're offered a super cheap deal it may be because you're heading straight into cyclone or monsoon season. If you are heading into the Australian bush make sure it's not in peak fire season. Use your common sense and think of what will make the most beautiful experience for you and your participants. Check local weather patterns and have contingencies ready if outdoor plans are marked by rainfall. Of course these days especially we can't predict the weather, just use your head.

Take photos throughout the retreat in a non-intrusive manner. It's great to have someone along who can do this for you, see if you can strike a deal with a local photographer who needs a weekend away. Or a friend or other staff member could do it for you. Get permission from the folks in the photos and let them know they may be used for social media, on your website or future retreat promotions. Most people are happy to, but don't presume, ask for permission. These photos can also be used to create an album that you can take to classes or workshops that encourages people to book into future retreats.

And finally…get yourself some great reviews. Ask your participants to write a testimonial in a little book at the retreat, a review on your Facebook or Trip Advisor page. Videomonials are also a really powerful way of promoting your retreats. If you have testimonials on your website be sure to put a face to the comment.

Ask Yourself

Why do you want to run retreats?
Where do you want to run retreats?
Do you want to offer an earthy, mid-range or elite option?
How can you ensure your retreat is an incredible, memorable experience for all the right reasons?
Will you run the retreat alone or with a partner?

Try This

Write a list of deep experiences that you can offer people…as many as you can. Then circle which ones are totally in line with your brand.

Set solid intentions for your retreat. How do you want people to feel at the beginning, middle and end? How do *you* want to feel? What do you want the energy to be like?

Decide the pricing, costing and venue. Is your retreat high end, budget or mid range? Does this suit your business audience or target market?

Write a list of the boundaries for your retreat. It doesn't want to read like a dictatorship, but think of the most important things to support you and your participants. Be kind but firm in your wording.

Write clear directions, a Google map and have a contact number readily available if they get lost and need to contact you. Or set up a seamless, reliable, friendly service to transport them to where they need to go.

Write a refund and cancellation policy.

Do a realistic costing, pricing and break even financial sheet on the retreat, and work out what you need to charge from there to make it financially viable. Think food, accommodation, equipment, time, marketing, your personal travel and accommodation costs and add ons like massage, day trips etc.

Write a standard form you can use again in the future that includes personal details, a disclaimer, emergency contact, dietary requirements, allergies, conditions and medications.

Understand that however organised you may be, things can wrong and you'll need to deal with any problems calmly, clearly, and directly. No one wants to see an hysterical leader!

Products

'Quality is never an accident; it is always the result of high intention, sincere effort, intelligent direction and skilful execution; it represents the wise choice of many alternatives.'
- William A. Foster

Products in wellbeing may include tangible items like books, tarot cards, clothing, candles, nurture or beauty lines, singing bowls, organic produce, statues and so on. Or products can also refer to your intangible offerings like mp3s, e-books, podcasts, e-courses and ideas. Basically anything that fills a need in the wellbeing marketplace. Product lines are a group of products that work together to enhance your brand, and support the spiritual and wellbeing lifestyle of your clients.

Make sure that creating products is an essential part of your business model before moving forward, because they can tie up an enormous amount of your time, energy and money that could be spent elsewhere in your business. If done well, a product line can offer you an additional source of income that enhances your brand. The spa industry in particular has done very well with tangible products like skincare as they give the client the opportunity to experience salon grade treatments at home in between sessions. There is no reason why home-based businesses can't take advantage of this as well; from coaches selling their books, to massage therapists selling essential oil blends, to healers selling crystals. Just keep it clear, purposeful and aligned. And don't be shy about offering it to the client at the end of the session. There is no need to go all shopping channel on them, but if you really believe your products can support them, why not offer them?

Digital or intangible products can also offer amazing support for your clients. If you are running a meditation course, why not create an app or mp3 that they can use at home to practice? Perhaps you could create an e-book to guide your clients through stress management techniques. Creating digital products will take a bit of research and effort to deliver at a professional standard, but I would thoroughly recommend investigating which digital products would enhance your business as we are moving well and truly into the digital age. Remember you don't need to do everything, just do a bit of research, experiment and go with what suits your brand, your business and you. I would go so far as to say if you want to get really out there in the world then a digital product of some description is an absolute must.

In terms of tangible products, you will need to decide whether you will create products yourself, or whether you will bring in products from other suppliers wholesale, and sell them to your clients at retail price. Creating a product line yourself requires a lot of research and development, and there are moral and legal obligations in creating many therapeutic lines, so be sure to investigate all requirements thoroughly. If you are bringing products in from the outside, make sure you have tried and tested them yourself, and they are of the quality you want to be associated with your business. As always you would only produce or promote products that are strongly tied to your core message and brand.

Products may be stand-alone, or tie in with other services you offer. For instance if your core message was about female sensuality, you might create or sell massage oils, candles, and ambient music. If you have a yoga studio you might want to bring in mats, props and a small clothing range. Or you may want to create a line of stand-alone skincare and nurture products like cleansers, moisturisers, bath salts, masks and scrubs. Remember as always less is more. I recently saw two stalls of homemade skin products at my local market. One had a table full to overflowing with about fifty different skincare products in white plastic pump packs with busy labels on the front. Many of the testers were also messy with globs of product running down the front, or dried at the end of the pump bit. The other stall had two moisturisers, two cleansers, a clay face mask and a bowl of rustic homemade soap. They were in brown glass jars with simple white labels with black print. The testers were in smaller glass jars in front. The simple blackboard sign said they were made with the rainwater from the Otway's National Park and essential oils. The scent from the soaps was totally pure and uplifting, I can still smell it as I'm writing this.

You can guess which product I bought. I know that the person selling the wider range may think they are offering more, but they are in fact just confusing their clients. I know there is no way that this person can put as much love, research and care into fifty products as the other stall holder can into six. Your packaging is also crucial because you can assume that clients buying natural skincare know glass is easier to recycle than plastic, looks and feels purer, will protect ingredients from UV rays and won't leach chemicals into the product like some plastic bottles can. The packaging is also very much about the *feel* of your business.

If you are running a retail store, obviously your product line will need to be a lot more varied, but once again try not to get too carried away so that your store ends up looking like a junk shop. There is a fine line between a joyful exploration of nooks and crannies and a dust bowl. Remember good energy flow and abundance doesn't thrive with too much clutter, and many of these items are sacred, and need to be treated with respect. Rather than go with a cheap line of mass-produced statues, try to source your sacred icons from ethical suppliers in Nepal, Tibet or India. There are a lot of fair-trade companies now offering beautiful traditional and spiritual products. There are also some wonderful local artists creating sacred gifts like dream catchers from reclaimed wood, feathers and crystals. Try also to stay away from artificially perfumed candles, lotions and oils as these are actually toxic. Stick to high-grade essential oils instead. Cleanse the space, your crystals and merchandise often to keep the energy of the store clear and flowing freely. Your store should have an overall feel or theme, from the name to the goods you offer.

Retail products are usually bought at wholesale prices and are marked up 100% plus tax, apart from things like books, CDs and DVDs which come with a recommended retail price and will not have a very high mark-up or profit margin. They also need to be taken care of as no one wants to buy a dog-eared book for a present and customers can tend to want to flick through them. Take your time with research and try to source products that are high quality, unusual, reasonably priced and deeply sacred. Wherever possible source products with stories or meaning attached and showcase these to your clients. Build your reputation on the authenticity of your shop and the care of your clients.

Get creative with your space to make each visit a sensory spiritual adventure for your customers, and invoke the feeling that what they purchase from you is special, unique and high vibration as it should be. Tell stories about the artisans, give the customer a hand massage with your latest organic range, use beautiful natural gift wrap with twine and leaves or feathers, offer handouts on crystals, singing bowls or how to read tarot cards with each purchase. It is the little things that make a huge difference. You could also run workshops, talks, consultations or courses from your store with suggested products to continue the journey at home. Crystal workshops might offer a crystal start-up pack for chakras, massage courses an essential oil starter pack, tarot courses a unique tarot deck and so on. These are the little things that will get your customers to keep coming back, and you will also want to offer an online store on your website for your best sellers and workshop starter packs.

It is essential in a retail store to get a good turnover, because of your overhead costs including rent, utilities, staff, advertising, stock, insurance and so on. Rather than holding on to a lot of lines, do an evaluation at the end of each month on your best sellers and worst sellers and adjust your orders accordingly. Start with small purchases as you feel your way. Most suppliers will have a minimum order amount which can vary greatly. Although they will offer discounts for larger purchases and it can cut down on freight costs, it can be more costly to have 'dead stock' in your store. Just start by testing the waters and you can expand from there. Also don't get too overexcited and order a million because the first lot sold well, sometimes things move in cycles. Be especially careful of ordering too much if there is a use by date as with skincare products.

If you are supplying a store with your products I would avoid giving products on consignments where possible. If a store hasn't paid for it they are less likely to care for it, and I have seen many disputes through damaged statues, dog-eared books and sun-damaged stock that can't be repaired. If they want your treasures badly enough, and if you want them to value your work, make them pay for it. And shop owners, it is never a good idea to hold consignment stock because when you have other bills looming, it can be a struggle to pay the artist for goods already sold, and that's not good karma for anyone.

For many folks the online store is the most sensible option for tangible products. Whilst it does cut back on your expenses, bear in mind you will need a good website and marketing plan to get the same exposure you would get on the street. Then again, do it cleverly and you can take in orders from all over the world. Try to maintain your point of difference and engage customers by showing video of artisans making products, how to use your beautiful skincare range and so on.

Be creative, be experimental, and keep your business feet on the ground. Overload your business with digital or tangible products and your clients won't know which way to look. Work hard on the look, feel and quality of the products you create and promote and they will only enhance your reputation.

Ask Yourself

What products can you bring in to complement your business and increase your income?

Are each of your products ethical and valuable?

How much research are you prepared to do to create a high-quality product?

Can you keep your range cohesive and on brand?

What are the three major requirements of any products you introduce?

Try This

Think of three words you wish to describe your own product line and ensure all the packaging, branding and contents are aligned with this.

Remember less is more. For each product ask yourself what purpose does it serve, is there a product that can work better, how will this enhance the life of my clients? Fill space only where there are legitimate gaps, and save your money for products that are worthy.

Remember high quality doesn't have to mean high end, keep rummaging around and you will find some amazing products in the marketplace that can balance both price and quality. Of course super cheap is usually super crap, and you don't want that reflecting on your business.

If you are developing products like medicinal herbs, food or ingestible oils, be sure to check the legalities in your region and ensure you are following all necessary regulations

People often develop a product when they can't source what they want specifically themselves, or if they have a deep love for creating it. If that's your motivation, plan well and go for it.

Remember to focus your marketing on your point of difference or a particular feel. Creating a specific niche helps you stand out from the crowd, especially when the market is flooded with a particular product like natural skincare. Your tag might read something like 'the only skincare that…' or 'skincare from the depths of mother earth' and so on.

Engage the senses and let your customers know how your product is going to make them feel, even if it's not a tangible product. Digital products should aim to solve a problem. For instance your meditation app is going to make them feel like they have a meditation teacher to guide them in the palm of their hand.

Packages

*'Knowledge comes by taking things apart and analysing them.
But wisdom comes by putting things together.'*
- John A. Morrison

A great way of putting together some amazing packages is to use your mind mapping skills. Remember the golden rule is to tie all your work into one core message or brand, so start with your business name and brand promise at the centre of your mind map. The reason why it is so vital to bring everything back to your core message is to remind yourself and everyone else what you are all about. There is no point coming up with a mad concoction of packages that have nothing to do with who you are. That would only cheat you of your authentic self-expression and your clients of reaping the full benefit of your wisdom. Each package you put together should be intrinsically linked to who you are in essence, because otherwise, well what's the point?

So what do I mean when I talk about creating a package? A package could be a series of talks, webinars, trainings, workshops, e-courses, consultations or classes. You could also put together a package that blends your programs, products and services. Clients should pay less for a package than they would to purchase products or services individually. The trick with a package is fair energy exchange; being generous without selling yourself short. You are encouraging clients to commit by putting together something that is very appealing in content and in price. For each course in a series you would build on the last, deepening your clients' experience. People respond very well to levels in packages, because it gives them the sensation that they are progressing. Each level should have a similar framework for branding, but different content, exercises and expectations.

Once you have decided what packages might work for your clients, it is time to turn it into an *experience* instead. This is what makes you stand out from the crowd. For instance, if you wanted to combine your products and services you could run an aromatherapy workshop that included a full days' training, your latest aromatherapy book, and an essential oil starter kit. Or you could make it more exciting. You could run your workshop at a lavender farm, have your lunch out in the field and focus on all the scents around you, use essential oils in your food or drinks where appropriate, create an ancient ritual linked to particular oil and so on. There is no limit to what is possible, just choose a few profound experiences rather than totally overwhelm the senses (save the extra ideas for levels two, three and four). Simple experiences delivered with great love will give you an impeccable reputation and amazing recommendations. These are the things people talk about to their friends, family and colleagues in the real world and online.

Packages form a vital part of your business and marketing. They should be clear, cohesive and reinforce who you are and what you stand for. Next time you feel like heading off on a tangent, why not try putting together a new program within your niche instead? That way you can flex your creativity, engage your imagination and create something new, whilst staying true to your soul purpose.

Ask Yourself

How could you translate your brand promise into action by creating some innovative programs around it?

Could you extend your imagination and sense of playfulness by adding some depth to your programs?

What is the best program you ever attended and why?

Look back on courses you have done in the past and ask yourself why you did or didn't continue with them. What were the deciding factors? What stood out to you? What are three small or large things that would have made all the difference to you? Apply them to your own business.

Try This

Write your business name and brand promise at the centre of your mind map (check out the mind map section if you need help). Then break down all the words in your business name and brand promise, and translate them into a series of programs based on your knowledge and expertise. Imagine this is the last chance you will ever have to impart your knowledge to others and dig deep.

Try creating a series of three levels; a beginner series, an intermediate course and a mastermind. What would you put in each? What would you call it? How could you make it appealing, innovative and attractive? How long would each run for? Would they be evergreen (always available) or just run at certain times?

Take the time to really cost your programs to make sure there is a fair energy exchange.

If you tend to over give or undervalue your work, remember to think about giving from a place that feeds both you and your clients.

E-Courses

'If you think in terms of a year, plant a seed;
If you think in terms of ten years, plant trees;
If you think in terms of one hundred years, teach the people.'
- Confucius

There are some amazing e-course integrations these days that can help you deliver courses easily and efficiently right across the world. You are truly living in a global community and e-courses are a fabulous way of expanding your reach and widening your platform. Even if you prefer to teach in person, e-courses can help you build a following in target areas for your world tour. Or help students catch up on missed programs. You can integrate some great e-course platforms right into your website, and links to smaller free e-courses are a great way to expand your mailing list. I thoroughly recommend taking a look at how e-courses could work for your business.

The beauty of e-courses is that the information can be delivered and absorbed in the way that best suits your clients. There are four main types of learning; visual, auditory, read-write and kinaesthetic. Visual learners prefer to watch people, videos, pictures and graphics. Auditory learners like to hear information; they would be more likely to listen to podcasts, mp3s and audio lessons. Reading-writing learners love to read, fill in forms and write notes. Kinaesthetic learners are experiential and like to feel, try and touch to learn and are engaged in trying things out for themselves and applying what they have learned. Many of us enjoy a combination of these elements, and the beauty is that most e-courses now offer tools to cater for all learners. For each lesson your clients can decide whether to read the information, download the PDF for later, watch the video or listen to the audio. They can post questions or comments which you can respond to. They can learn alone at their own pace, or join in group discussions in Facebook groups, live sessions or audio calls.

You can decide the length of the course and how the lessons are scheduled. If the lessons are released all at once, students can either take the course intensively, or each lesson as it suits their schedule. If you want to run the group through at the same time, the lessons can be released on a weekly basis or whatever timeframe suits your course. If you are running a certificate course you may hold back on the next level until all work from the previous level has been handed in. Many e-courses that are eight weeks long may have seven core lessons with a catch-up week at the halfway point, which involves a review of what has been learned so far, and gives students an opportunity to catch up if they are feeling behind. It really is totally up to you, and it is the flexibility here that is so fantastic for your unique business.

For a paid e-course you will obviously need to spend more time on making it content rich and finessing the tech aspects. Your price should be reflective on your experience, the content, time it took to put it together, the length of the course, whether there is a recognised qualification at the end or not, and how much money you have spent on the technology. If you have really schmick professional video, flawless audio and impeccable content over an eight-week course, you may look at charging up to $2,500 but if you are running a basic course you may only charge from ninety to a couple of hundred dollars. You can look at other courses to see what people are charging, but I fully recommend being honest with yourself and your clients and charging what it is actually worth. Never rely on someone else's idea of value and worth to set your own prices. Neither over charge, nor sell yourself short. A six to eight-week course is a good framework in general, although you could certainly run a longer course, or a series that builds upon each previous course.

If you are just starting out you might even have a couple of freebies so people can get to know you, and while you get used to the technology. It is also a good way of building your list by integrating the course with your newsletter provider. As each person signs up, they are automatically added onto your mailing list. Remember to make your freebie really rich in value so it encourages people to take your paid course. If your freebie is not inspiring there will be little incentive to pay for the rest of your material. By the same token keep your very best stuff for the paid course.

The beauty of creating an e-course is that once it is up, it can be selling itself while you are asleep. You can travel, work remotely and still be building your brand and your business. Although of course you will need to promote it and stay engaged with attendees. Try creating a Facebook group for clients who sign up to a paid e-course as a great way to build connection and community. Just be sure to keep the guidelines here clear.

Your course can be evergreen (available all year around) or it may only run once a year on a specific date. The benefit of having it evergreen means anyone can buy it at anytime and you can keep it in your portfolio of services. The benefit of a course that only runs once a year is that it may encourage people to sign up, or they will miss out and have to wait another year to take part. If you are doing it this way you will need to have a serious marketing launch planned well in advance and affiliates to help you build numbers, or you could find yourself with three people enrolled and twelve months until you offer it again. I recommend making it evergreen for beginners, but it is entirely up to you. You could always offer a special price on the launch day for an evergreen course that only lasts for forty-eight hours to encourage people to sign up then and there. If you want to test run an e-course you could run a special pilot program price to iron out any kinks in delivery and content.

Get super clear on your course outline and break it down into weekly lessons with bullet points for each lesson. Make sure your topic centres on your niche and expertise, and the styling is conducive to your message. Keep your folks engaged as soon as they sign up for the course by offering a free preparation lesson that is on brand; get them excited about what is to come. The first official lesson should include a warm welcome, introduction, and overview on what you'll be covering. Make sure you include a really powerful subject and exercise for your clients to work through. Not hard, just powerful and engaging. Remember they have paid for this course and if the first week is all outline and not much content they will start to worry; the following weeks should become deeper still, and each lesson should refer to the relevance of the last lesson and the next lesson to come to give your attendees a feeling of continuity. The final lesson should pull everything together and come to a powerful conclusion of all they have learned.

Invite your attendees to engage throughout the course by discussing how they are finding the exercises in the course comments or Facebook group. At the end of the course thank your participants profusely, encourage them to keep up the practice and ask them to share your course link on social media or leave a review if they have enjoyed it. This is also a great time to let them know about your other services or follow-up e-courses to deepen their journey.

Ask Yourself

What would you love to share?
What does your tribe need to know the most right now?
How could e-courses open up time and space and help you connect to a wider audience?
How could e-courses free up some time and space for your life and family?
How could you create a powerful passive income that supports your work?

Try This

Be sure to link your newsletter provider with your course provider so you are gathering emails as people sign up.

Make your content rich, warm and easy to understand.

Don't be frightened by the tech aspects of running an e-course. Start easy and then build up. Course Craft has a really easy format if you want to give it a go. You can try it outside your website or get it integrated. I do recommend trying a few and seeing what works best for you.

If you want to make e-courses a major part of your products and services, then invest in some good audio systems, a microphone, a professional videographer and a graphic designer to help with your branding.

Try putting together an e-course on your favourite topic or expertise. Create an outline, a seven-week lesson plan, content and exercises for your students. It should have a beginning, middle and end, and fulfil all learning objectives. Keep exercises simple and relevant and be sure to listen to feedback. You will need a landing page to excite and a sales page to get people engaged.

Create a pricing plan that works for you. Remember sometimes bite size courses inexpensively priced may earn you as much (or more) money than one big e-course that is more expensive. Choose the model that works for you and your audience; if you are targeting high-end clients, you wouldn't sell them a cheap course.

Be prepared to update your courses to ensure the content is still relevant and fresh. You could encourage others to go back and retake the course and add a link to follow-on courses at the end.

Transitioning from Work to Your Business

'The strongest of all warriors are these two; time and patience.'
- Leo Tolstoy

I am often asked how to transition from a full-time job into a wellness career and it's a great question. My answer is slowly, methodically and determinedly. Although you probably want to have a mad fit, chuck it all in and start tomorrow, if you can just wait, if you can just be a little patient, I promise you long term you'll be far better off. When I first started my wellbeing career back in 1996, I pulled the pin on my full-time job and dove in headfirst. Bad mistake. I decided that the universe would support me, clients would come streaming in and thus a brilliant career would be born. I learned the hard way that the universe rewards planning, dedication, clarity and action. Not immature faith without preparation, or the abdicating of responsibility whilst expecting all the rewards of success. Ouch. This not only knocked my confidence as a practitioner, it made me doubt my career choice and feel abandoned by spirit. It also left me with a load of credit card debt that I had to go back to work to pay off. So a year later I was back in the job I had left and worse off financially. I take full responsibility for those decisions and the outcome, so please learn from my mistakes.

If you are in a job now, thank your lucky stars. There is no shame in having a full-time or part-time job to help you build, support or prepare a business. Use the spare time and money you have now to pay for your training, set up your website, your social media, make contacts, plan, start to build an audience, buy any equipment you might need, run a few classes and workshops to test the market, and save up funds. That way when you step out of your old workplace you will be stepping into a new one, not just a wing and a prayer. The more established you are, the more successful you will be.

If you are lucky enough your workplace may even help you transition by allowing you to drop one or two days when you are ready, so you have the time to expand your business bit by bit. As one grows, the other recedes.

Actually you would use the same method if you wanted to change your niche in your business. Let's say you are a massage practitioner who wants to create a massage training school. There's no need to pull the plug. Just keep seeing your massage clients whilst you are getting your massage school website up, start talking at expos, writing blogs and positioning yourself as an expert. Get any further certifications necessary, research and put one foot in front of the other. Make the transition as easy as possible.

The only other caution I would offer is not to overextend yourself financially in other areas so that you end up obligated to stay at your current job for longer than necessary. If you are thinking of buying a new house or car for instance, could you wait or buy something simpler that supports your business vision, rather than tie yourself into high payment obligations that cripple your dream? Sometimes when you are in a job you don't really love, you can also tend to compensate yourself by spending too much on clothes, travel, eating out or other indulgences. I know it's hard, but try to remember your reason for staying, and give yourself lovely treats that don't cost the earth, or lengthen your time in your job. You are there for one purpose only; to get your soul work rolling, so the sooner that happens, the sooner you are out of there. By all means take rest and have a holiday too. This is not about forsaking your own wellbeing on the road to supporting others. In short have a plan, follow through and you will be on your way in no time. After all, what are a couple of years if it means setting yourself up for a successful future?

Ask Yourself

Are you willing to wait if it means a more successful business in the long run?

Can you see how creating a framework to walk into will support and sustain you?

What expenses or addictions could you cut back on to ensure you move forward sooner rather than later?

Where are you sabotaging yourself financially to the detriment of your dreams?

Try This

Understand that the ego may be sabotaging you by trying to get you to quit your job before it is time. If you really can't stand where you work think about changing jobs, but remember sometimes it's better the devil you know. Staying in a job that you know well means there will be more time and energy to spend on your own business out of hours.

Give yourself a time limit on when you will be out of your old job. Make a plan. What will you achieve by when, to ensure your smooth transition? Knowing that you have a countdown in place will help you follow through and lend a sense of urgency and reality to what you are aiming for.

Work out your replacement income. How much will you have to earn in your soul business to be able to drop a day in your current job? It doesn't have to match dollar for dollar, but it does have to be a realistic figure.

Ask yourself if the contacts in your old job could help your new career. If you work in the corporate world for instance, you could ask them if they want you to put a mindfulness program together for them. This leads to experience, extra income and something for the resume. They may even want you to continue when you've finished your old role. If you are a massage therapist contemplate giving free samples in your last weeks, and hand out business cards to engage potential clients.

Make a list of everything you could do now to set yourself up for success in the future. Work through it thoroughly and methodically.

One day it will be time for the big leap, so knit yourself a net and jump off that cliff with confidence.

Pricing, Value, Generosity & Worth

'Too many people undervalue what they are, and overvalue what they are not.'
- Malcolm Forbes

I am often asked how to set prices for products and services in wellbeing. Rather than give you figures, which will change over time, here are the main things you need to consider:

Pricing, Costing and Break Even

You need to do your sums. You need to treat money with respect by taking a long look at how much money you need to start up, what your outgoing and ongoing costs are and how much you need to earn to thrive. I often see wellbeing practitioners not wanting to look at this because they don't want to have their bubble burst. There is absolutely no reason why looking at your costs should mean the end of your dream. Far from it – this should signal the beginning of your planning. Let's say you want to open a yoga studio, but it will cost you $27,500 a year for lease, plus utilities, plus insurance, plus start-up equipment, website etc. Try to divide your start-up costs or what you need to get going (website, fliers, equipment, everything you can think of) from your ongoing costs like rent, utilities and so on. Work out how much money you need to launch and how much you need as a buffer zone while your business builds, to cover cash flow and any unforeseen expenses. Then work out how much you need to earn per week at your studio just to break even *and* how much you need to earn to create a wage. Then ask yourself how many yoga classes you would need to hold a week, with how many people at what price to break even, and how many you would need to make a profit.

Then ask yourself if it's viable on your current model, and if not don't lose heart, but fire up and go searching for solutions.

Could you pay a little more for a larger space that could hold practitioner rooms that you could hire out? Could you leave a Sunday free so other practitioners could rent it for one-day workshops? Could you provide more services yourself like workshops and consultations? Could other teachers with different specialties (like kids yoga or pre-natal yoga) rent the space by the hour? Or could you look for a room in a co-op or corporate building where there is already a client base? Should you stay at the community centre a little longer until you build more of an audience for your workshop and classes? Could you build a home studio? Maybe you'd really like to teach in a resort in the Maldives? And so on. If the sums don't add up, don't get deflated but search for solutions. To me it's a great opportunity to get clear on what you love, what direction you wish to go in and what your vision is. Make sure you're not just living through an old vision, whilst in reality your goals have changed. Your search for a solution may just bring about a whole new vision more aligned with your spirit than you dreamed possible. Please, please, please don't ignore your sums, because I've done it before and trust me it can get really ugly! Treating money with integrity on your spiritual path is vital. And if you are a not for profit the same thing goes, only ten-fold. The more you have the more you can give, so don't self-sabotage, take responsibility.

Value and Worth

Examine the amount of value you are putting into what you do and what you think that is worth. This is where really great packages come into play. Stop thinking of it personally in terms of what you are worth (because of course that is infinitely abundant and we don't have a currency huge enough for that) and think about what your product, service, content or package is worth. Think about the hours spent creating it, the love in it, the energy, the nitty gritty content, the experience, and decide what you think that is worth. What monetary value feels right?

We all love value for money. If you attended a course that was packed full of information and fantastic value for money, you would leave an amazing advocate for that event. If you left feeling ripped off, well.... It's really easy to create a fantastic-sounding course, but if you don't follow through on what's promised, the value is not there. You need to be fastidious about the level of value, content, information, solutions and joy at your workshops. By the same token if the cost of your gift bags, travel time, rent and so on is bleeding the profits from your workshops you may be undervaluing yourself.

One of the main tenants of my business is generosity. I believe by giving my wisdom, knowledge and experience freely with love across social media it comes back to me tenfold. And it does. In consultations, workshops and talks I always give great value for money, and then some. There is a huge difference between generosity and poverty consciousness. Poverty consciousness is about giving away more than you can afford to; physically, mentally, emotionally, spiritually, energetically, financially or timewise. Generosity always comes from a full tank and fills your energy even more. Your heart feels overflowing to bursting with the great joy of being able to share your gifts. If you feel depleted from giving, something is out of whack and needs examining.

I would rather give something away for free, than sell it too cheap. There's nothing wrong with giving a free talk to expand your reach, let people know about your products and services and build your mailing list. Either do it for free or charge something reasonable. If you consistently send things out too cheaply you are going to affect your brand and your reputation. If people want what you have to offer, if you provide great value, they will pay for it. Free events, talks, e-courses and webinars are a great idea to build your audience and your mailing list, but too much free stuff and your clients won't bother paying you for anything. You can see this is a huge problem at the moment across the wellness industry, so don't be fooled. When you pay, you get the best work available and the same goes for your clients, because if you're charging money, you know you'd better deliver value. Make sure your clients know that although free stuff offers a great snippet of who you are, the real stuff happens in paid consults, workshops and events.

Market Prices

Okay this is a tricky one. Whilst I do believe it is good to know what other practitioners are charging, it really is up to you to create your own price based on what your product or service is worth. If you are checking what others are charging, make sure you look at models similar to yours. For instance if you have a beautiful organic skincare range sold at exclusive spas, retreats and health food stores, you wouldn't compare prices with a product on supermarket shelves. I'm sure you know that not all organic skincare ranges are created equal too. You also need to take into account packaging, production and distribution expenses amongst other ongoing business costs. If you are new at coaching you probably won't charge the same amount as another practitioner with fifteen years' experience. You may be cheaper if you work from a home studio than if you are renting premises. So by all means be aware of what others are charging and then go with what is right for you. Be careful not to invest in a poverty consciousness mindset just because others around you are. If local massage therapists are all charging $80, but you use high-grade essential oils, have invested in a lot of further study and really believe you offer a unique, valuable experience, by all means take your prices up to $120 or whatever. In the end it's what feels right.

Business Model

My business model is to be able to reach as many people as possible, so I am happy for my prices to be reasonable. If I am talking to five thousand people, then I will still make great money, which goes back into my business, my life, my family, industry education, future projects and my bank. If your business model is to see twenty clients a week from home, then you need to work out what price you need to charge to make a great wage for yourself. If you are positioning yourself for individuals, your pricing will be quite different to if you were positioning yourself to corporate empires.

Your Delivery

If you are delivering e-courses your prices may be quite different to those if you are delivering workshops that involve travel, venue hire and other expenses, because the overheads are lower. That doesn't mean that e-course fees should be negligible as it still takes knowledge, experience, time and wisdom to put them together. Personally I like to work with people in person so generally my e-courses run at the same cost as live events to encourage people to come along in person. Obviously if your e-course is very simple you would charge less than if you had a really professional setup with optional downloads, video, audio and technology features. If your workshop venue is in a hall or a five-star resort, you will adjust your prices accordingly.

Karma

Now by karma I don't mean what you deserve because you've been good or bad. Trust me I've been both! I mean your unique experience in this lifetime; who you are called to serve and what feels intrinsically aligned with your soul in this lifetime. It is vitally important to me that I can offer a space for those who may otherwise feel they will be left behind, but I don't invite poverty consciousness either. There is free advice every day on social media, you can buy this book at a great price and work through on your own, or you can borrow it from the library. When you want to come to a workshop it is totally affordable. If you don't have the money right now you can save up and pay, and what a triumph that will feel like, because when people pay for something they value they feel proud and become richer for the experience.

    At the beginning of my journey I was very much in a poverty consciousness state of mind, always asking if I could pay off courses, which teachers usually agreed to. Let me totally cringe here as I say when I came toward the end of the course and I still had to pay for it, well I felt a little reluctant, maybe I even started to pick unfounded holes in it. Maybe I resented having to pay for it, when I had all the information already and was ready to move on to the next thing. Super cringe…I knew it wasn't right even at that time. The first time a teacher said no to me paying off a course I was a little offended, but actually it was the greatest gift she could have given me. I really wanted it, saved up, and lo and behold the universe sent extra work and money my way, and when I enrolled paying upfront I felt a huge surge of energy and pride. When clients pay they feel proud, the energy is clear for both of you, and you are holding them in an abundant vision.

It may be your karma in this lifetime to work with high-level pricing for an elite clientele, do community work for a not for profit or offer subsidised art therapy to the community. I say go for it, whatever is aligned with you, whatever feels right in your body, your heart and your soul. Look back at your life and ask yourself what clues there are on how you wish to work. Your choices about what you charge are totally up to you, just be honest about them.

Promotions, Early-Bird, Add-Ons and Rewards

Another way to thank faithful clients, entice booking commitments and build your brand is to offer rewards. Early-bird pricing options rewards commitment from your attendees, and lets you know early how many folks are coming ahead of time. Offer add-ons or bonuses like gift bags, samples, a free e-course, a pdf of tips and tools, a podcast and so on. Anything that is in line with your niche that adds authentic value and makes the customer feel recognised and appreciated. Promotions may be seasonal, celebrate your business birthday (or theirs), coincide with an event, celebrate a festival and so on. Check out your calendar for ideas. Get creative, have some fun, make it sweet, make it human and thoughtful and you will stay on their mind long after the event.

Opt-in offers are great for getting people on your mailing list too, but just one offer and make it juicy, but not desperate. If you're confident in what you offer even just saying sign up for free tips and tools may be enough, but those newsletters better pack a punch.

Remember that your clients need to earn any bonuses too. They are a reward for being a loyal, valued client, spending money with you and for recommending you. It's not fair if people who never invest in you get these things too, then they are getting rewarded for not spending with you, and that energy is not good for anyone! So set something special aside for your faithful followers, and make sure they know you value their service.

Swapping and Bartering

Okay, this is a pretty old-school practice and not one I would recommend. The only exception is if you are finishing your training and require a certain amount of hours of practice to get your certification. In this case if you are unable to charge or have to charge a smaller amount you could barter, but make it clear that this is for a limited time only and regular prices will resume shortly. With bartering more often than not someone gets more out of the treatment. Or complications can arise when one practitioner usually charges more than another, or if you decide you don't want to swap with that person any more. If you admire someone's work and respect their practice, then pay for it. Bartering keeps you in a poverty conscious mentality. So get that cash out, look the practitioner in the eye, and say 'thanks so much I really value what you have given me', and hand it over baby. Be prepared to pay and be paid to respect yourself and your fellow practitioners.

Ask Yourself

Are you valuing your services enough?
    Are you providing good value for money?
    What are your customers leaving you with?
    Are you delivering the experience you promised?
    Are your clients feeling joyful and empowered by the value in your services?
    Can you detach from what others charge and price your own services according to what feels right to you?

Try This

Do your sums and learn to look at your finances honestly, and then ask yourself what you can do to make a difference here. There is always an answer.

Go over your courses and examine your nitty gritty content. Ask yourself is there great value for money here or is there a lot of fluff? Make regular updates to ensure the information is still relevant.

Check your offerings and make sure you're not over or under giving.

Think of three great add-ons you could offer as a reward when people buy early, book into a course or buy a product. These should be easy and cheap for you to put together, but packed with value.

What kind of promotions or competitions could you run to get people to engage with your products and services?

Play around with several price points on your products and services and see what prices *feel* good to you.

Check that your prices are audience appropriate. If you are offering elite training programs a cheap price tag may worry your attendees.

Evaluate, Review and Respond

'Don't spend time beating on a wall, hoping to transform it into a door.'
- Coco Chanel

Although it is something you may want to avoid, evaluating and reviewing how your business is evolving is absolutely essential to your success. It offers you the opportunity to cast a clear eye over how things are going and make any adjustments necessary. I think people often avoid this because they are afraid of what they are going to see, but trust me if you think what you are going to see is bad now, it will be even worse in five years' time of looking the other way. There is great power in taking responsibility for your business direction and choices. It allows you to be responsive, rather than reactive to any problems. It may just be that a few tweaks are needed, or you need to focus more on your online programs than your consultations, or you may need to pick up a little part-time work to fund your business when you're just starting out. Information is power and it keeps you firmly in the driver's seat.

Think of all the beautiful blessings that could occur by looking thoughtfully at your business. Perhaps you will see more efficient ways of working that allow you to spend more time with friends and family. Maybe you will see a new opportunity you had previously missed. What if you could begin to work more creatively? You may notice a complication in your booking system that is turning clients off, when a few simple tweaks could put it right. Change your attitude so that any evaluation of how you are going is empowering and loving. Try to take a step back and see what is working and aligned, and what is not. If there is a program that is really true to your heart, but it doesn't seem to be succeeding, there is no need to ditch it straight away. Ask yourself what is missing, and think of all the ways you can get it off the ground. Perhaps you have been spending too much time in other areas; maybe you are not giving it enough time, money or energy to grow. Maybe your language around it is unclear or you are hiding it under other programs because it feels so precious to you.

Look at what is working too, and how you can take advantage of that by increasing or deepening your programs in that area. Take the time to celebrate your wins and achievements. Use evaluation as a positive tool for self-growth and resilience. Instead of saying I can't, or feeling defeated when things don't go your way, ask yourself how can I? Look for solutions and roads through any problems. Ask for help and outsource if you need to. Tap into that infinite source of strength and wisdom that is the universe, and remember there is always, always, always a way out from any problems, but the sooner you see them, the easier that road will be.

Ask Yourself

Can you see the power in being in charge of your business?
Can you make any evaluations with a firm but loving hand?
Can you look at things laterally to try to solve them?
When is the last time you sat back and had a look at the overall picture of your business and where it is working or not?
Are you taking the time to celebrate your wins and what is working?
How can you deepen and expand on your successes?
How can you use evaluations to get clearer on your purpose?

Try This

Break your business down into sections to evaluate it. Look at your products and/or services, your marketing, your planning, your social media, your website and your financials. Where do you see gaps in attention or knowledge and how can you remedy these through coaching, further education, more time, money, effort and so on?

After every event do an evaluation. How much time, money and energy did you put into this event? Break it down into hours, dollars and how energising or depleting it was for you. Then ask yourself what you received in return. Did you make a profit, should you have charged more, did it leave you feeling energised or depleted, could you do things more efficiently? Was there growth on the last event if you have done something similar before? Then write down all the ways you could improve the experience for yourself and your clients next time. This is not a harsh, critical voice that lists all your errors, but a mature, insightful one that takes into account what *did* work as well as what didn't.

If one particular aspect or program hasn't been working for a while, take some time to sit in meditation, tune into the body and the breath, and ask yourself if you really want to continue or if there is a new program you need to bring forth now. Evaluation should be as intuitive as it is analytical, and I would always tune into the body to double check your decisions.

List all the things that *are* working in your business for you physically, mentally, emotionally, spiritually and financially. Evaluation is as much about acknowledgement and celebration as anything else.

Mind Mapping and Soul Mapping

'Think left and think right and think low and think high.
Oh the thinks you can think up if only you try.'
- Dr Seuss

Mind mapping is a fantastic visual tool for getting all your ideas down on paper. If this map comes from deep within, it becomes a soul map for moving forward with purpose. Often when you simply list everything you want to do it can be a little overwhelming and disordered. You can feel snowed under by trying to match this with that, and seeing what might come first. It is also easy to get carried away with ideas, rather than forming a whole integral picture of what you want to achieve. Mind mapping keeps you on point and stops you getting distracted. If it isn't on your mind map, or doesn't radiate out naturally from the central purpose, you shouldn't do it. It also ensures if you are hungry for a new project, you can go back to your mind map and take something from there to develop, rather than pluck a crazy idea from outer space. It ensures all your actions and intentions derive from one focal point, which is of course your soul purpose. Everything that stems from that radiates out like rays of the sun from its bright, vibrant centre. It is perhaps the best planning tool you can use, and is what Deepak Chopra uses to write his books, and if it's good enough for Deepak, it's good enough for me. So how can you create a mind map that is a guiding force for your business?

Materials

Get a large piece of white paper, and a marker pen, you can use colours if you like but don't get so carried away with the decoration that you forget the content! You can certainly do this online and there are a lot of templates available, but when it comes to anything inspired, studies show writing by hand engages the brain, creativity and content better than using your computer. You can always transfer it to digital later if you like. Make sure you have adequate quiet time to give your full focus to the task, because your future lies on these pages.

Begin

At the centre of the paper draw a circle, and in there write your purpose or intention. For example let's say you are an art therapist with a passion for helping women connect to their creativity through art. At the centre circle you might put your business name and your intention or purpose (this may also become your business by-line).

The Creative HeART
Women blossoming through creative art

Then extending out from this centre circle, you draw lines leading to other separate circles that might say; retreat, consultations, workshops, classes, and book. Then from each of these individual circles, more lines extend out. For instance from the workshop globe you may have extensions that speak to your favourite themes or types of art; like clay therapy, dance and movement, drawing, colour therapy and story telling. These would become your workshop subjects. You can continue on from here, but I always start another page at this point because otherwise as you can imagine, your map starts to become quite complex and can be overwhelming to look at. If you keep it simple for your primary map, then you can see at a glance what you are intending to do and how everything stems from your core purpose. Then you can deepen each section on a fresh page that gives you the material and outline for your teaching. So you would start a new page with storytelling at the centre circle for the storytelling workshop, and lines that lead out for each lesson in that workshop. Each lesson would use storytelling as a way of reconnecting women to their creativity, because after all that's your core purpose. If you can keep your plan this simple in structure, and really deepen the content you will get great results.

Social Media Map

You can use mind maps for your social media plan too. Start as before with your core purpose at the centre circle and then draw lines out to further circles indicating the social platforms you intend to use. For art therapy these may be Facebook, Pinterest, Instagram and YouTube. Check the social media section in this book and highlight some of the ideas you could use on each platform, or get creative and make up a few possibilities of your own. For instance from YouTube you could extend to circles that show; art demonstrations, you talking about art therapy and how it helps develop creativity, you doing a piece of your own work, a classroom at work, clips from your retreat, a showcase of good materials to use, a student's progress over time in your course, a creative dance video, music therapy and so on. On your YouTube channel you can collect videos of loads of creative art therapy materials and clips you can share. Then do the same breakdown for ideas on other social media platforms. So when you are feeling a little overwhelmed by how to express what you do on social media, you just come back to the map and choose, create and curate content that is all aligned with your purpose. You can take it as deep and varied as you like within your unique calling. The deeper you go, the more you'll find.

Values Map

Again start with; you guessed it, your purpose circle. Then extending out from here, draw your values circles. For instance you may have integrity, honesty, passion, commitment, courage, love, warmth, generosity, or whatever is important to you and the fulfilment of your purpose at the highest level. Then extend out from each quality and list why these are important or what each of them means. This is an incredibly powerful exercise to take pride in who you are and what you stand for, and for any staff working for your business to understand what you're all about and what qualities are expected in all dealings with clients. You can also showcase these qualities in your social media and marketing.

Clarity Map

Start with your purpose circle and branch out into further circles labelled what, how, why, where, when and who. Then brainstorm for each of these, by extending your map out. This should help you brainstorm what you are going to do, how you are going to achieve it, why its important to you, where you will deliver your work from, when you want to bring each component in, and who you want to offer your work to. It's a bird's-eye view of your overall picture.

Content Map

If you're trying to work out what to include in a course, workshop or retreat, set the intention at the centre circle and let all your ideas pour out from there.

Mind mapping is a great way of brainstorming ideas for your business. You can also use sticky notes all over a wall or floor, a pin board or whiteboard so you can easily edit as you go. Sometimes it is necessary to do the work then think or meditate on it for a couple of days, come back to it and adjust where necessary.

Customer Service

'You learn when you listen.
You earn when you listen; not just money, but respect.'
- Harvey Mackay

I am absolutely fastidious about customer service. When I used to work in retail I always strived for perfection with my customer service, and expected staff to do the same. It is even more important when it comes to customer service in wellbeing. You are dealing with people's hopes and dreams; their physical, mental, emotional and spiritual vulnerabilities. They need to feel safe, professionally guided, seen and heard. They want value for money, positive results and tangible growth. They want to be treated with respect and dignity. They want to be understood. They want someone to 'get them' and to guide them through the minefield from where they are, to where they want to grow, live or be.

If companies spent as much time and money on customer service as they do on sales techniques, they would find success in both areas a whole lot easier. A successful business has been, is, and always will be about building relationships. Not to 'get something' but to serve first and foremost; to connect. Clients these days are super savvy and more than a little cynical, and will sniff the sell behind the language in a heartbeat. Your best chance of success is great word of mouth in the real world, and powerful social proof online, and to do that your customer service needs to be impeccable. It doesn't matter whether you are a start-up or long established business, a customer service overhaul will make a radical difference in how you are perceived.

Customer service starts with the first contact whether that is online, via email or phone. When someone writes a comment on your posts always respond, otherwise it's a little like someone at a party saying 'I really like your dress' and you just standing there staring at them. This is how conversations get started online. Say something that matters, that connects. If someone endorses you on LinkedIn or on Facebook shoot them a quick thank you or response. Manners take very little time and earn you a reputation of being approachable, warm and professional. In a time-poor world, the fact that you took the time will mean a lot, and that's the kind of thing people mention to others. Responses to phone calls and emails should be within 24 hours wherever possible, less if you can. Try not to get involved in lengthy consuming discourses that go nowhere, but also avoid being curt, dismissive or making presumptions that people are wasting your time. Remember when people contact you they are trying to get an idea of who you are before they commit to booking time with you, so be as warm and welcoming as you can, but remember its not a great idea to diagnose or advise in a short conversation without the whole picture. Say something like 'It would be great to have the time to take a whole rounded look at your wellness so I can really help you, would you like to make an appointment?' Or 'the best way to experience the class would be to come along and see how it makes you feel, why not come along on Thursday?' Being really clear about what clients need to bring and what to expect from a session sets them up for success. Never pretend to be someone you're not, or be able to solve something you can't just to get the business. I will happily refer clients to someone else if they want something I can't or won't provide.

Next is a warm welcome when people arrive at your classes, spa, retreat or consult room or sign up to your newsletter. It's the little things that make a difference. So for a consult you may have a candle going, a cup of water with a slice of lemon and mint, an herbal tea, soft music and so on. Make sure your client is comfortable, has everything he/she needs and is ready to go. Communication is everything, so if there are any problems, be honest and deal with them straight away.

Punctuality is absolutely vital. Nothing says your time isn't valuable to me like keeping someone waiting. If a client is running late, make sure the time is taken off their session, rather than penalising all the following clients. Trust me, it is much better to make one client take responsibility, than to expect five other clients and your reputation to take it. The same is true of classes. You should arrive well before your clients, set up the space and be ready to teach. Rushing in at the last minute and fumbling around sets a really poor tone. If you can't get there on time, change the class time to a more realistic time slot. If your babysitter runs late every week, get a new one. Ask yourself how you would feel in your customers' shoes, and you must presume they need to start and finish on time, because they have somewhere else to go. If clients are consistently running late to class or appointments, have a word. I have a rule in my yoga classes that if you are not there on time, you need to wait outside the class for ten minutes until the meditation is over. My students used to call it the naughty step. People actually love boundaries, but they'll test you where they can.

Ensure the environment is safe, aesthetically pleasing and welcoming. After the first consult you may like to follow up with great to have you there, work with you etc, and look forward to seeing you next time. If you have referenced anything in the session, be sure to follow up and send them the details. Then the session is closed until the next appointment time. Keep your boundaries tight by not being in constant contact between sessions as this can breed dependence. You can guide them to your email list, Facebook pages or groups and encourage them to sign up for another appointment while they are with you so they feel supported. I know some coaches do offer email support in between sessions, but just be careful you don't overdo it here. I am happy for clients to shoot me any questions, or contact me when they are having a crisis of confidence, but encouraging someone to look to you for every answer isn't healthy either.

I am a firm believer that the customer is not always right. Some people are difficult, refuse to grow, don't want to take responsibility, or just plain love conflict and drama.

There is no need to kowtow or quake in your boots that they could hurt you or your reputation. Just put down your racquet and step off the court. No need to play. Trust in the good reputation you have built so far and carry on as normal. Gathering social proof via great testimonials and endorsements also means that the odd bad review will be just like a drop in the ocean, and people will see it for what it is. If you ever hear someone speaking negatively about another practitioner who you know is fantastic, then stand up and say so. This storm will pass (more on this in the difficult clients section). Do ask yourself though how this occurred. You know somewhere in there you opened a door for this, or it is a test on your boundaries, so check that out and be honest with yourself. Best to learn wholly and early, because you don't want to board that train again if you can help it.

The level of customer service you provide is in direct alignment with how much you care about your work, professional recognition in the industry, a positive result for your clients and an amazing reputation for your business. This is the truth, no matter how you try to dress it up. If you have lost focus because you are tired, are having personal problems or feel you have lost direction, step away for a while. Don't ever, ever take your stuff into your business. Take a holiday, have a few days off, see another practitioner, meditate, calm, nourish, take some time to come back to balance and resolve things. Look after yourself. Never try to battle through, because one way or another it will come out in your customer care and results. At its roots excellent customer service is about cultivating mutual respect in a sacred space. It pivots on allowing your clients their sovereignty, whilst fulfilling your promise to the best of your abilities. No more and certainly no less. Put great care and great love into what you do and your professional reputation, business and soul will bloom and prosper.

Ask Yourself

Could my customer service do with an overhaul?
Am I getting back to my clients in a timely manner?
Am I always punctual?
How are my boundaries with clients?
Is the environment I am providing clear energetically and environmentally?
How professional do I look to my peers in the industry?
If someone referred me could they be sure of the same standard of treatment every time?
What three words would you use to describe your customer service?

Try This

Write up a customer service manual. Yes, even (or especially) if you are a sole trader. A manual is written purposefully in line with the ethics of your business in mind. It doesn't need to be scripted, but it does need to offer clear guidelines for you and any staff on what is and isn't acceptable for excellent customer experience. It should also include how to deal with difficult customers, so you can respond to something written from a clear, concise space rather than react from fear or anger. The aim is to create something that honours both you and your clients. This is absolutely vital if you have staff working for you.

Look back over your last five client requests via email, phone or social media. How long was it before you responded to their query? Did you listen carefully and respond specifically to their questions? What first impression did they receive about your business?

Look at your social media and see if you are consistently responding to comments and reviews or are you leaving your clients hanging?

Ask for reviews and testimonials about your business for your marketing. This is a great way of finding out how your customers perceive your service.

Deal with any issues immediately; how you handle any difficulties will make for either bad publicity or a totally devoted customer if you turn things around.

Get some surveys out there and see how customers are finding your products and services.

Difficult Clients

'Never waste your time trying to explain who you are to people who are committed to misunderstanding you.'
- Dream Hampton

Okay we need to have this conversation because I know that you have had or may have difficult clients in the future, and trust me you want to know how to deal with them with grace should the situation arise. No need to feed it, or live in fear of it, but a mature response starts with a mature understanding. Some of these are full on, and some are small things. It is essential to keep the boundaries and the energy in your business as clear as possible, so that your work has more potency and the environment is the most optimal learning situation for everyone. That means all clients feel respected, heard and clear on what is and isn't acceptable. You can't leave any problems for the group to resolve, because you're the authority in these interactions, and the onus is on you to resolve any problems that arise. That doesn't mean you have to march around the boundaries on patrol, yelling 'aha' at every transgression; sometimes a little leeway and compassion is needed. A firm but gentle voice will usually do the trick. But leave issues unaddressed and they will impact you, the client in question, other attendees and pretty soon you will have a situation on your hands. The best thing to do above all else is to have a policy guide or outline for clients at the beginning of your course or workshop, and then you can refer back to that if there is a problem. I thoroughly recommend being really honest about your business or event and who it is, and isn't suitable for. This will save you a whole world of grief later on. Don't ever just take clients in to fill the course. Make sure they are your people through and through. For sure sell all the benefits of the course, and also be prepared to have a section that says 'this isn't for you if…' So check out some possible circumstances below and how you might deal with them should the need arise. If you have had some other experiences, write a policy for next time too so the universe knows you got that lesson and you're building boundaries now.

The Latecomer

Arrive ten minutes late to a coaching session with a cup of coffee in your hand and I know where you have just come from. Its not rocket science. In that small gesture you have told me my time is not valuable, you want to control the session, you probably won't follow through, you don't like people telling you what to do, you want to suppress your truth, you're not ready to be coached, or you're scared to death. That's a bit harsh, isn't it? Well I could go on…Actually some people are just late to class or an appointment because of unexpected road works, an accident or something truly unavoidable, but the truth is most people are late for a myriad of other reasons. If someone is late to a session, they will usually hope you'll run that same amount of time over, so it's better to say upfront, 'you're a little late today Anna, but we'll have to finish on time as I have another client coming in straight after you.' You don't want one late client to throw out your day and run late for everyone else or you'll get a reputation for not being punctual. Keep the time tight and the energy stays clean and clear. If it happens more than once feel free to ask your client why they think they are always running late to sessions.

The Early Comer

How can this be a problem? Well it's all relative. Five minutes early to an appointment, ten minutes early to a talk or workshop or a yoga class to settle quietly into your mat is fine. However when clients arrive excessively early and want to stay late it can be a drain on your time, energy and focus, or even eat into your prep time. For an appointment some responses might be, 'Hi Jenny, just take a seat and I'll be with you shortly,' then retreat to your room and continue to prep over details for the consultation. Or 'Hi Jenny you're 15 minutes early today, we could get started straight away if you like and then we can finish up 15 minutes earlier if you like.' If someone is coming early to a class constantly and asking for lots of information, while you're trying to prepare you could say, 'Wow Claire, it seems like you're really curious about qi gong, I'd love to talk to you about it now, but I need to set up the room, have you thought about a one on one session or signing up for my talk/workshop next month? I think you'd really enjoy it and we'd have time to dig deeper then.' Use your instinct and always be warm with your response, but you don't want to be spending twenty minutes before every class counselling someone and creating a dependent relationship.

The One Who Doesn't Want to Pay

When I was teaching yoga in Melbourne, my students would pay me in full two weeks before the end of term one to secure their place for term two. All the classes were full, and there were people on the waiting list. I didn't put these payment systems in place *when* I was successful. This is how I *became* successful. When I moved down to the coast I had people turn up to class and tell me 'sorry I didn't bring the money this week, I'll pay you next week' with a casual flick of the wrist as they headed out the door. Meanwhile I stood there open mouthed. I know plenty of wellbeing teachers who habitually take payment whenever, however this really isn't good practice. And it's absolutely not necessary for you to do it too just because there's a *perceived* culture around it in your area or industry.

It's usually not the people who don't have money who don't want to pay. So you could explain to the class that all payments must be made at the beginning of term and if they are experiencing financial difficulty to please come and talk to you privately to make other arrangements. Don't ever let your clients set the prices, payments or tone of your financial contract. Ever got into the habit of making allowances, and then seen a client pay $1,000 outright for a training program when they said they couldn't afford your $150 workshop? I have.

You need to be gentle but clear about your financial expectations. I would also fully encourage you to set up pre-payments for classes, consultations or events so you can get that commitment in early, because after all you deserve to be financially supported for all your hard work. Don't you? This is where automated payment services are so fantastic. Clients pay, they get the ticket, course, or download instantly. Or they pay for your consultation before they even get to the treatment room, so they just need to walk in and get started. All you have to do is focus on the work. And you know exactly who is coming to what. Money equals commitment and respect, and there is no doubt you teach people how to treat you with both.

It's up to you if you want to offer any payment plans for retreats, training or larger purchases. My advice if you do so is to ensure the final payment is made well before completion, because once people have the knowledge they came for, there is little incentive to continue to pay and something can always come up that takes priority. Make sure that client does not receive the qualification or full course until all payments have been honoured. If you have to chase someone for money I can guarantee you'll end up the bad guy. So don't let it happen in the first place. As an industry we need to be regarded as a professional body, and part of that is being paid for our knowledge and expertise. If you go to a hairdresser, a clothes shop, a hotel, a dentist or a restaurant you expect to pay, and in wellbeing it is no different. Personally I don't allow payment plans because it feels too much like taking financial responsibility for someone else, creates extra admin and is a pain in the bum if you have to chase it. I have managed gyms and you would not believe the amount of default payments that go on, it is absolutely exhausting, annoying and very uncomfortable to chase it up. If it feels good to you to offer a payment plan, then do it, but keep those boundaries crystal clear and have appropriate contracts in place. If all this sounds a bit harsh or cynical, think of it this way. Money is energy just like anything else, and in order to keep the energy clean and clear you need to sweep up after yourself.

If the boundaries are clear from the outset, then there is an obvious choice and you are sending a message to the universe that you only want clients who can pay easily and happily for your knowledge, experience and wisdom. I choose to empower my clients to find their own financial strength by saving up and making their own value choices. And I don't need to compensate for that, and neither do you because you have more important things to do than chase up money; like sharing your bliss for instance.

The Victim

Sometimes you get a client in your workshop who wants to play the victim, ignores all the tips and tools you're giving out, and just keeps going back to their sad stories. This can affect the energy of the entire workshop so it's best to address it in your introduction. Let your clients know that although moving forward is not always easy, it is essential for change, and we can all choose to be a victim and be disempowered, or to empower our spirit through acting despite our fears. Sometimes you just have to act your way through to create change. If they are arguing the point by nominating extreme situations like starving children in Africa, ask if that is the case in their life, and if they say no, you just say the best thing we can do is focus on our own backyard. When we heal ourselves, we are empowered to go ahead and help starving children in Africa if we want.

So it's fine to be gentle but honest and say to that person, it really feels as though you're not taking in these workshop tips, because you keep referring back to your problems, but if you engage these tools, you'll be able to move to what's beyond your blocks. If they continue, you could say, so what is the solution to that, or how could you act your way out of it do you think? What are three things you could do this week that would make a change? And if they refer to others such as 'I'd love to but my husband..' you can just gently remind them that it is ultimately just about them and as they commit to change, the world around them will change too. Or you could get them to write down every single reason why they can't do it and then why they are going to do it anyway. Say this is a crossroads and you can either head down the victims road where everything is wrong and nothing is right, or you can head down the action road which may have a few rocks on it, but will change your life. Because there is only one thing worse than being stuck today and that's being stuck in five, ten or twenty years' time. If they are determined to stay where they are, that's a personal choice you must respect, so don't get tangled in the rescuing.

The Angry Client

You know anger is really a cover for something else like fear or hurt right? If someone appears angry, there is nothing wrong with saying gently, it seems like you're really angry about something, what do you think that is about? How can you resolve that feeling now? A softened tone, slow movement and space can do wonders for a bit of anger. Often naming a problem can diffuse it straight away. I find addressing the obvious helps you to get straight to the good stuff so it doesn't hang around as a barrier to action. Of course if there is a lot of aggression or any physical threat, just back right away!

The One Who Knows Everything Already

Ever run a workshop to have someone pipe up every two minutes with 'Oh yes, the ancient Indians use those techniques too, but they do it this way' or 'Oh that's not the way I was taught in my six-month immersion into leadership training with the powerful women technique', or try to reinterpret your instructions to others with a few extra additions of their own? In my field of teaching teachers I need to be especially careful here. I'm sure each workshop you lead is specially crafted with cohesive skills that come together into one fabulous final result. A lot of the time extra information can be a distraction at best, or sabotage the whole group at worst. It can be a fine balance between allowing others to express themselves freely and fully and letting the focus of the day slide. So again I always set up boundaries at the beginning of the day asking teachers to step into a space of receiving, focus on their own personal experience and not to surrogate or step in to rescue other participants, or try to find answers on others' behalf. Another way can be to ask them to step into the body and experience the day at a visceral or intuitive level to get the most out of the class, and to look for internal inspiration, rather than evaluating and seeking solutions through the mind. If an occasion arises through the day I just say, 'Claire, can you let Jane find the solution herself?' or if someone is generalising about an issue, 'How does that feel to you personally? How are your body and your breath when you think of that?' Bringing other subjects or knowledge to a discussion can be a way of deflecting the learning available, and can overload participants, so it's important to keep steering the ship with love.

The One Who Wants to Dominate the Time in the Group

Some people will speak up and engage more, and other people are quiet and like to listen, but are still taking it all in. If someone is dominating a group you may need to say 'thanks for that Jenny, it's great to hear your feelings, let's see what others have to say'. You can also break people into smaller groups and nominate a facilitator who hasn't said much to lead. Or say to the group 'we are hearing some great stuff from these participants, but I was just wondering what everyone else thinks?' The introverts shouldn't be forced but invited to speak, and as great listeners they can often have incredible insights to share that may otherwise be missed. You may also dig a little deeper with the things being said by the dominator, like asking 'how did that make you feel in your body', to ensure they are really embodying the learning at a deeper level. When people talk a lot it creates Vata energy and can whip the group up a lot, especially into the mental or emotional realm, so feel free to call silent time through an exercise, lunch prep or even do a meditation or a minute's silence. You may offer a listening exercise where participants listen very carefully to their words as they speak them, slow down their speech, become more observant, or even sense how each word feels as it falls upon the cells of the body. This heightened state of awareness will ground things really beautifully. If clients struggle with this it could be interesting to explore why silence or quietness is an issue.

Direct Attack

Again set boundaries and guidelines at the beginning of any workshop or retreat that state that every participant including you is to be treated with the utmost respect. Personal attack is absolutely not on and not to be tolerated at any time. You are well within your boundaries for asking someone to apologise and adjust or leave. It is up to you to create a safe space for yourself and attendees, and you don't want people feeling so uncomfortable that they have to meditate with one eye open. If you have experienced attack online, block, report, ignore. That's it, no second chances, no appeals, nothing. Draw a line. Opinion is one thing, attack is another and you know when it has happened, even if it is sneaky and subtle. Move away from any Facebook groups that contain this energy and let any group administrators know immediately if there has been a genuine personal attack on you. Then make a choice whether you want to stay or leave. Bullying has absolutely no place in this world.

Someone Accusing You of Being Inauthentic or Out of Integrity

Ouch! That's a real stinger. Is there anything worse than being accused of being inauthentic or out of integrity? Not really, and that's why it's a great prodding stick for those who use it. At the end of the day you know whether this is true or not. No one else gets to define who you are. If you do make a mistake, or have acted out of integrity, that doesn't make you a bad person either. You can absolutely be a woman or man of total integrity even when you have made mistakes. There is no person on this planet who hasn't acted out of integrity at one time or another in their life, from emotional manipulation to unconscious action. Just examine it, make amends where necessary and move on, but never admit to something you haven't done, or take responsibility for someone else's stuff. If someone is trying to paint you with this or even talking to others about you, hold fast, hold strong, stay true. Something about you is triggering their fears and you don't need to hold this or compensate for it in any way. Keep moving forward with your plans, debrief with someone you trust, and never let it turn you away from your dreams. Keep building your integrity and let anything else wash over you. In practical terms you can respond to any complaints by saying

'I'm sorry you feel that way', or if someone catches you off guard just say, 'that's really interesting I've never heard that before', or 'I think you may have a projected a false idea of me, but thanks for your feedback'. Then as hard as it is, because you'll want to defend yourself, just walk away, detach, ignore and trust in your own integrity and reputation to pull you through.

If You're Stuck

Call the universe to help. If you are struggling with a client and need a hand, send out an immediate call to the universe. I did this once on a retreat in my early years where I had two women being incredibly disruptive. I went straight to the beach and said 'Universe, I need you RIGHT NOW. Let me be really clear. If these two women want to stay and fully participate, engage and enjoy, let them stay. If they are going to disrupt the energy of the retreat or any other participants, I want them gone NOW.' Isn't it amazing how urgency can really help you clarify what you need? I went back to the retreat centre and within five minutes they came to me and said they were going home, and I was like thank you universe! The rest of the retreat went beautifully. So you're never alone, just get everyone to do an activity and remove yourself to create time and space to centre, and ask for a solution. Above all set an intention for the kind of people you want to come before you launch any event. Be very specific. Man did I learn that lesson.

Ask Yourself

What are the difficulties that seem to come up with your clients and are you learning the lessons around these?

Can you deal with difficult situations calmly and clearly without demonising or shaming anyone?

Can you back yourself where necessary?

Can you treat all clients with love and compassion, even if they push your buttons?

Are you willing to back yourself as much as you are willing to question yourself?

Try This

Create a page for etiquette on your website, in any course descriptions, in your brochures or retreats and at the beginning of any workshop. Make sure clients are really clear on expectations of how they, you and others are to be treated. At live events literally ask everyone to put up their hand if they agree to this.

After any problems always sit by yourself afterwards, meditate and contemplate how you could do things better next time. Debrief with a trusted friend, colleague or professional. Not just a whinge session, but to become aware of how it arose and how to handle it if it occurs again. Extract as much awareness and wisdom from it as you can. The more you learn now, the less likely you are to have to take another lesson in the future.

Handle any issues immediately, gently and firmly. Naming what is happening without blaming will take the sting out of it and allow you to find solutions. Such as, 'hey guys it's really important to bring your self-awareness to the process and there seems to be a lot of blaming going on, so what do you think this is really about?'

Professional Conduct and Ethics

'Accountability breeds responsibility'
- Steven Covey

I often say that practitioners are the guardians of their own conduct and I mean it. I have no interest in policing others, but here are some principles I believe in to ensure you are running a professional practice. Feel free to make your own code of conduct that resonates with your soul.

Be Honest

Okay, so I am a coach myself. I love authentic coaching. I feel it has incredible practical tools to bring to the world of wellness and personal development. There are however some coaching practices that verge on dishonesty and manipulation. I'm all for positive affirmations and intentions, but not lies. So if it hasn't happened yet, you haven't done it. Use language to excite, invite, entice; but never to mislead or invoke fear. Keep your marketing ethical. Marketing deals with psychology, so you need to be super astute here to where you may be manipulating people in a negative way. Never ever let anyone feel less than if they don't come to you or buy what you're selling. This should be a no brainer. Also please be aware that trying to read people and give them what you think they want to hear to make them buy, is going to subvert your true work and begins the relationship from a place of misguided strategy. Tell the truth. Tap into your authentic message from the heart and soul and offer people that. There is nothing missing in your infinite capabilities that you need to make up for with lies or manipulation. In all your consultations, classes, workshops, courses or retreats only ever promise what you can deliver; then go over and above to impress, delight and absorb people.

Be Compassionate

Be gentle, warm and kind. The Brahma Kumaris have a saying that 'encouragement and a light touch is usually the best way'. If you show frustration, disappointment and impatience with a client's growth, they will pull back. Instead ask a kind but firm question about what they feel is happening. Make it a co-creation of success for both parties.

You Have the Right to Say No

If you have a client that is difficult, self-sabotaging, combative, disrespectful, intentionally non-responsive, always running late, disruptive in class or anything else that doesn't sit right with you, you have every right to stop seeing them. Don't waste your time and their money continuing. Make the choice to work with people who are your dream clients and let the rest go. It is totally fine to be clear on this when marketing classes and courses too. Coaching often encourages clients to sign a contract about expectations and promises to follow through, which I think is a great idea. Then you can start a conversation about self-responsibility and remind the clients about the commitments they made to themselves when they started if they are not following through on promises.

Create a Safe Space

Creating a safe and gentle place for any growth is vital. If clients don't feel safe physically, mentally, emotionally or spiritually, they won't open up or let go, and the truth will be harder to get to. I once had a massage in the living room of a practitioner whose teenage son came through at one point! There was to be no relaxing from that point on, because although I didn't feel in danger, I certainly didn't feel safe enough to let go. What a blessing it is to walk into a space where you feel totally nurtured and safe.

Everyone Has Their Own Timing

Try not to let your ego get in the way when it comes to seeing results from your clients. Some clients will get it straight away and go off like a rocket, and other people will take longer to integrate change. Understand the difference between a client who is self-sabotaging and one who just moves a little slower than others, but is determined to succeed.

Healthy Boundaries

It is possible to have a client become a friend, but you need to know this is a rarity rather than a certainty. I have had a few bad experiences with this one. In my experience it is only possible if that person is at the same learning phase as you. If you see clients outside the practice room there is a chance they will still want to see you as a practitioner/teacher and will often expect you to stay in that role. They may be shocked or disappointed if you are not the idea of perfection they expected to see, or are reluctant to minister to them outside business hours. During sessions keep your timing tight to respect your own and your client's energy, and so as not to keep anyone waiting. If they arrive late the appointment is not extended.

Allow Your Clients Sovereignty

I'm not a huge fan of the follow-up call after appointments. It can tend to create co-dependency and the impression your client can't cope without you. Why not try sending self-help hints and tips in your newsletters instead, which offers backup support if and when they need it. There is a whole load of ways to create an integrative system in this day and age through social media, e-courses etc, which supports your client in between sessions. Always honour the choices your client makes for his or herself as to what will work best for them. You are simply a facilitator for them to reach their goals and they, not you, know best, even if you may not think so at the time. Never seek to override their will or you may find it backfires in a million ways, including on your reputation.

Keep Your Office in Order

Non-negotiable legalities are business insurance, association membership, taxation records, client history notes, bank records, expense receipts, licensing renewals where appropriate, business names, business domains, education and IP obligations where appropriate. Be acutely aware of any legalities specific to your business. If you run a messy office you'll run a messy business.

Keep Notes

Be sure to keep confidential notes on each treatment; including any problem areas, advancement or improvement and take-home instructions for the client. This will be essential if you want to work in a clinic or have practitioner insurance. Notes should be securely stowed for privacy and never, ever shared.

Legalities

I can't offer legal advice because I'm not qualified to do so. It is your responsibility to ensure all your legal obligations are fulfilled and up to date. If you are unsure what this means contact a legal professional or your association for advice. Unless you are qualified to do so, do not diagnose or give a medical opinion. Never advise anyone to stop seeing their medical practitioner or stop taking prescribed medication.

Hygiene

Please refer to the guidelines posted by your industry association and follow through. I'm sure we've all had some scary experiences of used massage towels before that don't bear repeating. I don't care how expensive laundering is; don't give me those towels lined with someone else's skin cells....ewwww!

Energetic Impeccability

Always ensure you are in a good place energetically to conduct a healing by keeping your own energy clean and clear. If you can't balance yourself, or are feeling physically, mentally, emotionally or spiritually unwell, it is better to reschedule the treatment. Ensure you clear the space and yourself in between clients even if you feel it was 'a good clear session'. In the same way physical hygiene is important, energetic hygiene is equally so, and people don't want or need to deal with other people's stuff in their own healing session.

Your Words Carry Power

As a professional guide or teacher, remember people will take what you say very seriously. I know people who are still hung up on something a teacher said to them twenty years ago. With any message you impart, be sure it comes as a nudge from spirit, not a nudge from your ego. Always leave your client in a space of feeling positive. It is easy to pick up on the doubts and fears, but reporting all this back to your client will only tell them what they are not. By all means be honest where you see problems, but also tell them the potential you see in them and offer them practical tools on how to make changes. Leave everyone who comes to you with light and a sense of confidence moving forward.

The Four Agreements

The Four Agreements by Don Miguel Ruiz are wonderful principles to integrate into your life and business. The Nia dance trainings use these as guidelines, and they can certainly help to give your clients a gentle list of expectations that you can refer back to, should issues arise in the individual or between two participants. *The Four Agreements* from the same book are as follows;

1. Be impeccable with your word

Speak with integrity. Say only what you mean. Avoid using the word to speak against yourself or gossip about others. Use the power of your word in the direction of truth and love.

2. Don't take anything personally

Nothing others do is because of you. What they say and do is a projection of their own reality, their own dream. When you are immune to the opinions and actions of others, you won't be the victim of needless suffering.

3. Don't make assumptions

Find the courage to ask questions and express what you really want. Communicate with others as clearly as you can to avoid misunderstandings, sadness and drama. With just this one agreement you can completely transform your life.

4. Always do your best

Even if it is less than what is asked of you. Your best is going to change moment to moment; it will be different when you are healthy as opposed to sick. Under any circumstances simply do your best, and you will avoid self-judgement, self-abuse and regret.

Licensing

'Walk where your heart leads you.'
- Gao Xingjian

Usually when you have finished your training you are able to set up your own business and go ahead and teach. Some practices however require that you purchase a yearly license as well. Licensing is effectively leasing someone else's brand for a fixed period of time, usually by the year. The great thing about this is you get to use their branding, logo and marketing materials, as long as you pay your license fees and abide by their conditions. If they have a powerful marketing campaign in place and brand recognition is strong, this can give your business a huge kick-start. There are quite a few licensed practices in fitness, health and wellbeing now, so before you decide to undertake any training in a new modality, make sure you check to see if you need a license to practice it. There are both benefits and drawbacks to working under a license agreement, so do your research and choose whether this is the right course of action for you.

If you study a general fitness course you should be able to teach various techniques to a range of demographics, developing your own style, specialising where you like and adding your own unique flavour. You need to belong to an association and have insurance, but other than that you are free to teach in your way. If you study a licensed practice, you may only be qualified to teach that particular style depending how specialised it is. If you decide you don't want to renew that license, your qualification may also become defunct until or unless you renew. That means your insurance will no longer be valid. You can't just decide to teach another style, you may need to go back and enrol in another course altogether.

A license has both fabulous benefits and constraints, so before you enter into a license agreement think about whether licensing would suit your personality. If you like to be in control, create your own systems and processes, lead the field and initiate new programs, being a licensed practitioner may feel smothering or constraining to you. If you like to be a part of a community, be led, inspired, collaborate, and work under established systems it may suit you perfectly. Do your own research, and sit with it. If you do decide to go with a licensed practice, don't forget to build your brand at the same time by blogging on specialties that interest you, giving talks or running workshops that help you create your niche and be seen as a wellbeing expert. Who knows, your licensor may even notice you standing out and ask you to speak at one of their gatherings, mentor new practitioners or lead a demonstration at a wellness expo.

You will need to look really carefully at what is required of you under the license agreement and think about whether you are able to abide by the terms and conditions, because there are ethical and legal obligations involved. As you can imagine people are pretty particular about keeping the integrity of their brand in good shape, so rules can be strict and they kind of need to be. So see how much room to move you have with the license. Ask a few questions, send a few emails. If I decided to add this to my class would that be okay, and if I decided to do that, would that be out of bounds, or this is what I want to specialise in, would that be a good fit? Better to ask and know rather than find out after your training, or to miss out on training based on misconceptions.

If you decide to license your own brand out to others, I want you to check in first. Be really, really clear about what this means in terms of your responsibilities to your licensed practitioners. Don't think of it as an easy way to make money because it isn't. There are loads of legal and business implications, it takes plenty of infrastructure, marketing, maintenance, admin and communication. If you are going to provide licenses to others, I would be very particular about who they were going to as well, because those people will hold your brand in the palm of their hands. If you have a course on offer I would make sure there was a strong application process in place, so you're not just letting any old person in, and you know exactly who is going to be holding your brand. A bad, immature or inexperienced teacher can leave your brand in shreds, especially if you're just starting to build your reputation. Be very clear in your training paperwork that you have the right to refuse or remove license where you feel the individual does not meet accepted standards. A difficult conversation and strong boundaries in the beginning can save a lot of drama in the future.

A franchise is a type of license where this is especially true. Let's say you had a fantastic spa business model and were going to offer franchisees the opportunity to purchase. Have a really thorough look into their background and who they are, get references from people they have worked with, check their social media accounts and so on to explore their energy and philosophy. Don't just rely on what they say. There's no need to get ASIO involved, but really think about your reputation rather than just selling off as many as you can. Your franchisees may be just looking for easy business models, and you need to check that they are aligned with your brand before you hand it over to them. It may take a little longer but it's worth the effort. You'll end up with advocates who will go the extra mile to preserve and promote your brand at the highest levels. If franchising is your end goal, make sure your business model has all the necessary nitty gritty frameworks in place, so they can be replicated and adhered to with ease. Have regular evaluation processes in place like mystery customers, customer feedback forms and respond to any problems swiftly and professionally. Speak to a licensing specialist, lawyer and someone who has bought and sold franchises before to get a realistic idea of what is involved.

As a License Holder

Check that your chosen modality is approved by associations in your industry so you can be confident of getting association membership and insurance cover.

To check exactly what the licensor expects of you – look thoroughly at the legal obligations.

Ensure the licensor gives you adequate marketing support to sustain, promote and grow your business.

Ask yourself if the cost of the license is fair and sustainable for your business.

If you are looking at a franchise like a spa outlet, make sure you are aware of the fit out costs as well, compulsory annual conference fees and maintenance standard costs (you'd be surprised to find the extras add up to thousands each year).

How much creative freedom does it allow you? Some licenses are quite generous here, others are very strict so be clear, ask questions before you commit.

Don't make the mistake of thinking with a license you can just sit back, do nothing and watch your business grow. You will still need to do the hard yards of any business venture with building reputation, customer service, communication, etc...

Remember to build your own brand at the same time as any licensed practice you teach, that way if it collapses, or changes in such a way that you no longer wish to be a part of, you have a strong professional profile and can build on that rather than start from scratch.

Make sure you are energetically and ethically aligned with the group you are joining. Check out their website, social media, teachers' pages and so on. Feel the vibe.

Remember you can create community in other ways than being part of a licensed group.

If You are Licensing Out Your Creation

Remember to triple check all your details and legalities are in place.

Be sure you are in it for the long haul or you may face legal action yourself.

Understand the level of commitment you are making.

Make sure you are giving your licensed practitioners value for money and their marketing money's worth.

Be very clear about everything they get for their license fee and make sure you follow through on your promises.

Make sure your IP, trademarks and social media are in place.

Do your research.

Make sure your communication strategies are high level.

Make sure your brand is strong and resilient and you are consistently driving the marketing and expansion of your brand in the marketplace.

Make sure your business model is foolproof; strong and simple wins every time.

Have systems for checking your ideals are being upheld.

Decide who it is you want to hold your precious brand.

Make regular visits and check-ins to ensure your brand and reputation is being upheld

Get involved; ask for feedback from your licensees. Get that information before the unknowns affect your business.

Make a good old-fashioned pro and con list about whether you should become a licensor.

Research, research, research.

Business Names and Intellectual Property

'Your identity is your most valuable possession. Protect it.'
- Elastigirl

For many of us the idea of intellectual property and ownership over a name or brand can trigger the guilt impulses. In spiritual training you are taught not to grasp, hang on to or covet things, so how can you turn this inconsistency into something that feels okay in your bones? There is incredible power in a name. There is amazing intention in words. What if you were being asked to name and claim what you do, and plant a flag to who you are, and what you are here to share in this lifetime? Are you ready to lay it all on the line? There is some universal reason why this is happening. Synchronicity, evolution and growth don't just occur in the spiritual realms or around spiritual topics. There is a reason why social media is taking off and it's not all about the ego. There is a deeper intention behind why we are being called to name who we are and what we do. Could it be the universe wants us to stand up? Could the time for skirting around the edges and avoiding be over? Is there a deeper calling behind this? I think so, and the more I see spiritual folks squirm around naming who they are and what they do, the surer I am it's a call to action. It's not about ownership for its own sake; it's about owning your message and taking that commitment public. So before we get the judgement stick out around intellectual property, let's see what opportunities it's gifting us.

In a world where there are more and more practices emerging for the healing of the planet you need to be super clear on who you are and what you do, to make it easy for your tribe to find you. So how do you choose a name that is aligned with who you are? I chose Wildlotus® as my wellbeing business name because whilst I believe wholeheartedly in the sacred, it is part of my personal experience and core philosophy that you don't need to be perfect to begin your journey. Start where you are or you may never start at all. I am not an ascetic; I am committed to teaching spiritual practices for a modern age. I feel that if you make things too out there, insurmountable or strict, people may never have the chance to start. Wildlotus was the best name for me because I was a bit of a wild child, I don't like a holier than thou attitude, and I feel it's where the ego meets the spirit in a space of love. To me that love is what brings change, acceptance and our capacity to grow. I chose Spirit in Business® as the name for my new business because I feel it is important to keep our spirit alive in our business, and because I believe there is much for our spirit to learn from business in order to be heard. The two to me are not separate, but work on an interchangeable energy of authentic self-expression.

You can choose your name based on what you do; eg 'Blissful Massage', or who you are, eg 'Women Leading Change'. More and more the emphasis is on telling people who you are; connecting people to an action, a feeling, a sensation. Think about it for a moment. Would you be more likely to tap into a website or social media campaign called 'Successful Business Women' or 'Women Leading Change'? How does each one make you feel? For me the first one feels clear but very business oriented, maybe self-serving or corporate. Women leading change still feels professional to me, but it also feels innovative, purposeful and powerful. It feels like a movement rather than a static body. Which one would you want to be involved in, tell your friends about or invite people to join?

Your clients should be able to get a really clear idea of who you are from your business name, so dig deep and meditate on it. Let go of any fear of judgement and tell the truth. What words, feelings or movement do you love? What verbs resonate with you? Play with words. Think of how you want your clients to *feel* and create language around that. Can you see yourself being happy with this for many years to come? Sit in the body and ask yourself does this feel true to me? Once you have found a name its time to take it out into the world.

Registering a Business Name

If you use your own name straight up then there is no need to register it as a business name in Australia, but if you use Matthew Jones Massage or Trish Jepson Healing Centre you will have to register it. If you are using a business name such as Healing Haven you should search the business names register to see if it is available and the IP database to be sure it isn't trademarked. Have a list of names ready, keep searching and tweak until you find something that feels right to you. Don't just plug in any old thing; think about what will serve you long term in your business, has a strong feeling sense attached and feels right in your heart and soul.

Trademark

Once you have your business name you should consider registering a trademark on that name nationally and/or internationally, because the business name alone won't give you a trademark. If you are planning big things this is especially important because if you have worked hard for many years building a name for yourself, but you don't trademark it, anyone can come along, trademark that name and legally stop you from using it. It doesn't mean you need to be remotely litigious yourself if you own the trademark, it just means no one can stop you from using the brand you have worked so hard to build. It's not as expensive as you might think, so it's well worth looking into. Trademarks have a use it or lose it policy though, so once you have registered your trademark you will need to start using it on your website and in your marketing. This is a good thing really as it means people can't just park on a trademark without using it as they can on a domain.

Domain Names

Your domain name is your url or website address. There are many companies that offer domain name searches and registration. Please note that you must have an ABN to register an Australia .au website address. You can register your domain name for up to ten years, but most people just do it for one to three years at a time. Be sure to keep your contact details up to date with your domain provider and pay renewals before time. If it expires anyone else can purchase it, and many people pay to have a particular domain name watched so they can be notified as soon as it becomes available. Before you begin your search have a heap of alternative names at the ready and a credit card ready to buy. There's no point searching a heap of domain sites because if it's not available on one it won't be available on any others. Do some research about which provider you would like to use. The cheapest isn't always the best, as sometimes you may be able to register for a pittance, but need to pay add-on costs to have your domain do what another more expensive version does automatically. I would recommend registering your own name as a url as well as your business name. It's not that expensive, and if you decide later to go with your own name you know it's still available. That way if your direction changes and your website name no longer covers the craft you teach, it will be easy to change direction.

If you don't have a website yet make sure you at least buy a domain name now; it's not expensive and if you want to be out there in the future you need to make plans for it today even if you're just starting. In five years if you decide you want to create a webpage, the chances are your name will be gone. Even for small, grassroots, beautiful earthy businesses, a website is crucial. Think of what it will gift you; a presence in the world, an opportunity to say who you are and what you do from the heart, a blog to give your loving advice to people who need it, a chance to express yourself and a vibrant business with heart.

Social Media Names

Once you have decided on your social media platforms it is also important to use your business name, or own name on your account, and to personalise your url address here too. Then you can create links from your website to your social media platforms, and people using these platforms can recognise you and your voice. Think of it this way – if you don't claim your business name on social media platforms, and someone else does, your clients may think what they are watching is you, when it isn't. If there is someone else out there teaching things that don't align with your philosophy, you don't really want to be connected with that, and your clients may find it confusing because they are getting mixed messages.

Alignment

You will want to align your names as much as possible across all platforms. That means your website address, your social media addresses and your professional pages. I couldn't get the spirit in business url because someone else was sitting on it, so I went with spirit in biz;

www.spiritinbiz.com.au
www.facebook.com/spiritinbiz
www.pinterest.com/spiritinbiz
www.instagram.com/spiritinbusiness
www.linkedin.com/company/spirit-in-business
www.linkedin.com/in/ginnywest
www.twitter.com/spiritinbiz
Twitter (handle @spiritinbiz)

Just do the best you can and remember there probably will be some overlap at some point because there are so many people getting onto these platforms. I think we will all become better over time at understanding this and differentiating voices, so the moral here is to be really clear on who you are, what you believe, your niche and what you have that will help others.

As far as 'ownership' is concerned, don't allow your ego to become involved and go into a panic if someone seems to be swinging up alongside you. At the end of the day all you can really own is your voice. At the same time honour your path and respect the gifts spirit has given you by performing due diligence in your business.

Continuing Education

'The beautiful thing about learning is that no one can take it away from you.'
- BB King

I am a huge believer in education. As in any profession, once you are qualified your learning has only just begun. Formal education, reading, conferences, expos, festivals, industry talks, workshops and research should be an active and regular part of your career. Further to that and just as important is your personal and spiritual development. That means taking the time to integrate, understand and assimilate your practice at a personal level. As a wise guru once said 'yoga is not a mask you can put on, it has to grow out of you like hairs'. It is the same for any of the healing arts. Wisdom comes only when outside knowledge has been internalised and truly understood at a deeper level. That way rather than turn to textbooks or other people's words for your answers you can respond to any questions from infinite knowledge deep in your soul. Knowledge and intuition together are a powerful blend. If you have truly walked the process yourself, you can speak with great authenticity, authority and compassion.

It is a requirement of many associations that you upgrade your skills once a year with further study. Your insurance may become invalid without these upgrades so be sure to do your homework on what is required to fulfil your obligations. First-aid updates are also an essential component, so have those marked in your calendar every year. Rather than seeing any skill upgrade as a drain on your time or money, dig deep, have a look around and get excited about it. Gone are the days of boring workshops, and there are some amazing creative, spiritual and personal development programs that can fulfil your obligations. They can deepen and extend your knowledge, provide inspiration and bring new gifts to yourself and your clients. And remember much training can be used as a tax deduction. Be choosy when you are trying to decide which courses to take, and make sure it is aligned with your soul.

Whilst I fully believe in investing in the right courses, it can be very costly and time consuming to run from one course to another. Ask yourself is this course going to directly influence where you want to be in ten years' time personally and professionally or not, and make your choice from there. Will it feed your heart and soul? Concentrate your knowledge in your niche or heartland. Get to know the school or person running the course, not just from the course description but look at their social media, read their blogs and try and get a feel for who they are. Do you like their content, their communication style, and their philosophy? Feel free to pick up the phone, have a chat, and ask questions about what to expect. Do they resonate with you, are they qualified in what they are doing, and are they highly regarded? You may also want to fine-tune particular skills that are in line with your purpose like speaking, writing, consulting or teaching. And then there are the social media and marketing skills and so on.

If you have ever felt fraud or imposter guilt that you don't have the necessary skills, knowledge or wisdom to be successful, a combination of education and experience will help allay many of your fears. Please bear in mind that you will always need to deepen your own spiritual practices with the divine in daily meditation, and thoroughly embody what you have learned by trying to integrate it into your daily life. This is about owning your own leadership skills and sovereignty. Otherwise you may always feel a little imposter guilt. It can't just be about carrying around ideas. You'll need to *know* and demonstrate to empower others. Education expands your horizons, deepens your knowledge and enhances your confidence. You will then be able to go on to educate others either formally, or through tiny morsels of wisdom that fall like raindrops from the depths of your being.

Ask Yourself

Are you really clear on your legal obligations for further study from your insurance and association membership?

What have been the best and worst educational experiences you have ever had?

Have you taken the time between trainings to integrate, assimilate and understand how they have impacted you on a physical, mental, emotional and spiritual level?

Are you spending enough time on your own spiritual development?

Where are the gaps in your knowledge right now?

Try This

Before enrolling in any course or education, tune in. Ask yourself what it is you need the most right now. If you are really clear on what you are looking for it will be easier to find.

Do some research into any courses you are thinking of taking. Is it on brand for you? Will it deepen your skill set in your niche? Will you get sufficient return on your investment physically, mentally, emotionally, spiritually and financially?

Research any courses to ensure they are approved by your association or insurance provider so you will be able to get insurance to teach or practice.

The health industry has become a lot stricter on what level of education is required to offer private health rebates, so if this is crucial to your practice make sure your education providers meet all requirements.

Ask the education provider whether you will be issued with a certificate or diploma, get really clear on costs, payment plans, and assessment requirements before you commit.

Research the reputation of the education provider and remember you usually get what you pay for.

Be mindful of online education in wellbeing, especially physical practices such as yoga, massage or even kinesiology. Many industry specific associations won't acknowledge pure online education and will require a certain percentage of your studies to be face to face to gain credits. Do your research. If getting time to study is a factor it might be worth doing a four-week intensive or short module bursts, or weekend workshops instead.

Collaboration and Partnerships

'Collaboration is about being who you are and speaking what you see.'
- Lynn Serafinn

Collaborating with a like-minded soul, or souls, in wellbeing can be an absolutely wonderful experience. Someone to share the journey, offer support and advice, problem solve, get excited and create with. There are lots of ways to collaborate from formal partnerships to getting a group of practitioners together for a retreat, to creating a workshop with a friend. Before you begin you need to be really fastidious about the people you collaborate with, because their reputation will rub off on yours and vice versa. You need to sit down together and talk about who you are, what is most important to you, what your deal breakers are, and how you want your clients to feel at the end of their experience. You need to know each other's work inside out, and make sure it is compatible so you are not sending your clients mixed messages. Ideally collaborators should be on equal footing; a similar level of education, experience and spiritual maturity, so that the input is equal.

For larger projects, apps like Evernote are a great help because you can divide the work fairly at the beginning, and set tasks for each collaborator to complete by a certain time. As each task is completed, the other members are notified, and they can also see who isn't getting through their work by deadlines. Having it in black and white makes it a lot easier to manage, see any gaps and encourage those falling behind to start fulfilling their roles. Of course there is room for negotiation, if one member is sick perhaps you can take some of their tasks this time, and they can take more of the load on the next project or less of the profit on this one. I know it sounds harsh but it is absolutely vital that the energy is kept balanced, and if one partner isn't happy to make up any time lost, or doesn't feel obliged to do so, it may be time to take a look at their overall input and have a chat about it. You need to be mature enough to have the awkward conversations like 'I feel I'm putting in a lot more time than you', or 'it makes me feel off balance when you don't arrive early enough for the workshop set up', or 'I feel you're taking over or sitting back too much'. There needs to be an equal exchange of time, energy and money so that no one feels depleted and the energy remains clear.

Remember that any profits will need to be divided, so be sure you are taking into account all costs, and what all contributors are being paid. If someone has a larger role than the others they should be paid more, and this should be clear from the outset. You need to keep all the energy for your fabulous work. Keep the boundaries as clear cut as you can in the beginning and there will always be a reference point to refer back to. I know to some people this will seem too rigid and I understand, but the better the structure, the cleaner your energy, and the happier everyone will be in the long run. For larger project this is absolutely essential. Remember creativity thrives on structure, and when everyone knows what they are doing when and why, they will be able to add their own unique flavour to it. No one can produce their best work when the walls are falling down.

In collaboration you will need to be a really great listener, take others' creative input seriously and respectfully, and communicate gently and clearly your own wants and needs. Start each collaborative project meeting with a meditation to really connect to the soul of what you are creating here. If it is divinely guided there will be nuances, messages and illuminations you will want to pick up on. Ask yourselves how you might be able to take your work to a deeper level and encourage each other to go deeper and further for your clients so they come away with a mind-blowing experience. What makes your work stand out from other collaborations? What is your point of difference? Make sure you have great structures, systems and integrations around any booking system so it is as simple as sharing a link from all parties.

Remember there is a big difference between creating a collaborative project from the outset together and being asked to speak at an event as a contributor. If you are asked to speak you will have to abide by the guidelines and expectations of the organiser, so don't be surprised if your million suggestions for the event are not implemented! Perhaps you would be better off creating your own event.

There is no need to collaborate on projects if you work better alone, as a contributor or as a leader. You can still create great connections that make you feel part of a larger whole. You can network at wellbeing events, speak at industry conferences or expos, talk over any problems with fellow practitioners, use other practitioner's goodies in your gift bags, cross-promote services, write for a wellbeing publication and so on. There is no need to feel isolated just because you work alone.

Make sure any collaboration or partnerships help you deepen and align with your purpose, and be sure to allow others to express their dharma freely too. If you can't all express yourselves to the depths of your being, something needs adjusting. Partnerships and collaborations can be absolutely amazing, loving and dynamic. They can also be a bloody disaster; so do your homework, ground your plans, examine options with love and mutual respect, and make the choice from the highest part of your being. Make sure everyone is on the same page, and that the love for what you do, and the results you want for your clients, are at the forefront of any endeavour.

Ask Yourself

Is it truly part of your calling to work with a partner, or is it just because you are scared to launch something on your own?

What support can you call on from colleagues, sister industries and professional bodies without having to create a formal partnership?

Can you express yourself fully in partnerships you have formed?

In collaborations are you and your partners being given equal time to speak and be heard?

Can you deal with any difficulties honestly, gently and truthfully?

Are you doing your fair share of the work?

Try This

For every partnership you will need a contract drawn up. This is absolutely essential, *especially* if you are best friends.

Trust your gut. If something doesn't seem right at the beginning STOP. No matter how awkward it may be to say no, things can get really messy financially and emotionally fast in the wrong partnerships, so be brave and cut your losses early. You'll save a lot more heartache and friendships in the long term.

Check in with your body. Imagine working alongside this person or these people. How does it feel? Not just in the mind, but in your skin, your breath, and your posture. Sit down quietly, visualise and take the time to feel the future cast. If it feels amazing, go ahead.

Be mindful that even if you love the person you are working with their husband, wife or partner may also want to be involved because of financial commitments, so boundaries will need to be clear. You don't want a third party heavily influencing the business, especially if they have different ideas and little knowledge of the industry. Or they may be absolutely gorgeous, but just not a business person.

Ensure every partner has up to date qualifications, insurance and is a member of a professional wellbeing association, or this may affect your own insurance.

If you are having trouble with a business partner, never ever discuss it with other people in the industry. Share with your partner, a close friend under strict confidence or see a kinesiologist to sort it out energetically. If anyone tries to get you to expand on what happened, simply smile and say it didn't work out, even if you are itching to put your case forward.

Sit down and have the difficult conversations before you begin. What will you do if one of you wants to get out, how will you make decisions about bringing other people on board, how will you use your time and money in the business, how will the profits be split, how much money will you keep and how much will go back into the business, when will you begin to pay yourselves a wage and so on.

Be really clear on what each of you want to create individually, then bring it together and see if it works. Test run it by trying case scenarios out with each other to see if the fit translates into programs, products or services. Push through any discomfort with this and do it anyway.

Get yourself a neutral mediator for any problems that arise. Personally I would also clear stuff energetically before you begin the partnership with a kinesiology session for the two of you.

Take responsibility for yourself. Being in a partnership is going to bring up your fears, communication hurdles and self-worth issues. Do what you need to in order to approach any problems from the soul not the ego.

It is a really great exercise for you and your partner to individually write down what your core message is, who you really want to work with, what energy or qualities you want to surround your work, what your deal breakers are, and where you want to be in five years' time. Then come together, swap sheets, really absorb who your partner is and what they want to achieve and see if you align. It can be such a beautiful thing.

One Last Thing

'The end is inherent in the means.'
- Mahatma Ghandi

We are at the interface of a need to deepen our soul work and a need to deepen our understanding of technology. One without the other will not see us thrive. Once upon a time you may have thought it impossible to be deceptive or unethical in your voice, but you may have also noticed manipulative language creeping into many digital platforms. The more you ignore this, the more immune you become to it, or perhaps you even start using some of that language yourself. Promises of six-figure businesses, scarcity or failure triggers are all specifically designed to agitate fear in people to force them to buy.

It is psychological manipulation at its worst. You don't want to draw people into your programs this way, because the energy of how you draw people to you sits in your work, and endorses those methods for others.

You need to believe you can gather your tribe from your soul; by speaking honestly from the depths of your being. By letting people know who you are and how you can serve. You need to listen well too and make sure you're being drawn to other programs for the right reasons. Tune up your intuition, unplug from your ego and ask yourself is there deep spirit in this person's work, and will it feed my heart, soul and purpose? If the answer is yes, immerse yourself.

In order to move forward authentically and impeccably as spiritual leaders we cannot repeat mistakes from the past. The technological age has barely begun, so let's get really clear early on as to how we will conduct ourselves. It is never too late to change. Technology in itself is not destructive, how we use it is totally up to us. It offers incredible tools for integrity, creativity and community. For spreading love, light and joy across the planet.

The same can be said for money. Own and welcome your abundance, but don't make it your driving force. If you want to know what a world driven *purely* by money looks like, take a look around you. However, let me be really clear here. There is absolutely nothing wrong with celebrating wealth, earning money and being rewarded for your hard work. The more soul driven and authentic your work becomes, the more you'll invoke a natural flow of abundance from the universe. This wealth is sustainable as it comes from infinite source and will build upon itself, requiring less effort, not more as time goes on. Your heart makes you worthy so never turn abundance away.

The truth is this is all you need; a strong connection to your soul purpose, a really clear step by step plan on how to execute that, a beautiful ethical marketing plan to take your soul work out into the world, commitment and action. Plan and act with love. One foot in front of the other, one step at a time; that's it. I wish you all my love, I wish you all success, I wish you all peace, I wish you all joy and I beg you one last thing. Lay your life and soul in the arms of the universe and trust your heart with every fibre of your being.

Ginny West xx